SHOWDOWN WITH
NUCLEAR IRAN

OTHER BOOKS BY MICHAEL D. EVANS

Beyond Iraq: The Next Move

The American Prophecies

SHOWDOWN WITH NUCLEAR IRAN

RADICAL ISLAM'S MESSIANIC MISSION TO DESTROY ISRAEL AND CRIPPLE THE UNITED STATES

MICHAEL D. EVANS

with

JEROME R. CORSI, PH.D.

NELSON CURRENT

A Subsidiary of Thomas Nelson, Inc.

Published in Nashville, Tennessee, by Nelson Current, a division of a wholly owned subsidiary (Nelson Communications, Inc.) of Thomas Nelson, Inc.

Nelson Current books may be purchased in bulk for educational, business, fundraising, or sales pro-motional use. For information, please e-mail SpecialMarkets@thomasnelson.com.

Scripture taken from the HOLY BIBLE, NEW INTERNATIONAL VERSION®. NIV®. Copyright © 1973, 1978, 1984 by International Bible Society. Used by permission of Zondervan. All rights reserved.

Library of Congress Cataloging-in-Publication Data

Evans, Mike, 1947–
    Showdown with nuclear Iran : Radical Islam's messianic mission to destroy Israel and cripple the United States / Michael D. Evans with Jerome R. Corsi.
        p. cm.
    Includes bibliographical references and index.
    ISBN 10: 1-59555-075-5
    ISBN 13: 978-1-59555-075-0
    1. Nuclear weapons—Iran. 2. Iran—Military policy. 3. Nuclear nonproliferation—Iran—International cooperation. 4. Nuclear arms control—Iran. 5. National security—Middle East. 6. Iran—Military relations—Israel. 7. Israel—Military relations—Iran. 8. Iran—Military rela-tions—United States. 9. United States—Military relations—Iran. I. Corsi, Jerome R. II. Title.
U264.5.I7E93 2006
327.1'7470955—dc22   2006024661

Printed in the United States of America

06 07 08 09 10 QW 5 4 3 2 1

*I dedicate this book
to the late Menachem Begin,
Prime Minister of Israel.*

*He was, without question,
one of Israel's greatest leaders.*

*My own life has been enriched
by the rare privilege of friendship
with this brilliant man.*

"War is a blessing for the world and for every nation."
— AYATOLLAH KHOMEINI,
12 DECEMBER 1984

CONTENTS

SHOWDOWN WITH NUCLEAR IRAN

Preface

ISRAEL, IRAN, AND THE CURRENT CRISIS

I'm in northern Israel, which is under a rocket attack by the Hezbollah terrorists of southern Lebanon on this bright summer day. A few days ago armed Iranian militants staged a raid into northern Israel, ambushing an Israel Defense Force patrol, killing three soldiers, and abducting two as hostages for ransom. When Israel sent in an armored column to rescue its soldiers, Hezbollah unleashed a pre-planned missile attack across the entire northern border. At the moment I write this, more than a million Israelis are living in bomb shelters, driven there by more than 2,000 missile hits this week.

I look across a deserted intersection in the normally bustling seaside town of Nahariya, where I've come to comfort the Goldwasser family, whose thirty-one-year-old reservist son, Ehud, was one of the two kidnapped soldiers. Ehud's wife showed me her wedding album. They'd been married just nine months. My heart broke, and I wept with this brave man's family. They are still in shock at his capture. Hezbollah wants to trade the kidnapped soldiers for Palestinian terrorists being held in Israeli prisons.

Israel is such a small and close-knit country that I was not surprised when we were joined at the Goldwasser home by the fathers of two other kidnapped soldiers, Eldad Regev, who was kidnapped with Ehud, and Gilad Shalit, who was abducted from his post near the Gaza Strip two weeks earlier by Hamas infiltrators. Neither was I surprised to learn that Ehud's younger brother is a special forces soldier waiting for the word to go into Lebanon with his unit to join the search for his brother.

I am accompanied on this trip by the camera crew, field producer, and a close friend from the States. We are filming a television special based on this book that will tell the story in pictures of Iran's involvement in the Israel-Lebanon War. Our next stop is Nahariya's Government Hospital, where the patients have been moved underground to protect them from rocket fire. It's the only hospital this close to the northern border and so has taken in 463 wounded so far, thirty-three of them soldiers. Even inside the building we can hear Israeli artillery firing into Lebanon, which is just eight miles away.

Before leaving town for the border, we pause for a moment a few blocks from the hospital to ponder the wreckage of an apartment destroyed by a direct hit from a Katyusha rocket. Its owner was killed while sitting on her porch.

We ride for some twenty minutes toward the northern front, passing the hulks of two crashed helicopters and glimpsing fires on the distant hills caused by our artillery shells. We pass the farming village of Meron. Seven-year-old Omer Pesachov of Nahariya came here to stay with his grandmother, Yehudit Itzkovitch, to be safe from the Katyushas. They were killed in her kitchen by a direct hit.

From Meron we ride a few moments farther north and join soldiers manning a battery of giant mobile artillery. We press palms to ears as the crew fires round after round of heavy shells at the Hezbollah rocket launchers across the border. I pray that innocent Lebanese civilians escape the consequences of Hezbollah deliberately placing its launchers among their homes. Despite this despicable use of human shields, I know that Israel has no choice but to fight back at an enemy that respects no human life in its fanaticism, not even the lives of its own people.

Despite the Katyushas falling as never before, we decide the safest place to stay for the night is Haifa. This beautiful bayside city had become Hezbollah's prime target, not because of its industry, but because its mixed Jewish and Arab population has made it Israel's symbol of peaceful coexistence. Civilians from both groups are among the victims.

As darkness falls, I stand with the earth shaking beneath my feet from the guns pounding and think how ironic it is that the peaceful Galilee of the scriptures was being brought to the very brink of Armageddon by Hezbollah, a proxy of the Iranian government, on its unholy mission to destroy Israel in the name of world jihad.

○
○ ○

Visiting the city's main Rambam Hospital the next morning with Mayor Yona Yahav, we meet a survivor of a direct hit on a local railway maintenance shed. Eight of his fellow workers were killed. The terrorists packed a Katyusha warhead with dozens of ball bearings to maximize the lethality and damage. The wounded man's life was saved at the last minute by a surgeon who extracted one of the steel balls from his heart.

After staying a while, we make for the exit only to hear the air raid sirens wail once again. We hustle back inside to the shelter to wait out another attack. Next to a bomb shelter, the best place to wait out a rocket attack is a hospital, I suppose. Amid the chaos, I can't help but think how Iran has masterminded this crisis to divert international attention from its nuclear weapons program. Iran's hope is to distract the G8 nations which include Canada, France, Germany, Italy, Japan, Russia, the UK, and the US, from their attempt to keep Iran from carrying out its declared plan to wipe Israel off the map. The tactic seems to be working.

Iran's proxy in Lebanon, Hezbollah warlord Hassan Nasrallah, has promised to deliver "surprises" to Israel—like the shore-to-ship missile Iranian Revolutionary Guards fired at an Israel Navy ship off the coast of Beirut, killing four sailors. Iran's long-range Katyushas have brought all of northern Israel within killing range, as far south as Tiberias on the Sea of Galilee. These missiles cannot be guided, only aimed toward the general direction of as many Israeli civilian targets as possible.

We wait for the all-clear, and my thoughts move to an image I saw on Israeli television the previous night. The show was a discussion of the options for the safe return of Hezbollah and Hamas' Israeli hostages. The moderator was interviewing Hayim Avraham, whose son had been captured with two comrades by Hezbollah in October 2000. In January 2004, Israel traded some 400 Hezbollah terrorist prisoners for the three soldiers' bodies. My heart tore as I saw the weeping Avraham shout into the camera, "They kidnapped my son and they murdered him! And now the liberal media and the UN are screaming for Israel to show restraint. Shut up, Kofi Annan! You're killing us!"

At last, we leave the hospital and ascend Mount Carmel, the same site where Elijah prophesied, for an interdenominational peace service. But there is no peace. Air raid sirens twice interrupt our worship, and the congregation moves swiftly to the church bomb shelter.

Later in the day, Mayor Yahav accompanies us to Haifa's Emergency Command Center, which is fielding some 6,000 calls each day during the crisis. A few blocks away we view a small, three-story apartment building that took a direct hit from a Katyusha and collapsed into rubble. I pick up a fragment of shrapnel and remember a similar scene on a Beirut beachfront in October 1983. By grim coincidence, I had been there on a similar newsgathering mission on the day a Hezbollah suicide bomber had detonated himself outside a US Marines barracks, murdering 241 of our peacekeepers. It was now twenty-three years later, but the same terrorists were still packing their bombs with ball bearings for maximum carnage.

o

o o

In the evening, we head for Jerusalem. For once, the city is far from the front line, though our drive is slowed several times by impromptu roadblocks responding to alerts for possible attacks by suicide bombers. Before we reach the capital, the car radio announces the capture of a terrorist suspect and the cancellation of the alert. Earlier in Haifa we had counted six air raid alerts before we left, resulting in six missile hits and several casualties, but at least no deaths. All in all, there were twenty-eight rocket attacks in the North during this long day of destruction.

I think about the wife of the man whose heart was pierced by the deadly ball bearing from the rocket. She told me how he had phoned her in the middle of the night from his hospital bed during an air raid alert, unable to breathe as the sirens sounded. The doctors had saved his heart from the rocket, but it will take much more time to overcome the fear.

The common answer given by everyone we interviewed was that it makes no difference to the terrorists whether their victims are Jews or Christians or even fellow Muslims—just as it makes no difference to the terrorists whether their target is "the Great Satan" America or "the Little Satan" Israel. Both countries are in the terrorists' sights and are slated for destruction in their perverted dreams of world jihad. Wrapped up in the turmoil of the Mideast for the last three decades, I cannot avoid the thought that this same terrorism will move west toward America for another 9/11 unless it is stopped here and now by Israel.

I turn on this thought as we pass Ben-Gurion Airport on the highway to Jerusalem and my eye catches the unmistakable shape of a giant C-5 Galaxy on a distant runway. The US Air Force transport has apparently just arrived to replenish supplies Israel needs in its fight against Hezbollah. It is a heartwarming sight. For the first time in my life, a US president completely supports Israel's struggle. Every other president, at one time or another, caved to the pressures of oil-market manipulation by Arab leaders, all of whom have been openly hostile to Israel and whose own countries are repressive Islamic dictatorships.

Ascending the Judean Hills to Israel's capital, the highway passes a dozen roadside memorials to its 1948 War of Independence: the preserved hulks of homemade armored buses and trucks destroyed by Arab marauders as they tried to lift the siege of Jerusalem. I am struck once again by the incomprehensible thought that Israel is still fighting its War of Independence fifty-eight years later.

For nearly six decades, Israelis have been struggling to survive in the face of near total Arab hostility. At last America has a president who understands this daunting reality and who stands up to a world whose media cries crocodile tears over the "occupation" of the Palestinians—as if Palestinian terrorism began after the Six Day War in 1967.

Bush knows that Israel accepted the two-state solution voted on by the UN in November 1947, creating the two nations of

Israel and Palestine, and that the Palestinians and their fellow Arabs rejected this peaceful solution to the conflict. He knows that it took several decades and more wars for Egypt and then Jordan to make peace with Israel, while the Palestinians still delude themselves that suicide bombers and Kassam missiles will destroy the Jewish state. He knows that Iran created Hezbollah in 1982 as its proxy in the battle against Israel and that Teheran is using Hezbollah and sacrificing hundreds of innocent Lebanese to distract the world while it pursues nuclear weapons.

Bush also knows that Iran has simultaneously begun an assault on two DCs: Jerusalem DC (David's Capital) and Washington DC. The Islamists of Teheran fully believe they have the power to build nuclear arms and use them to take over the entire Middle East by terrorizing it, undermining moderates, and pursuing the demented belief that global jihad will hasten the arrival of the so-called Twelfth Imam, the Mahdi, to establish Muslim rule over the entire world. Bush realizes that Iran's unhinged, fanatic President Mahmoud Ahmadinejad is striving not only for a world without Israel but also for a world without America.

○
○ ○

In Israel's capital we begin an intensive round of interviews with political and military leaders for their input on the crisis.

Reservist Major General Yossi Peled, a former head of the Israel Defense Forces Northern Command and a knowledgeable adversary of Hezbollah, tells me, "The IDF's mission today is to strike at Hezbollah with such force that the movement won't survive. Even though Iran is hiding behind Hezbollah, we must focus on the immediate threats against Israel. And these are coming from Hezbollah, Lebanon, and Syria."

Peled knows more than most Israelis about "immediate threats." He survived the Holocaust as a young boy in Belgium, when his mother placed him in the care of a Christian family who raised him as their own. She survived the Nazi Auschwitz death camp, reclaimed her son, and brought him to Israel, where he grew up to be a great defender of his people.

The Lord knows how difficult this is on the actual battlefield, but it has also become harder in the battlefield of public opinion where the news media "reporting" from Lebanon have been engaged in dumbing down the world, taking as gospel everything they are fed by Hezbollah, while turning a blind eye on Hezbollah's use of civilians as human shields. These networks have been serving as Hezbollah's agents of indoctrination, painting the poor Lebanese as "martyrs" on the one hand, while barely acknowledging the suffering of the Israeli civilians on the other.

Media expert Mitchell Bard made the point quite clearly: "A CNN reporter is taken to an area of Beirut and told that the rubble of buildings is a result of Israeli air strikes on civilian targets. The reporter repeats the allegation as fact. He has no way of knowing what was in the buildings, whether it was a rocket workshop, a hiding place for Katyushas, the home of a Hezbollah leader, or a command center. In fact, he doesn't even know if Israel was responsible for the destruction that he is shown. In waging their propaganda war, Israel's enemies count on journalists to report first and research later, if at all, and CNN and other media outlets have fallen into their trap."

Bard recalled perhaps the most dramatic example of Arab disinformation from the previous war in Lebanon, when the *Washington Post* published a photo on 2 August 1982 of a Lebanese baby that appeared to have lost both its arms. "The UPI caption said that the seven-month-old had been severely burned when an Israeli jet accidentally hit a Christian residential area. The photo disgusted President Reagan and was one reason he subsequently called for Israel to halt its attacks. The photo and the caption, however, were inaccurate. The baby, in fact, did not lose its arms, and the burns the child suffered were the result of a PLO attack on East Beirut."

Despite Western journalists and talking heads "reporting" from their five-star hotel rooms on unchecked casualty statistics supplied by Hezbollah, it goes without saying that there would be no Lebanese casualties if Hezbollah had not perpetrated an unprovoked attack on Israel in the first place. And how many poignant interviews have the US media conducted with Lebanese civilians and their relatives in the States, compared with how many interviews with some of the more than one million Israelis living in bomb shelters, or their relatives abroad?

"Similarly," Bard points out, "every report has focused on the Americans living in Lebanon, while no one seems interested in the thousands of Americans living in Israel. It is terrible that tourists and students are having to be evacuated from Lebanon, but what about those same groups in Israel? What about the hundreds of students on summer tours and programs in Israel, many of whom were in the North when the violence escalated?"

Former Prime Minister Binyamin Netanyahu, besides being the author of four books on fighting terrorism, is the leader of Israel's opposition Likud Party. He notes with satisfaction that the international community appears to be lining up with the US to pressure Hezbollah's patrons, Iran and Syria. Israel has already signaled its readiness to consider the stationing of a multinational force in southern Lebanon, which can happen "once Israel breaks Hezbollah's ability to terrorize our population militarily."

Netanyahu was one of the first to articulate Iran's complicity in

Islam's worldwide jihad, calling the 9/11 attacks "America's wakeup call from Hell." In recent testimony before a Senate committee, he warned that Iran would use Hezbollah attacks on Israel to divert attention from its nuclear ambitions. "For now, they're winning," he said but noted that, "These insane people hate Christians as much as they hate Jews."

This point is echoed by General Peled, who says Israel's Jews are now in effect in the position of fighting to save America's Christians, since the battle had shifted to a decisive confrontation between Iran's proxy, Hezbollah, and Israel, which the Islamists consider America's proxy in the region, "the Little Satan."

Israel's former UN Ambassador Dore Gold focused on the infamous speech delivered by Iran's Ahmadinejad, in which he declared that Iran would "wipe Israel off of the map." But Gold, who heads the Jerusalem Center for Public Affairs think-tank, also points out that, like Hitler, Ahmadinejad is aiming at bigger conquest: first the Middle East, then an Islamic-dominated world without "the Great Satan," the United States. Gold noted that the Iranians have not only supplied their Hezbollah proxy with Fajr missiles capable of hitting Haifa some 70 kilometers inside Israel but are also extending the range of their own Shahab-3 missiles so they can reach Europe. "Defeating Iran's opening shot in this Middle Eastern war is not just Israel's interest," he concluded, "but the collective interest of the entire civilized world."

This point was also stressed by Minister Isaac Herzog, who, until the Hezbollah aggression, was preparing to celebrate the record recovery of Israel's tourism industry after years of slump due to Palestinian terrorism. Israel and other moderate nations must oppose Iran, he said, calling it "this extreme lunatic coalition, this axis of evil that ranges from Teheran to Damascus to the Hezbollah." He agreed that Iran had initiated the current crisis to divert attention from its nuclear program and said this is because Teheran is approaching nuclear self-sufficiency. "We do not have years left," Herzog said, "but months."

Former Mossad chief Danny Yatom confirms that members of Iran's Revolutionary Guards have been launching Hezbollah's longer-range rockets, like the ones that have been hitting Haifa. "The finger that pulled the trigger was an Iranian finger," he says, noting that the rank and file Hezbollah terrorists have been entrusted by their Iranian patrons with firing the shorter-range Katyushas but not the more complicated longer-range Fajr missiles. These, he adds, are not as portable as the Katyushas but must be launched from fixed sites, e.g., the houses of innocent Lebanese villagers. Israel has no choice but to destroy these missile sites in order to protect its own civilians, a cold calculation Hezbollah takes into account by deliberately using civilians as disposable human shields, then crying foul about Israel targeting civilians.

While Yatom is confident that Israel will soon prevail over Hezbollah in Lebanon, he is raising the alarm over Iran's accelerating nuclear weapons program, which he is certain it will try to deploy. Iran must be stopped: "If there is no intervention, and we sit idle, then the Iranians will be able to achieve their nuclear capability in a few years, a very short period of time, as a matter of fact. Because we have to take into consideration that, once the Iranians have in their possession a nuclear bomb or a nuclear attacking capability, they will consider using it against Israel."

It is a sobering thought as we return to our Jerusalem hotel and prepare to return to America. As we pack, the television news announces the latest casualties of the Hezbollah missile fire: a fifteen-year-old Muslim girl, killed when a rocket struck her home near a mosque in the Galilee village of Maghar, home to Druze as well as Arab Christians and Muslims. In downtown Haifa, an elderly man collapsed and died of a heart attack as he ran toward a bomb shelter, and another fifty people were wounded throughout northern Israel.

We watch as the camera pans over the Hezbollah quarter of Beirut, an exclusive zone which the terrorist organization had sealed off from the rest of the city and which the Israel Air Force has reduced to rubble in an effort to kill Hezbollah leader Hassan Nasrallah. The scene clearly shows how the government of Lebanon bears responsibility for the Hezbollah aggression. It allowed Hezbollah to establish itself as a state-within-a-state, providing it with official legitimacy and allowing its attacks to proceed unhindered.

Hezbollah obtained its stockpile of some 12,000 missiles along Israel's northern border because the Lebanese government allowed this weaponry to be delivered by air from Teheran and over land from Damascus. Hezbollah's aggression would not have been possible were it not for the failure of the Lebanese government to fulfill its obligation as a sovereign state to extend its control over its own territory and disarm Hezbollah, as called for by Security Council Resolutions 425 and 1559.

Hezbollah and Hamas, backed by Iran and Syria, are driven by an extremist jihadist ideology which calls for the immediate destruction of Israel. But, as Gold points out, the war cry is not limited to Israel, and the world will ignore it at its peril, for the recent actions of the Hezbollah-Hamas-Iran-Syria axis are merely the opening moves in an international strategy to wage holy war against the entire "infidel" Western world so that Islam may conquer the globe.

In the post-9/11 reality, security authorities worldwide are preoccupied with protecting their populations against the threat of ever more terrible scenarios: preventing weapons of mass destruction that could strike down entire cities by spreading some hideous plague, or detonating a suitcase-sized nuclear device. And the one country that today represents the worst threat to world security in terms of its proven record of support for Islamist terrorism and defiant pursuit of a nuclear capability is Iran.

No one should think Iran's "Islamic revolution" is over. The Islamic republic's present rulers have not abandoned the world view of their founder, Grand Ayatollah Ruhollah Khomeini, who declared Saudi Arabia's rulers unfit to be the guardians of Islam's holiest cities, Mecca and Medina, and who first branded the US "the Great Satan."

Sanctions have not stopped Iran from exporting its Islamic revolution to Shi'ite-controlled Lebanon and sponsoring Hezbollah terrorism against Israel. And now the International Atomic Energy Agency is sounding the alarm about Iran's nuclear development.

Iran seems to be on the verge of becoming a nuclear power despite the best efforts of the US and the world community to prevent it. The time for diplomacy is running out, while Iran's nuclear arms program approaches critical mass.

"When I read the recent [intelligence] reports regarding Iran, I saw a monster in the making," said Dr. Yuval Steinitz, chair of the Israeli Knesset's foreign and defense committee. He is concerned that Iran's ability to build a nuclear bomb may be as little as a year away. "There is only one option that is worse than military action," he said, "and that is to sit by and do nothing."

The questions we face are very real and very disturbing:

- Just who is Iranian President Mahmoud Ahmadinejad?

- How does his belief in the Twelfth Imam (the Mahdi) influence his presidency?

- Is he willing to precipitate an apocalyptic event with worldwide repercussions to prepare for the return of the Mahdi?

- How will Israel respond to Iran's nuclear proliferation?

- Is there a way to thwart Iran's advance in the nuclear arms race?

- Will diplomacy work?

- How will the United States respond if sanctions against Iran are ineffective?

- What would happen if Israel or America were to attack Iran's nuclear facilities?

- What are the roles of Russia, China, Pakistan, and other nations in the conflict?

- How much time do we really have until the showdown with nuclear Iran is upon us?

We will explore these and other questions in the pages that follow. One thing is certain right now: We are at a historic moment where the very survival of the Jewish state hangs in the balance. Iran is determined to tighten the vise—pursuing nuclear weapons on a fast track, while unleashing Hezbollah and Hamas to crank up the pressure. Israel can survive, but only if the Jewish state remains steadfast in the determination to defend itself at all costs and America is ultimately willing to back up its most valued ally in the Middle East. Facing the religious zealots who control the Iranian regime, a conflict of biblical proportions is building.

To see what may be in store, the prologue that immediately follows offers a fictional glimpse at the very possible horrors ahead.

MICHAEL D. EVANS
22 July 2006, Israel

Prologue

OPERATION: MAHDI

SOMEWHERE BETWEEN ALEXANDRIA, EGYPT AND GAZA

It had been a long night for Abdul al-Jawad. The monotonous trek from Alexandria to Rafah, near the border with Gaza, gave him too much time to think about his role in the coordinated apocalyptic events that were about to unfold—the events that would bring about the collapse of the revolution's two most hated foes, the "Great Satan" (America) and the "Little Satan" (Israel).

Abdul smiled and silently saluted Iran's president as his words flowed like cool, sparkling water through the channels of his mind. The Zionist regime was a rotten, dry tree that would be eliminated by one storm. Its existence had harmed the dignity of Islamic nations far too long. The United States was a plague that had hatched plots against Iran, Iraq, Syria, and Lebanon in an attempt to bring the entire Middle East under the control of the Zionists. Abdul was confident that its machinations would not succeed.

In joyful anticipation, Abdul reached through the open window and slapped his hand against the side of the truck. The Arabic characters on the side read "Building Materials." He knew what was really inside and chuckled when he thought of the irony.

Abdul reached into his pocket and pulled out a pack of Gauloises. He much preferred these Western European cigarettes to the more-popular American brands. The flare from the match illuminated the cab of the truck, and in the brief glow, Abdul could see the sleeping form of his oldest son, Abdullah. He reached over and lightly stroked the teen's hair and whispered, "Sleep, son. Tomorrow, a new day will dawn for Islam."

Abdul thought that day had come years earlier when his uncle, Sheikh Abdul Rahman, and his radical Muslim Brotherhood executed what was to be the first of a series of deadly attacks in America. Abdul grinned as he thought about how stupid the Americans had been. They welcomed his uncle into their country, completely oblivious to the fact that they were taking a snake into their bosom.

Of course, everyone thought his Uncle Abdul had failed. *Not so*. He had merely galvanized Osama bin Laden into planning and executing the most deadly attack ever on US soil. That's the one thing the Americans didn't understand about the *shaheed*; these martyrs were content to wait and plot for years, until the time was right.

As he drove through the night toward Gaza, the prophecies of Ayatollah Khomeini also floated through his mind. Khomeini had predicted that first the Shah of Iran, Mohammad Reza Shah Pahlavi, would be dethroned; an Islamic revolution would be birthed in Iran; and then the Soviet Union would fall. This would be followed by the collapse of Saddam Hussein's regime, and his country would be burned by fire. Next would come the annihilation of Israel and the collapse of the United States. Abdul believed he had been chosen by Allah to prepare the way for the age of the Mahdi, when Shi'ite Islam would spread across the world to destroy all other apostate religions. "At last, I am preparing the way," Abdul rejoiced.

Abdul, a Shi'ite, believed in the second coming of the Mahdi, the Twelfth Imam, who disappeared centuries ago down a well in Qom, Iran. This messianic vision required a world apocalypse to bring his return. "If an apocalypse would usher in the Mahdi," he thought, "then we will shut the mouth of Satan for all eternity."

His mind wandered back to the days when he was chosen to become one of the Grand Ayatollah's "Children of the Imam," the youngsters that were destined for training in the ways of martyrdom. In July 1981, he was part of a group of approximately 150 hand-picked and trained young men who graduated from Iran's most elite and secret training camp. These dedicated devotees of the Grand Ayatollah Ruhollah Khomeini were thoroughly prepared for service to the Imam.

As they filed across the parade grounds during their graduation ceremony, each student was presented with a framed portrait of Khomeini, a copy of the Qur'an, and a leather armband containing a verse from the Qur'an that purportedly protected the wearer from evil. The ceremony was ominously silent. There were no celebrations with family, no shouts of congratulations, not one word of publicity. The camp and its trainees were shrouded in secrecy.

Two weeks following the furtive graduation ceremony, Abdul and the other cadets were presented to Khomeini. Following the meeting, each graduate fell heir to a plastic-covered piece of the Ayatollah's turban. This graduating class, endowed with the task of exporting the revolution to an unsuspecting world, had apparently been granted Khomeini's seal of approval. The young men were ready to return to their homelands and spread the gospel of Khomeini's Islamic revolution.

Suddenly, Abdul was jerked back to the present. There it was—the laser signal from the *wadi*. His al-Qaeda contact, Hamid, was waiting for him. Abdul eased the big truck and trailer loaded with its deadly cargo onto the edge of the road. He crushed the stub of his cigarette into the cab floor, opened the door, and greeted the man with the traditional greeting, the left hand on the right shoulder and a kiss on each cheek.

Over Hamid's shoulder, Abdul could see the lights from the Bedouin tents where his Hamas and al-Qaeda brothers waited to take charge of the cargo. As Abdul followed Nasser across the sands to the tents, he breathed the oath he had taken as one of the Children of the Imam: "In the name of Allah the Avenger and in the name of Imam Khomeini I swear on the Holy Book to perform my sacred duty as a Child of the Imam and a Soldier of Islam in our Holy War to restore to this world the Light of Divine Justice. May Allah be my Guide on the Path of Jihad."

At his graduation from the secret training camp in Iran, Abdul had received a red headband identifying him as a "Volunteer for Martyrdom." Tonight, the coveted headband was taped inside his *galabea*, next to his heart. He was ready to meet his destiny. His only wish was that he had a headband blessed by the Imam to present to his son. Abdul reached inside his *galabea*, untaped the red headband, and slipped it over his brow.

Abdul didn't see the man armed with a silenced pistol slip out of the shadows and fall into step behind him and Hamid. Nor did he feel the bullet that bore through the back of his skull. And, mercifully, Abdul never knew that his beloved son was the target of an assassin's bullet as he slept.

It would be days before a pack of wild dogs uncovered the bodies of Abdul al-Jawad and his son. In the feeding frenzy that followed, the treasured headband, a remnant of Abdul's days as one of Khomeini's "Children of the Imam," was torn to shreds.

WHITE HOUSE PRESS CONFERENCE

In Washington DC, President Jack Hedges was just finishing a press conference in the East Room with the president of France. The two heads of state were ecstatic over the outcome of negotiations between the EU, the US, Russia, China, and Iran.

For months after Iran confirmed that it did, indeed, possess a nuclear bomb, the world had lived in fear that President Hamahdi would launch an attack against Israel and/or America. Today, they had proved to the world that there was no reason for such paranoia.

Fielding a question from an Egyptian reporter, the French President René Valois replied, "There was no reason for the world to live in fear. Yes, they do have the bomb, but détente worked, negotiations worked. We can all sleep more easily tonight knowing that Iran is now a part of the family of nations."

WHITE HOUSE STATE DINNER, WASHINGTON DC

The president of the United States raised his champagne flute in salute to President Valois. It had been a long and arduous day of negotiations on a nuclear test ban policy with Iran. With a hint of a smile, the president whispered his thanks to God that although the road had been long and hard, reasonable minds had at last prevailed, in spite of the bloodshed.

President Hedges unwillingly relived the months preceding the negotiations with Iran. Hundreds of sleeper cells across the nation had been activated. Suicide bombings in America had mirrored the deadly attacks in the heart of Jerusalem during Yasser Arafat's *intifada* days. Buses and commuter trains became rolling targets for explosives-laden *shaheeds* (martyrs) intent on bringing America to her knees through fear.

Churches, schools, and shopping malls in New York City, Los Angeles, Chicago, Dallas, and Atlanta were selected for destruction by the merciless suicide bombers during peak attendance hours. It had been a deadly and bloody time, unlike anything Americans had ever endured.

Now, America and the world could breathe a sigh of relief that a nuclear holocaust precipitated by President Hamahdi had been averted.

ONE YEAR EARLIER, IN KARACHI, PAKISTAN

Brigadier General Hossein Shirazi was paying a rare midnight visit to Mr. Nabih Osmani. Osmani was the director general of Pakistan Shipping Lines in the port city of Karachi, on the east side of the Arabian Sea. General Shirazi was reveling in his new role as commander of the Iranian Air Force. Osmani knew that Shirazi's new responsibilities included full charge of Iran's ballistic missile program, a key component in Iran's plan to become a global Islamic superpower.

Shirazi sank into one of the plush chairs in Osmani's office and accepted the glass of tea from Osmani's servant. A taciturn man, General Shirazi went directly to the point. "We have some particular specifications for one of the new container ships you are building," he said, referring to one of six new bulk container ships to be built completely in Pakistan.

Osmani had made a name for himself the previous year by exceeding his goal of successfully transporting over 600,000 containers even with his outdated fleet. Osmani had put Pakistan on the map as a major exporter. Osmani was, himself, a supporter of the revolution. He had graduated from one of the *madrassas* in Pakistan, and had even fought beside bin Laden's son in Iraq.

"What will you require?" Osmani asked politely.

Shirazi explained that he wanted a special compartment built on the cargo deck. "It needs to fit these dimensions," he explained, handing a page of specifications to Osmani, "about twice the length of your largest container, and about twice as high."

Osmani quickly did the calculations. The largest standard container was commonly eight feet wide, almost nine feet tall, forty feet long, and could weigh up to twenty tons. Could Shirazi's special container be destined to transport a military vehicle, maybe even a missile launcher? If Shirazi was involved, that was more than likely.

"Will this special container need to be off-loaded?" Osmani asked.

He knew that dock-side cranes were built to handle standard-size containers. It was unlikely that an ordinary crane would be able to handle this massive container, especially if it had to be moved several times before reaching its final destination.

"No," Shirazi replied. "It will be a permanent fixture of the ship. Another thing; we need the compartment to be made with a lead lining and a door that opens at the front end."

Pulling a handful of technical sketches from his briefcase, Shirazi continued, "You will have to construct the compartment so you can completely cover it with your normal container load. We want the compartment to be totally hidden from air or satellite surveillance. We also want you to design your deck so we can deploy a vehicle from the compartment. You must be able to quickly and completely clear the deck above the container."

Osmani, the engineer turned multimillionaire, made sketches in his mind while calculating how he might accommodate the general's request. He figured if Shirazi were planning to launch a missile, it would be fired at sea. But it didn't matter. Osmani knew his only job would be to build whatever Shirazi instructed, preferably without asking why.

RAFAH, EGYPT, NEAR THE GAZA BORDER

Shrouded from air surveillance just outside Rafah was what appeared to be an ordinary community of Bedouins. Inside the tented compound, a specially trained Revolutionary Guard team of seven engineers and two scientists was hard at work. Despite the shaggy camels staked outside the tents, inside was some of the most advanced scientific monitoring equipment in the world. The scientists had been well-trained for this job before being dispatched to Egypt, posing as a group of archaeologists searching for clues to ancient civilizations. They unpacked the contents of the two lead-lined containers with extreme care. The team needed no instructions on how the components were to be assembled.

Once assembled, the unit was packed inside a semi-truck trailer and checked to make sure everything was operational. Two engineers and one scientist stayed behind in Rafah; the others prepared to return to Cairo for their trip back to Iran.

The specially adapted Shahab-3 missile with its launch trailer occupied its own tent. At the appointed time, the covering would be pulled aside, the missile would be fueled, and its deadly cargo would be readied for launch. The unit was ready for delivery; all the team needed was final instructions.

ABOARD OSMANI'S FREIGHTER, SHADOW-3

The *Shadow-3*, one of Nabih Osmani's prized new container ships, had dropped anchor outside the Port of New York just as darkness fell. Sailing under the Panamanian flag afforded a certain measure of anonymity and blurred the paper trail that could lead back to its Pakistani owners. Hidden aboard the ship in a specially-built, lead-lined container was the revolution's gift to the American people. The captain and the team of Revolutionary Guards onboard were all dedicated *shaheeds*. Each knew he might have to pay the ultimate price to attain Paradise. The unsuspecting crew readied the ship for inspection by the Port Authority the following morning.

The encoded message was received by the ship's captain at 6:00 AM EST in Washington DC. After a cursory glance, the captain handed the envelope to the Revolutionary Guard commander in charge of the special cargo. With a curt nod, the commander turned sharply and went to ready his crew. The six-man team, handpicked by none other than President Hamahdi, had practiced daily since setting sail from Karachi.

One team member manned the giant overhead crane positioned amidships. With a practiced hand, he swiftly plucked one of the four empty containers that concealed the special compartment from prying eyes and dropped it in the ocean. The other three decoy containers rapidly followed. Two team members moved to the panel that controlled the hydraulic door on the special container. Each man punched in his portion of the code needed to activate the giant door.

As it swung up and out of the way, the fourth man raced inside and eased into the seat of the Russian-built missile launcher, technically identified as an MAZ 534 transport erector launcher. As the huge launcher crept slowly forward, the erector began its slow rise, lifting the fifty-three-foot-long Shahab-3 missile skyward. Countdown to launch began.

To the unsuspecting population across the northeastern United States, it was simply six o'clock on another mundane Wednesday morning in April. School children were being roused from their warm beds; moms were setting out cereal bowls and making lunches; dads were grabbing their first cup of coffee before the long commute to work; and congressional members were preparing for the long Passover/Easter weekend. People readied for their workday all across the eastern seaboard.

In California, it was 3:00 AM. In a few hours, the alarms of those workers with long commutes on the Los Angeles freeways would begin to squawk. No one anywhere in America knew at that moment the United States was about to be the target of a nuclear missile attack that would totally incapacitate the nation. Nor would they suspect that the one-missile attack was the first of a two-blow assault.

At exactly 6:30 AM EST, the word was given to ignite the solid-fuel missile. With the push of a button, the missile roared to life and slowly lifted from the ship's deck. A surveillance satellite circling overhead photographed the launch and sent the digital pictures hurtling earthward. The young man who might have issued the warning was momentarily distracted. He was downloading a new song to his iPod.

Emerging from their hiding place in the safety of the lead-lined container, the Revolutionary Guard commander saluted the missile with its deadly cargo before turning back to his team. He barked an order in Farsi and the team sprang into action. As the missile disappeared over the horizon, the cumbersome launcher was rolled back into its compartment and tarpaulins draped overhead to conceal it from view. The plan had worked perfectly.

In less than a second after the launch, alarm bells went off in the Cheyenne Mountains Operation Center of the North American Aerospace Defense Command (NORAD). On the large central display, the point of the launch in the Atlantic was flashing. The center's computers displayed the trajectory and impact point—near the western Beltway of Washington DC. Impact time was predicted at three minutes, forty-nine seconds from launch.

The NORAD operations center was thrown into frenzy as personnel rushed to their duty stations and started studying their computer displays.

Air Force Brigadier General Jack Simpson, the chief duty officer, immediately called Admiral Timothy Keating, the commander of NORAD, who was out of the center at the moment, but nearby. Admiral Keating ordered General Simpson to call the White House immediately, as well as the Chief Duty Officer at the Pentagon. Alerted by the call, the president's chief of staff rose from his desk to head toward the Oval Office, rushing to alert the president. But time had run out.

The Shehab-3 "shooting star" missile carried a one-ton 550-kiloton enriched-uranium nuclear warhead. The missile with its deadly payload was right on target, heading for Washington DC. Traveling at a speed of 4,300 MPH, the Shahab-3 traveled for about 180 seconds before detonating at an altitude of nearly 80,000 feet, some fifteen miles above Washington DC. This lone Shahab missile exploded at just the right altitude and reacted with the earth's atmosphere.

In scientific circles, the missile-one detonation was known as an EMP attack, or Electromagnetic Pulse. The warhead detonated above the earth as programmed, instantly producing a barrage of gamma rays that radiated down to the earth's surface at the speed of light. Billions of electrons were scattered at high energies, ionizing the atmosphere and generating a powerful electrical field. The EMP was so brief a flash that no damage was done to the human bodies or the buildings through which the pulse passed. In fact, the actual nuclear blast was barely a flash visible to the naked eye.

US satellite sensors picked up the blast and signaled the NORAD Operations Center. It was unclear exactly what had happened, but when General Simpson called the White House again, there was no signal on the line. It was as if someone had ripped up the phone lines. The same results were evident for the calls to the Pentagon.

In a radius moving out from Washington at the speed of light, the EMP reached instantly across a radius of several hundred miles, as far as to the outskirts of Boston. Instantly, the pulse destroyed all generators within a direct line of sight. As failures in the electric grid cascaded, in a matter of minutes every electrical grid covering Washington, Philadelphia, and New York was knocked offline. The White House, the Pentagon, the CIA, and the National Security Agency were rendered inoperable. Isolated communications pockets within these centers that were shielded were still semi-functional. The problem was that connecting with anyone was nearly impossible.

Every computer in the blast radius went dark in a flash. Hundreds of thousands of people were trapped in elevators. Chain-reaction car accidents were repeated across the northeastern section of the country as every traffic light in Washington, Philadelphia, and New York, as well as the countryside and small towns in between, went dead. Most cars in the blast radius came to abrupt halts as the electronics (upon which systems as basic as fuel injectors function) ceased to work.

Cell phones in the area affected by the blast became worthless, and military high priority top-secret systems were useless, including those connecting out of the CIA and the National Security Agency. Reaching NORAD in Washington was impossible.

Nothing that depended upon electricity or electronics worked. In the flash of an instant, key cities in the northeastern United States went black, rendering 150 years of technological advancement worthless.

Washington, Philadelphia, and Boston were reduced to a technological state that pre-dated the invention of the telephone or the light bulb. Hospital patients died when doctors were stopped in mid-operation and surgical equipment, including respirators, quit functioning. Thousands of airline passengers fell miles to frightful deaths as airplane engines flying through this zone failed and sophisticated jetliners fell from high altitudes. Power failures in the eastern US were rapidly triggering system failures all the way to California.

The panic was immediate. All command communications reaching from Washington to our military forces around the world just shut down. Attempts to bring them back were fruitless.

The world's superpower with its advanced technological prowess was rendered helpless by the explosion of one relatively low-yield nuclear warhead high over Washington. The attack had come from what had been long-perceived as a third-rate Middle East power. The Iranians had figured out how to come in under the radar and launch a successful sneak-attack on America. Like the attack on 9/11, they had discovered a way to use America's own technology against her and disarm her otherwise sophisticated state-of-the-art, missile-defense systems.

Nationwide panic followed quickly. With no communications, transportation, refrigeration, water resources, or medical help, a crisis of pandemic proportions had gripped the United States. Nobody in America was communicating, not above the distance the sound of their voices would carry. Was America under attack? If so, how would our government or military determine who had attacked us? We could launch a nuclear counterattack, but who was the target? And how could we find a way to make our missile systems work without electricity or electronics? And how would Americans know that the horror had just begun?

ABOARD OSMANI'S FREIGHTER, GRAND AYATOLLAH

All preparations for phase two of the attack had been completed. The Revolutionary Guard team stood silently by, eyes glued to the chronometer as the seconds ticked away. Their encoded instructions had been received: "Launch at 6:30 AM EST." Like their counterparts aboard the *Shadow-3,* this team, too, had practiced daily since departing from Karachi. Now they were 250 miles off the coast of Norfolk, Virginia, aboard the *Grand Ayatollah* and ready to fire.

During the night hours, the deck of the container ship had been cleared, exposing the doors of the secret compartment. The men knew that by sunrise, there would no longer be a need to hide their deadly cargo.

At 5:00 AM EST, the giant doors were opened and the huge Soviet-built MAZ 534 transport erector launcher crept into view. Identical to the launcher aboard the *Shadow-3,* this vehicle, too, carried a Shahab-3 missile. With a measured step, the ship's captain approached the team commander and handed him the final GPS coordinates to be programmed into the guidance system— the White House, Washington DC. The commander couldn't help but smile as he looked at the piece of paper. "Thanks be to Allah for the Internet," he thought. "Even the most extraordinary information is available with only a few keystrokes." The countdown to launch had begun.

The entire crew aboard the *Grand Ayatollah* gathered on the deck. Unrolling their prayer mats, each man faced Mecca and began to pray.

At precisely 6:29 AM EST, the fateful coordinates were programmed into the Shahab-3 missile, and the commander stood at the ready to push the launch button. He counted down, "10, 9, 8, 7, 6," all the way to "Launch." As the missile roared into the atmosphere and toward its target in central Washington DC, the men cried as one, "*Allah Akbar!* Death to America!"

WASHINGTON DC

President Hedges was in the Oval Office reading the morning newspapers. Suddenly, all the lights in the Oval Office went out, evidently in a power failure. In seconds, his Secret Service detail armed with flashlights and drawn weapons burst into the Oval Office. Grabbing the president by the arms, they rushed him toward the secure bunker beneath the White House. He was still unaware that the blackout covered much of the country. He would have only minutes to wonder.

At approximately 6:38 AM, the Shahab-3 found its mark. In less than one second, a huge mushroom cloud billowed skyward from the center of Washington DC. A fireball, enveloping every-thing in its path, literally vaporized the seat of government for the world's largest superpower. Temperatures began to rise to an unimaginable twenty million degrees Fahrenheit, and every-thing—structures, automobiles, landscapes, and people—simply disappeared. Underground bomb shelters at Ground Zero and for several miles outward collapsed from the impact. The Shahab-3 left a crater that rivaled the largest meteor ever to impact the earth.

RAFAH, EGYPT, NEAR THE GAZA BORDER

At the same time the *Grand Ayatollah* was reaching the launch point in the Atlantic, the tents covering the truck and trailer in the Bedouin compound near Rafah were rolled back. Slowly and menacingly, the erector on the portable missile launcher raised its murderous cargo. The Revolutionary Guard scientist was standing ready to punch in the coordinates of the next target: Tel Aviv.

The three men assigned to the truck knew that their mission was historic. They were the last three remaining in the compound, and there was no place to hide from the radiation poisoning to which they had been exposed over the past few days. These men would die with a smile, however, knowing they would be instrumental in ushering in the return of the Twelfth Imam. And their martyrdom would be just as sure as if they had strapped on suicide bombs and detonated themselves in a busy marketplace in Tel Aviv.

They watched as the seconds ticked down. The zero hour, or "h-hour," was calculated to synchronize with the exact instant as the detonation over Washington DC. As the minutes ticked toward 1:30 PM in Israel, the Iranian scientist loaded the final GPS coordinates for the center of Tel Aviv into the rocket.

The Shahab-3 missile, the 150-kiloton enriched-uranium warhead was ready to go. The countdown began. When his expensive Tag Hauer chronometer finally ticked down to the appointed hour, the scientist pushed the button. The three men watched as the missile streaked low over the beaches of the Mediterranean toward Tel Aviv. Israel was about to experience the same devastation that was, even now, occurring in Washington DC.

As the nuclear flash of a thousand suns exploded over Tel Aviv, it set in motion a process that the regime in Iran expected. Israel would be wiped off the map; Palestine would be returned to the Palestinians; and Jerusalem would belong to Allah alone.

While considered a "low-yield" atomic bomb by today's standards, the 150-kiloton atomic blast was still more than five times the magnitude of the atomic weapons dropped on Hiroshima and Nagasaki at the end of World War II. Tel Aviv would mimic both Japanese cities as it, too, realized the appointed destiny with atomic destruction.

Within the first second of the blast, a shock wave with a peak overpressure of twenty pounds per square inch extended four-tenths of a mile from Ground Zero.

The blast wave exploded the shining new Ministry of Defense as if it were a pile of kindling wood scattered by a huge wind. Instantly, all the military personnel within the complex were gone, wiping out without trace the entire cadre of top military officials on which the strategic defense of Israel depended. Adjoining the Ministry of Defense, the Azrieli Towers, one of Tel Aviv's most distinctive landmarks, were also blasted to smithereens.

Everything within the first four-tenths of a mile from Ground Zero was reduced in the blink of an eye to a flying pile of exploding debris, regardless how much steel and concrete had been used to reinforce construction against the worst imaginable natural hazards of earthquakes, tsunamis, and gale force winds.

A peak overpressure of twenty pounds per square inch is equivalent to winds of 500 miles per hour. This force is enough to demolish multi-story concrete-reinforced buildings, up to a radius of about 1.8 miles. By comparison, winds of a mere 75 miles per hour are enough to warrant hurricane status.

The thermal pulse emitted by the blast instantly vaporized some 250,000 of the approximately three million people who were still in Tel Aviv at the end of the business day. Those within a one-tenth mile radius of Ground Zero were dead before they had a chance to comprehend the meaning of the brightest flash they had ever seen in their lives.

Within that first instant after the detonation, the distinctive mushroom cloud and fireball of a nuclear explosion began rapidly expanding upwards.

Suddenly, all communications systems throughout Israel that depend on Tel Aviv for broadcast simply went dead. All national television stations and dozens of radio channels were instantly off the air. Cell phones throughout Israel malfunctioned, as the communication grids, satellite links, and switching systems on which they depended quit working. In the wink of an eye, Tel Aviv had suddenly gone silent to the rest of the world; without explanation, all communications and broadcasts simply dropped in mid-sentence.

Four seconds after detonation, the shock wave extended for at least a mile from Ground Zero, still traveling with a brutal force of ten pounds per square inch, even at the periphery of a mile radius, with a wind force velocity roughly equivalent to a strong 125 mile per hour hurricane blow.

Reaching west to the famous Tel Aviv beach, all the high-rise luxury hotels from Gordon Beach in the north to Ge'ula Beach in the south were blown apart, sending what looked like splinters of their concrete and steel-reinforced structures flying for miles out into the Mediterranean Sea and back into the shattered city.

As the shock wave spread in a deadly radius throughout Tel Aviv's downtown, everything in its path was destroyed. Buildings were blown apart and cars were lifted and thrown like toys. In the four seconds it took the shock wave to travel one mile toward the city's edge, nearly one million people were dead.

Those unlucky enough to survive the blast soon found they were severely injured and trapped in massive rubble from which they were unlikely to escape. In horror, survivors soon realized they were doomed to die, most of them alone and in agony, without any hope that rescue efforts could be organized in time.

At ten seconds after detonation, the shock wave had expanded to a radius of 2.5 miles, covering virtually the entire surface area of Tel Aviv, reaching all the way to Jaffa on the south side at the water's edge. The shock wave of the atomic blast that reached the city's edge at h-hour plus ten seconds still carried an impact of two pounds per square inch at the periphery, still enough to cause huge damage to reinforced steel buildings, bringing them to the point where, even if they withstood the shock, they would soon collapse.

As the shock wave moved out ten seconds from Ground Zero, an estimated 235,000 people were killed, with an additional 500,000 seriously injured. The casualty ratio was beginning for the first time to exceed the kill ratio from the blast. At the edge of Tel Aviv, those wearing darker clothes were more severely burned from the thermal pulse.

Within the city center, an inferno had begun to burn out of control. Combustible materials even at the city's edge burst into flames as deadly radiation, traveling at the speed of light, reached the city's outskirts. Throughout Tel Aviv at h-hour plus thirty minutes, a deadly and consuming firestorm raged out of control. Debris from partially destroyed buildings spontaneously combusted into flames from the still-rising, overwhelming heat generated by the blast and subsequent widespread fires. The inferno soon made Tel Aviv look like the horror of Dresden in the grips of the fire bombing raids of World War II.

As darkness drifted over Tel Aviv, one million people lay dead and another one million were severely injured. The remaining one million inhabitants of the city at h-hour were trapped in the rubble, at risk of being killed by the inferno which raged out of control, or falling victim to the radiation left over from the blast. Fewer than twenty-five percent of the injured would survive more than a week.

The very old and the very young would die first. Those survivors able to move around would not know what to do. Thousands would be trapped in elevators, sealed in what would soon become their tombs. Those survivors who were not at home when the blast occurred realized as night fell that they would probably never communicate with loved ones, even if they were alive. Survivors were doomed never to find out what had happened to husbands, wives, and children. For all but a few there were never any words said of "Goodbye" or "I love you."

Who would come to the rescue when the radiation was likely to kill all who dared enter the devastation without protective clothes? The survivors found themselves homeless, mostly without food or water. All hospitals had been destroyed. Even if a medical facility had been left intact, there was no way to transport the injured to medical treatment. Darkness descended upon what was left of Tel Aviv with no apparent answers available to anyone.

Word spread around the world that Tel Aviv had been wiped off the map by a nuclear attack. Western allies soon came to the realization that both Israel and America had been the simultaneous targets of a nuclear assault, with very different results. As news of the attack on Tel Aviv and America reached Muslim countries, people took to the streets in celebration that both "The Great Satan" and "The Little Satan" had been rendered powerless.

In Europe, people milled about in shocked disbelief of the events unfolding. Fear took hold as many began to ask, "Are we next?"

Literally in seconds, both America and Israel had suffered knock-out blows. Washington, the center of American government, was in the throes of the cruel aftermath of a nuclear attack. Tel Aviv, the center of Israel's economy, was destroyed beyond repair. The damage done to the economies of America and Israel was so enormous that no one could comprehend the true magnitude. The resulting psychological shock spreading across the globe promised to bring paralysis throughout the Free World for an indefinite period of time.

NATO HEADQUARTERS, BRUSSELS, BELGIUM

At NATO headquarters, the telephone rang in the office of the head of the Intelligence Division, Major-General Al Armbrister. "Armbrister here," he snapped. He was stunned when the decidedly Middle Eastern voice on the other end of the line screamed, "*Allah Akbar!* I have finally brought the Zionist Crusaders to their knees."

"Bin Laden," whispered the major general, "and I was sure it was the Iranians."

JERUSALEM, ISRAEL

The Knesset was still in session when the blast occurred. The reaction was instantaneous: Retaliate! But against whom? Speculation abounded that it was Iran, but who knew with certainty?

Should Israel launch an attack on Iran, just to strike back at the most likely aggressor? But, no, NATO was saying that bin Laden was responsible for the attack. Should an attack be aimed at Afghanistan or, perhaps, northern Pakistan? Pakistan's arsenal of atomic weapons would mean instant retaliation.

The prime minister and the Knesset debated the alternatives. What if the attack had nothing to do with Iran? After all, al-Qaeda had been active in Israel for months, perhaps years.

The whole world stood at DEFCON-1, the highest military alert. "Was a United States nuclear strike on Iran, China, or Russia imminent?" wondered the prime minister. "Would they come to our defense?" No one could say. All they knew was that the American president could not be reached.

In Europe, the NATO countries were not sure if they were

about to be attacked. What if the attack had come from Russia, or possibly China?

What had happened to the world on this unimaginably horrible day? Even those who could still communicate with one another did not know for sure. How should the nations of Europe respond? As night fell over Europe, confusion and panic spread. Fears of continued attacks prompted concerns that the nuclear-armed countries of England and France would attack some country, before they themselves were attacked.

TEHRAN, IRAN H-HOUR PLUS SIXTY MINUTES

The Iranian regime in Tehran received confirmation from the Revolutionary Guard commander on board the *Grand Ayatollah* that the Shahab missile launch was successful. Reports from Israel confirmed that the launch from Rafah was equally successful. Armed with this intelligence, President Hamahdi went into a top-secret meeting with Ayatollah Noorani and top leaders, including the Council of Guardians.

For the past week, tank transporters had carried Shahab-3 missiles armed with non-nuclear payloads to isolated and secure locations within Iran. This move was designed to protect the Shahab-3 missiles from air attack and, in addition, position them for additional strikes on American military bases throughout the region. Ayatollah Noorani ordered the next phase of the plan to be put into operation immediately.

President Hamahdi agreed. Secure communiqués were sent from government headquarters in Tehran to Hezbollah, Hamas, even al-Qaeda commanders in the field. Their instructions? Begin rocket attacks on Israel. President Hamahdi communicated with President Hassan in Syria, confirming the glorious victory that had brought the United States and Israel to their knees. "It has been ordained by Allah," Hamahdi gushed in victory, uncharacteristically unable to control his emotions.

"How many atomic weapons do you have left?" Hassan asked.

"We have three more," Hamahdi confirmed. "One is on a ship just off the coast of Los Angeles, a second is aboard the *Grand Ayatollah* aimed at New York City."

"Good," Hassan agreed. "And the third Shahab missile?"

"Aboard a ship in the Persian Gulf. Within the hour, we will launch an attack on the American military in the Middle East, as planned," Hamahdi confirmed.

"Good," Hassan nodded in agreement and replaced the phone in its cradle.

In Tehran, Hamahdi bowed before Allah, knowing that the attack had been according to divine plan. "The Grand Ayatollah Ruhollah Khomeini's predictions have proven true," he thought. "America and Israel, too, would fall under the press of Islam. *Velayat-e Faghih*, absolute cleric rule under our revered Ayatollah Noorani, is about to engulf Israel and America."

JERUSALEM, ISRAEL

The defense minister stood with tears running down his face. "Mr. Prime Minister," he stuttered, "we must launch now. Our sources tell us that Iran could have as many as sixty nuclear devices. We must act now!"

The prime minister stood before the somber Knesset members. "The decision has been reached, then?" With downcast eyes, they nodded silently.

The *Samson Option* was implemented. The nuclear warhead-laden missiles were now ascending from their silos, their targets known only to the prime minister and his closest advisors. Dimona, Project 700, the Zechariah Project, the Temple Weapons, each a part of Israel's vast nuclear arsenal, were destined for all-out retaliation.

1

THE REVOLUTION BEGINS

"Islam makes it incumbent on all adult males, provided they are not disabled and incapacitated, to prepare themselves for the conquest of other countries so that the writ of Islam is obeyed in every country of the world."

— AYATOLLAH KHOMEINI, 1948

"Iran has joined the club of nuclear nations. . . ."

— IRANIAN PRESIDENT
MAHMOUD AHMADINEJAD,
APRIL 2006

Y ou have just read a fictionalized account of events that could happen around the globe in the very near future. Much of what I've presented in the preceding prologue is based on facts gathered from decades of work as a confidant to Israeli leaders and as a journalist working in the Middle East. With Iran's long history of contempt for the United Nations and the International Atomic Energy Agency, the timetable for an apocalyptic event could accelerate at any moment.

The modern-day Islamic revolution was born on April Fool's Day in 1980 as Ayatollah Ruhollah Khomeini proclaimed it the "first day of the government of God" in Iran. That same year I wrote *Israel: America's Key to Survival*. The premise was that terrorism was spreading like a plague and that America would soon be in the hot zone.

I interviewed many of America's top generals. One of the most memorable interviews took place just outside of Washington DC, at the home of Air Force General Robert Huyser, who was deputy chief of staff for Plans and Operations. Huyser was sent to Iran on a fool's errand for President Jimmy Carter, a scheme to destabilize the Shah's government.

Huyser was a man of principle and moral clarity and believed that his mission was to support Prime Minister Shapour Bakhtiar and Iran's generals. Carter promised that the US would protect and provide all assets needed to shore up the government, which was increasingly endangered by violent protests against the regime of the Shah, Mohammed Reza Pahlavi. Despite America's history of support going back to World War II, Carter had no desire to see a pro-Shah regime in power. He preferred the Ayatollah, whom he seemed to regard as a Gandhi-like figure. The comparison made sense to a point: the Ayatollah opposed the Shah, who had a terrible record of human rights abuses. But that's where the comparison breaks down. Gandhi was nonviolent. The Ayatollah was anything but.

Huyser awoke when he realized what was really going on. His orders did not reflect the president's real intentions. While Carter was pressuring the Shah to make what he called "human rights concessions," the president was actually working through the US Embassy and the State Department to put Khomeini in power. At that point, Khomeini had been in exile in France for fourteen years.

On the ground in Iran, things only worsened for the government. Bakhtiar urged the Shah to leave. On 16 January 1979, the Shah and his family fled to Egypt as the protests brought the regime to its knees. They would never see their home again.

As for Khomeini, his exile was nearly over.

THE AYATOLLAH RETURNS

It is Thursday, 1 February 1979, and over one million people fill the streets of Tehran. The hordes are organized to greet a triumphal Khomeini as he returns to Iran. Roads for twenty-five miles around the airport are impassable, clogged with people and cars. Millions more are glued to televisions, awaiting the Ayatollah. All are hoping for a glimpse of the holy man.

A military guard at the airport stands ready to receive Khomeini, with the full support of President Jimmy Carter. After five and a half hours of flight from Paris, the Air France plane settles to the ground and taxies down the tarmac. The Ayatollah's bodyguards, a motley crew of thirty to forty highly-trained Libyans, deplane first, followed by Khomeini himself. As he steps onto Persian soil for the first time in fourteen years and into the bright Iranian morning, this is the dawn of more than just another day.

The Ayatollah boards a blue and white Chevrolet and joins a motorcade that pushes its tumultuous way through the heart of Tehran. His trip is anything but aimless. Khomeini tells his driver to take him to the Behesht-e Zahra cemetery, the resting place of many martyrs, victims of Iranian Army troops under the Shah. Supporters, some of whom assembled there as early as 3:00 AM, wait in eager anticipation. Khomeini's car stops, and he delivers a speech that changes everything.

"I must tell you that Mohammad Reza Pahlavi, that evil traitor, has gone," he says. "He fled and plundered everything. He destroyed our country and filled our cemeteries. He ruined our country's economy. Even the projects he carried out in the name of progress pushed the country toward decadence. He suppressed our culture, annihilated people and destroyed all our manpower resources."

But Khomeini's goal isn't to merely demonize the Shah. The Ayatollah is here to lay down the law. "We are saying this man, his government, his Majlis [parliament] are all illegal," he continues with profound authority. "If they were to continue to stay in power, we would treat them as criminals and would try them as criminals. I shall appoint my own government. I shall slap this government in the mouth. I shall determine the government with the backing of this nation, because this nation accepts me."[1]

It's a declaration of war on the government of Prime Minister Bakhtiar, whose days are now officially numbered. Khomeini plans to establish a cleric-dominated theocracy with himself as chief spiritual and political leader, and there is no place in that scheme for a Westernized leader like Bakhtiar. The mullahs had been preaching the need for an Islamic theocracy for over twenty years. Khomeini's speech is a clear decree that their time has arrived.

A grim scene quickly unfolds. Many of the generals who worked to stabilize the country are soon assassinated. Slower on his feet than the Shah, Bakhtiar flees to France but does not escape the revolution. Khomeini's assassins murder him in his new home—a token of another, more troubling reality. The Ayatollah's plans for Islamic revolution will not be contained by Iran's borders. The revolution's destiny is to spread across the globe, often by blood and terror.

Taking a cue from the French Revolution of 1789, hasty show trials pave the way for politically and religiously motivated executions. No opposition is brooked. Heretics and dissidents are imprisoned and killed. Mothers even turn in disloyal sons, which the Ayatollah publicly applauds.

Iranian students overrun the US embassy on 4 November 1979, taking fifty-two American diplomats and citizens captive. The hostages are held for 444 days through delicate political negotiations and an ill-fated and abortive attempt by the Carter administration to rescue them.

Considering his regrettable involvement, it is fitting that America would remember President Carter's performance amidst the crisis. He refused to solicit our allies' support to stop the Ayatollah from returning to Iran. He refused to give material support to Bakhtiar's government. And most devastating of all, he refused to publicly condemn Khomeini. His grand scheme of undermining the Shah exploded in his face. The events in Iran would ultimately destroy his political career and contribute to the birth of our current crisis with radical Islam. They would also pave the way for one of the world's most serious nuclear threats since the Soviet Union.

DREAM OF THE AYATOLLAH

There is a photograph of Khomeini on that historic flight back to Iran. Traveling through the night, Khomeini sat off by himself, in a comfortable first-class seat. The picture shows him in a moment of satisfied meditation. A deep inner joy appears to emanate from his face. In this instant, Ayatollah Khomeini is savoring the approaching moment when his life-long aspirations are finally about to be realized.

His eyes look down and to the right, distantly as if into the past, maybe into the future. He is seventy-nine years old, but he appears venerable, by no means senile. A trademark black turban sits on his head, his visage distinguished by a flowing white beard, his often fierce dark eyes highlighted by arching eyebrows. His lips are pursed in a private smile. His hands are folded quietly in his lap, gracing the folds of his long robe.

The photograph captures a moment of silent calm before the wild storm of public frenzy breaks upon him.[2]

Ayatollah Khomeini returned to bring his radical Islamic revolution to Iran. He believed this was the first step of his revolution sweeping across the world. Khomeini's heart burned with the vision that the West, led by the United States, would come under Islam's grip. Soon, the illegitimate state of Israel would be eliminated. He was convinced all other religions would give way to Islam and a Muslim theocracy would be established in every corner of the globe. Before 11 September 2001, such an idea sounded fantastical, even absurd to Westerners. It's much easier now to understand that when men like the Ayatollah speak, there are throngs of believers waiting to translate those words into deeds—some of them terrible to behold.

The power Ayatollah Khomeini held over the Iranian population was almost mystical in nature. He was a Shi'ite Muslim, a minority in a world where the vast majority of Islamic adherents are Sunni. (Iran is one of the few countries where Shi'ites are in the majority.)

The dispute between Sunnis and Shi'ites goes back to the death of the Prophet Mohammed, in the seventh century. The first Islamic theocracy was founded in Medina, a Saudi Arabian city north of Mecca. The Sunni branch of the religion believes that the first four caliphs are the rightful successors of Mohammed. The Shi'ites believe that only the fourth caliph, Ali, is the legitimate successor.

The distinctions don't stop there. In 941 AD, a religious leader known as the Mahdi, or the Twelfth Imam, supposedly disappeared down a well near Jamkaran, in Iran's Qom province. Shi'ites believe that he was hidden or "occulted" but will one day reemerge to oversee a millennial-style age of peace, justice, and true belief. Adherents have a messianic view that the way needs to be prepared for the return of the Twelfth Imam, much as many orthodox Jews await the appearance of the Messiah and evangelical Christians await the second coming of Jesus Christ. With the second coming of the Mahdi, Shi'ites expect to realize the final triumph of Islam worldwide.

That final triumph will not come without intense struggle. Khomeini believed that only a properly structured Islamic theocracy could create conditions needed for the return of the Twelfth Imam. As he and his followers saw it, Khomeini was on a mission from God. Divine destiny preordained that he would return to Iran. Divine destiny preordained that his theocracy would start in Iran and then sweep across the world—a motion that would entail apocalyptic wars that would eventually remove the infidel from the Holy Land and unseat America from its role of superpower.

But the Ayatollah died with his work unfinished. By the time of his death in 1989, Khomeini had succeeded only in establishing his theocracy in Iran. Yes, the mullahs were in firm grip of the radical Islamic Republic. But the Jews remained in Israel, and America still held a strong military presence in the Middle East.

Still, Khomeini had humiliated the United States. Khomeini held the American embassy hostages for a record 444 days and savored Carter's defeat as a great victory. On the day Ronald Reagan was inaugurated, Khomeini strategically released the hostages. He acknowledged both Carter's weakness and Reagan's strength.

The Reagan administration ultimately brought down the Berlin Wall and caused the Soviet Union to fall, events that most Americans never imagined they would live to see. Reagan also brought an end to the crisis caused by OPEC's oil embargo. Gone were the long gasoline lines that Americans suffered while Carter was in the White House. But Reagan could not bring down the Ayatollah. In the end, Reagan backed off, legitimately concerned that the Iran-Contra crisis of his second term could become his undoing. Two suicide attacks in 1983 drove the US out of Lebanon. Those events have become the yardstick for Iran's activities. Its leaders believe that if the heat is sufficient, America will retreat.

Khomeini set in motion the dream of a worldwide radical Islamic revolution. Even today, the emotion of Khomeini's 1979 revolution remains as strong as ever in Iran. Ayatollah Khomeini's successor, Ayatollah Khamenei, and Iran's president, Mahmoud Ahmadinejad, have picked up Khomeini's cause and are inspired by shared belief in the Mahdi. It is their divine mission to complete the radical Islamic revolution that Ayatollah Khomeini began.

The primary tool to achieve their goal? Nuclear weapons.

NUCLEAR CHESS MATCH

Iran is pursuing a secret nuclear weapons program, in defiance of world diplomats, the United Nations, and the International Atomic Energy Agency.

Israel and the United States have both announced that Iran will not be permitted to develop a deliverable nuclear weapon. If current diplomatic attempts to bring Iran into compliance with the inspection requests of the International Atomic Energy Agency do not work, then a preemptive military strike by Israel or the United States becomes increasingly likely.

Only increasing that possibility, President Ahmadinejad has declared to the world that he has a "mission from Allah" to fulfill the preconditions required to commence the second coming of the Mahdi. As such, Ahmadinejad's mission may well include bringing about the apocalypse he believes will pave the way for the return. Such a move would also fulfill the prophecies of Ayatollah Khomeini who foretold that Iran's destiny was to destroy Israel and the United States in a final apocalyptic war.

It's easy to see why the West is uneasy with Iran's pursuit of the bomb.

"We cannot let Iran, a leading sponsor of international terrorism, acquire nuclear weapons and the means to deliver them to Europe, most of central Asia and the Middle East, or beyond," said John R. Bolton, then-undersecretary for arms control and international security in August 2004. "Without serious, concerted, immediate intervention by the international community, Iran will be well on the road to doing so."[3]

Since it is likely one of Iran's first targets, Israel is just as concerned—if not more so. In January 2005, head of the Israeli Defense Force Intelligence Branch, Major General Aharon Ze'evi

Farkash, spoke to a group assembled at the National Security Studies Center at the University of Haifa. According to Farkash, "If Iran's uranium enrichment activities are not halted it could develop its first atomic bomb at some point between 2007 and 2009." He opined that Iran was about six months from being able to enrich uranium, a step he described as the "point of no return."

At the Washington Convention Center, on 24 May 2005, I sat across the table from Prime Minister Ariel Sharon during his last trip to Washington DC, and asked, "How dangerous do you consider Iran and its nuclear threat to be?"

Sharon: "Iran is an insane regime, and the center of world terror. Iran will make every effort possible to possess nuclear weapons. This is a danger to the Middle East, a danger to Europe, and a danger to America."

Several highly-placed sources told me that Ariel Sharon had given the order for the State of Israel to be ready by the end of March 2006 for a possible strike on uranium enrichment sites in Iran. Sharon said to me in that meeting, "Israel cannot accept a nuclear Iran, nor can America. We have the ability to deal with this, and we are making all the necessary preparations to be ready."

How soon will Iran have the bomb? Meir Dagan, the head of Mossad, the Israeli Intelligence Agency, told the Knesset in December 2005 that Iran is one to two years away, at the most, from having enriched uranium to build a bomb. Unfortunately, that estimate was off. In an announcement that temporarily sent the US stock market plunging in April 2006, Iran's former president, Akbar Hashemi Rafsanjani, reported to the Kuwaiti news agency, JUNA, that Iran was producing enriched uranium from 164 centrifuges. He did not identify the location of the processing plant(s). These statements were confirmed in a televised speech on the same day by President Ahmadinejad.

On 13 April 2006, Iran rebuffed a request by the United Nations nuclear agency chief to halt uranium enrichment. "Uranium enrichment is a line in the sand from which my nation shall not retreat," said Ahmadinejad.

Iran is currently capable of fast-tracking its centrifuge production. To manufacture nuclear weapons, it will take between 1,500 and 3,000 centrifuges. At that point, any attempts by Israel or the US to take out Iran's nuclear program with military force will create a nuclear disaster, contaminating the countryside and its oil fields and refineries.

Understandably Iran is trying to avoid such a situation. We should never forget that the Persians invented the game of chess. The intent of Ayatollah Khamenei is for Iranians to play the global chess match of diplomacy, summits, and international talk so that there is nothing the United States or Israel can do to stop them from developing nuclear weapons until it is too late. If Iran openly announced an intention to develop nuclear weapons, the world would intervene to prevent this from happening. So instead, following the path that Ayatollah Khomeini set when he was alive, Iran operates by stealth.

By claiming that Iran wanted nuclear power only for peaceful purposes (such as energy and medical research), Khomeini realized the West would be thrown into confusion. Countries such as France, Germany, and the United Kingdom would be cautious but desirous of obtaining favored access to Iran's oil and natural gas reserves. The French and Germans could also be bought with lucrative contracts to help build Iran's nuclear infrastructure.

The strategy Iran put in place was brilliant. By remaining a signatory to the Nuclear Non-Proliferation Treaty (NPT), Iran could claim a right to pursue nuclear fuel for peaceful purposes. The lie would not be discovered until too late. From the beginning, Ayatollah Khomeini had calculated that his radical revolutionaries would ultimately be able to checkmate the world. Then no country would be able to stop Iran from realizing its cherished goals—goals that Ayatollah Khomeini had predicted were destined by Allah to be fulfilled.

Now Ahmadinejad was in place as Iran's president. Religious zealots in Iran knew the day was growing close when a surprise nuclear attack to destroy Israel could be launched successfully.

AHMADINEJAD, TRUE BELIEVER

While working on this book, I met with Sharon's former chief of staff, General Moshe Ya'alon. General Ya'alon was the chief of staff of the Israel Defense Forces from 2002 to 2005. In discussing Iran's nuclear pursuit, he brought the underlying motivation back to belief in the Mahdi.

"Shi'ite Muslims believe that the Twelfth Imam, or Mahdi, the last in a line of saints descended from Ali, the founder of their sect, vanished down a well in 941 AD," he said. "According to their beliefs, he went into a state of 'occultation,' like the sun being hidden behind the clouds. After a stormy period of apocalyptic wars, the clouds will part, and the sun [the Mahdi] will be revealed. They believe that when he is released from his imprisonment, the entire world will submit to Islam."

This belief is the driving force behind Ahmadinejad, Ayatollah Khamenei, and the majority of the central figures in Iranian government.

Just days before I interviewed General Ya'alon, I watched a DVD recorded shortly after Ahmadinejad returned from the UN General Assembly meeting in New York in September 2005. The president is seen entering a house with Ayatollah Javadi Amoli, a senior conservative figure in Qom. They sit on a carpet and are served tea while talking about the money the government has allocated at the Mahdi's shrine at Jamkaran.

Ahmadinejad then turns to his recent UN address: "On the last day when I was speaking, one of our group told me that when I started to say '*bismullah Muhammad*,' he saw a green light come from around me, and I was placed inside this aura," he says. "I felt it myself. I felt that the atmosphere suddenly changed and for those twenty-seven to twenty-eight minutes, all the leaders of the world did not blink. When I say they didn't move an eyelid, I am not exaggerating. They were looking as if a hand were holding them there, and had just opened their eyes."[4]

At the close of his speech to the United Nations, Ahmadinejad called for the reappearance of the Twelfth Imam, the Mahdi. "O mighty Lord," he said, "I pray to you to hasten the emergence of your last repository, the promised one, that perfect human being, the one that will fill this world with justice and peace."[5]

Considering the apocalyptic connection with the Mahdi's expected return, for a head of state to hold these views is increasingly disturbing. The world may smirk as it hears the president of Iran talking about the return of the Mahdi. Just a bunch of religious foolishness? To him it's the truth, and he's dead serious about it. Not only does he believe it, but the tens of thousands of mullahs controlling ancient Persia believe it also. It is their mission from God.

When Ahmadinejad walked across American and Israeli flags painted on the pavement of a mosque and voted in Iran's ninth presidential election, the world was convinced there would be no possibility of his election. They were stunned when proven wrong. An ideologue emerged triumphant. Ahmadinejad is, without question, fueled by messianic religious fervor. He has rekindled revolutionary fires long extinguished. He believes that Iran's redemption will come through a combustible mixture of this Islamist ideology and deep suspicion of a world conspiracy propagated by the Crusaders and the Zionists (Americans and Israelis).

Would a radical Islamic regime be willing to accept even a suicidal nuclear holocaust, as long as Israel were destroyed and the West were crippled? If such an apocalypse brought about the conditions needed to cause the Twelfth Imam to return, would that justify an atomic attack on Israel?

Just a day after the president of Iran challenged the UN over uranium enrichment, Ahmadinejad proclaimed Israel a "permanent threat" to the region that would "soon" be liberated. "Like it or not," he said, "the Zionist regime is heading toward annihilation." He added that "Palestine will be freed soon."[6] The setting was an Islamic fundraising conference which Ahmadinejad was hosting for the Palestinian terror organizations Hamas and Islamic Jihad, with Iran's supreme leader Ayatollah Ali Khamenei and smiling Hezbollah members sitting on the front row.

Israel has already made clear its intention to stop Iran's nuclear ambition if it feels threatened. Hampered by a growing anti-war movement at home because of the situation in Iraq, the United States may find it harder to act. It may be forced to act nonetheless.

I fear the radical clerics ruling Iran are aware that their time is short, unless they can enforce their rule with nuclear weapons. Once Iran is in possession of a bomb or a missile, Israel or the United States will have to go to the brink of a thermonuclear exchange if either country expects to push a regime-change agenda in Iran. And here's the frightening thing: Considering the desire for a major and decisive apocalyptic event, perhaps that is exactly what Iran's president wants.

2

PURSUING THE HOLY BOMB

"For the last three years we have been doing intensive verification in Iran, and even after three years I am not yet in a position to make a judgment on the peaceful nature of Iran's nuclear program."

—MOHAMED ELBARADEI,
DIRECTOR-GENERAL
OF THE IAEA, JANUARY 2006

"The application of an atomic bomb would not leave anything in Israel."

—FORMER IRANIAN PRESIDENT
HASHEMI RAFSANJANI, 2001

I ran has moved with great determination to become a nuclear weapons power as fast as possible. The strategy employed to get to this goal has been both subtle and brilliant. If it were anything less, the plan would assuredly backfire.

Iran paid close attention to Israel's 1981 military strike against Iraq's Osirak nuclear reactor. The attack was relatively simple because Iraq had only one major nuclear facility. Iran resolved not to make this same mistake. As a defensive move, it decided to decentralize its nuclear facilities around the country. Many nuclear facilities could be embedded in population centers. To attack successfully, Israel or the United States would have to launch a multipronged strike which would be more tactically difficult to plan and implement successfully than a single-site attack.

Worse, with nuclear facilities inside Iran's cities, a military strike by Israel or the United States would cause civilian casualties. Would Israel and America be willing to kill thousands of Iranian civilians to take out Iran's nuclear facilities in a preemptive military attack? Clearly, this would raise the stakes against Iran's enemies.

Iran further determined that each separate nuclear installation would be devoted to a single purpose, a piece that could be fitted into the puzzle. This way, if a particular facility were attacked and destroyed, Iran would lose only the functionality fulfilled at that location. Some operations would be duplicated in other facilities;

others might be replaced by outsourcing the fulfillment to a friendly country, perhaps Pakistan or Russia. Components would remain functioning if they were not attacked or if the attack failed to fully knock the facility out of operation.

Decentralization and compartmentalization—any successful attack on any one facility would not knock Iran's total nuclear capabilities offline for long. Even if particular components were destroyed or were temporarily put out of service as a result of a military strike, Iran could rebuild the nuclear system quickly. It's the perfect plan.

FULL FUEL CYCLE: FROM ORE TO BOMBS

In February 2003, Iran announced the opening of a uranium mine at Saghand, in the Kavir desert near the central Iranian city of Yazd, some 300 miles south of Tehran.[1] A little more than a year later, in September 2004, Iran allowed the international press to tour the mine for the first time. Saghand is one of ten estimated uranium mines in Iran.[2] Ghasem Soleimani, the British-trained director of mining operations at the Energy Organization of Iran, reported on plans to begin extracting uranium ore from the mine in the first half of 2006. He claimed that "More than 77 percent of the work has been accomplished."[3] The mine reportedly has a capacity of 132,000 tons of uranium ore per year.

Uranium ore is processed into uranium ore concentrate, commonly called "yellowcake" at a separate yellowcake production plant located at Ardakan, less than forty miles from Yazd.

Iran's uranium processing facility is located at yet another site, at Isfahan, a central Iranian city, some 250 miles south of Tehran. The Nuclear Technology and Research Center in Isfahan is said to employ as many as three thousand scientists in a facility constructed about fifteen kilometers southeast of central Isfahan at a research complex constructed by the French under a 1975 agreement with Iran.[4] Isfahan also houses one of Iran's major universities, with some one thousand graduate students and approximately ten thousand undergraduates, in fields that include science, social science, and humanities.

On the eastern outskirts of Isfahan is the Uranium Conversion Facility, a cluster of buildings, surrounded by razor wire fencing, and protected by anti-aircraft guns and military patrols.[5] Here the yellowcake is processed into uranium hexafluoride gas, the first step required to convert uranium ore to the enriched state needed to run a nuclear power plant or to provide the weapons-grade uranium needed to make an atom bomb.

From Isfahan, the uranium hexafluoride gas is transported to yet another facility, this one near the small mountain town of Natanz, about ninety miles to the northeast of Isfahan. Here the uranium hexafluoride gas is enriched in rapidly spinning centrifuges, completing the "full fuel cycle" and ending the range of processes needed to get from uranium ore to highly enriched uranium. At lower grades of enrichment, the uranium can be used to fuel peaceful power plants. Highly enriched uranium can be fashioned into the metallic form needed to serve as the fissile core of an atom bomb.

The fuel enrichment plant is located several miles from the town, set off by a perimeter security fence and military guards. The plant houses two large underground halls built eight meters below ground. The halls are hardened by thick underground concrete reinforcing walls built to protect the facility. The construction was designed to house an advanced centrifuge complex of as many as 54,000 centrifuges.

Experts estimated that the fuel enrichment plant was prepared initially to house some 5,000 centrifuges, in the initial stage of the project scheduled for completion by the end of 2005 or early in 2006.[6] Operating at full capacity, 54,000 centrifuges would be capable of producing enough weapons-grade uranium to build over twenty weapons per year. When completed, the underground facilities are planned to have no visible aboveground signature, a move designed to complicate precise targeting of any munitions that could be used to attack the facility.

Precise satellite imagery of the nuclear facilities at both Isfahan and Natanz can be found online at GlobalSecurity.org. Multiple satellite views show the precise location of the operations. The photos document various phases of facility construction and concealment, from the time the facilities were first begun to very recently, on a continuously updated basis. Inspection of the satellite images reveals that the complexes are designed to include dormitory/housing facilities for those working at the plant. Also visible are various complexes of administrative and scientific buildings needed to operate the facility.

Even these publicly available satellite photos show the military defense and anti-aircraft installations designed to provide security. Inspection of the satellite images makes clear that Isfahan and Natanz are both sophisticated facilities. The Iranians paid careful attention to facility design both for the professional operation of nuclear activity and the military preparedness needed to protect the facilities from attack.

CAT AND MOUSE

Iran's uranium processing and its inevitable interaction with the outside world regarding it has been an elaborate game of cat and mouse.

In February 2004, an International Atomic Energy Agency (IAEA) report was leaked to the Associated Press suggesting that

Tehran was planning on processing 37 tons of yellowcake uranium oxide into uranium hexafluoride gas, estimated to make more than two hundred pounds of weapons-grade uranium. It was enough to make about five small atomic bombs once the gas was highly enriched.

The report caused a blow-up in the press. Ali Akbar Salehi, a senior advisor to Iran's Foreign Minister Kamal Kharrazi, reacted sharply when questioned about the report. "That we want to process 37 metric tons of uranium ore into hexafluoride gas is not a discovery," he told the international press. "The IAEA has been aware of Iran's plan to construct the Uranium Conversion Facility in Isfahan since it was a barren land. We haven't constructed the Isfahan facility to produce biscuits. . . ."[7]

Later that year, in September, Iran told the IAEA in a report little noticed at the time that the country planned to process some 40 tons of uranium into uranium hexafluoride gas.

But then just two months later, in November, Iran agreed to stop all uranium processing at both Isfahan and Natanz. The decision was made to comply with a condition set by the EU3 (the European Union countries of France, Germany, and the United Kingdom) for negotiations regarding IAEA requirements for facility inspection.

The IAEA wanted to determine that Iran was compliant with the provisions of the Nuclear Non-Proliferation Treaty prohibiting the development of nuclear weapons. To make sure it was playing by the rules, Iran was to submit to a standard of "transparency," meaning that all its facilities and operations should be open to IAEA inspection at times and places of the IAEA's choosing. This was important because Iran was limiting inspections—possibly to conceal nuclear weapons activities. If Iran were allowed to limit inspections to certain times and to certain facilities or particular areas within facilities, the "advanced warning" limitations would give workers the opportunity to "sanitize" operations prior to inspection.

But there was more going on than a simple shell game. International skeptics argued that Iran had only agreed to suspend uranium processing because Isfahan and Natanz were not yet complete in November 2004. More time was needed by Iran to finish facility construction and resolve technical problems. By agreeing to "stop" operations Iran was truly not ready to begin, they seized the opportunity to appear cooperative. Skeptics argued Iran's primary goal was simply to buy more time.

Sure enough, in May 2005, Mohammad Saeedi, head of the Atomic Energy Organization of Iran (AEOI), affirmed that 37 tons of yellowcake had been converted. This was an important announcement since work at the facility was supposed to have been suspended. It seemed as if work at Isfahan had never been suspended after all.[8]

To resolve this conflict, Saeedi explained to the international press that 37 tons had been processed, but before formally suspending nuclear processing at Isfahan the previous November. "We converted all the 37 tons of uranium concentrate known as yellowcake . . . at the Isfahan Uranium Conversion Facility before we suspended work there," Saeedi told the international press.[9]

In a separate statement, Hasan Rowhani, Iran's top nuclear negotiator, admitted that Iran had produced uranium hexafluoride gas. Rowhani also discussed the suspension of uranium processing in a way that suggested Iran's real intent was to work on the Isfahan and Natanz facilities. "It is true that we are currently under suspension," Rowhani commented, "but we conducted a lot of activities in 2004. Today, if we want to start enrichment, we have sufficient centrifuges at least for the early stages, while we didn't have such a capacity 25 months ago."[10]

The following month, Ahmadinejad was elected president and Iran's supreme leader Ayatollah Khamenei had everything in place to take the regime in the ultraconservative direction he believed would fulfill Ayatollah Khomeini's prophecy. Never had the moment been so right for Iran and so wrong for Israel and the United States.

BACK ONLINE

In August 2005, Iran openly resumed processing uranium at Isfahan, defiantly breaking their earlier promise to suspend uranium processing while the EU3 negotiations were proceeding.[11] What's more, Iran told the world that the negotiations were no longer important or worth continuing.[12] Iran appeared determined to pursue nuclear technology regardless of what the world community said, and its aggressive defiance was being met by confusion and inaction from the United States and European nations.

Despite the show of defiance, the Iranians were calculating carefully, taking one step at a time. Reopening Isfahan meant the Iranians were resuming uranium *processing*, defined as the refinement of uranium ore into uranium hexafluoride. By not opening Natanz, the Iranians technically were not yet engaging in uranium *enrichment*, defined as the process of converting uranium hexafluoride gas into highly enriched uranium (also called uranium-235). Carefully, the Iranians were moving their pieces on the chessboard, always with a view to being able soon to declare a surprise "checkmate."

In response, the IAEA fell into a series of crisis meetings. On 24 September 2005, at the urging of the United States, it voted to hold Iran in noncompliance with the Nuclear Non-Proliferation Treaty. This locked in place a key piece of the US strategy.

When the IAEA vote was taken, Iran was celebrating "Sacred

Defense Week," marking the twenty-fifth anniversary of the Iran-Iraq war. In Tehran, Foreign Minister Manouchehr Mottaki called the IAEA resolution "political, illegal, and illogical." On state-run television, Mottaki portrayed the EU3 as puppets of the United States, claiming that "the three European countries implemented a planned scenario already determined by the United States."[13]

That same week, John Bolton, the US ambassador to the UN, told the House International Relations Committee that now Iran had a choice to make. As Bolton explained, "Right now, in the aftermath of the IAEA resolution, it's unmistakably up to Iran to decide whether it's going to continue a policy of pursuing nuclear weapons, or whether it's going to give it up, as did the government of Libya."[14] Bolton and the rest of the world got Iran's decision in November.

On 17 November 2005, Reuters reported that Iran was preparing to process a new batch of 250 drums of yellowcake uranium at Isfahan.[15] This left no doubt about Iran's intentions. Iran evidently did not want to resume negotiations with the EU3 if resuming negotiations meant forfeiting the right to process uranium. The Iranian decision was particularly defiant, given that the IAEA was expected to meet in just a week to vote on the September resolution to take Iran to the Security Council.

Immediately, Russia put a proposal of its own on the table. To break the impasse, Russia offered to establish a joint venture with Iran to operate a uranium enrichment facility located in Russia; that way a more reliable nation could oversee the production. Enrichment was the next step in preparing the fuel for a nuclear reactor (or bomb), so theoretically this was a juicy carrot for the Iranians.[16]

Once again, the IAEA postponed a decision to take Iran to the United Nations Security Council for additional sanctions, preferring instead to give Russia time to develop more fully the alternative and to win Iranian acceptance of the idea.

Once again, Iran had calculated correctly. By taking the defiant path, Iran had thrown the IAEA and the EU3 into confusion. Rather than confront Iran, the first impulse was to retreat, hoping they could still work out a diplomatic solution.

Now the Iranians said they would negotiate again, but Iran would not give up the right to enrich uranium in their own country, not even to Russia. The Iranians would talk, but only as long as the talks were on their terms. With every move, Iran bought more time. With every start and stop, confusion set upon the United States and the Europeans, just as Ayatollah Khomeini had foretold decades earlier.

It was getting very hard to trust the Iranians.

A HISTORY OF CONCEALMENT AND DECEPTION

French diplomat Phillippe Errera drove this point home in a March 2005 speech in Tehran: "Iran has lost this trust not because of any discriminatory attitude toward it, nor because of any instrumentalization by 'third parties,' the United States or Israel, for example, but simply because of the revelation of close to twenty years of clandestine activities dealing with highly sensitive nuclear matters, and of secret cooperation with an international proliferation network linked to nuclear proliferation programs in Libya and North Korea, coupled with the absence of any civilian justification to its nuclear fuel cycle program; there is no functioning reactor in Iran today."[17]

Indeed, in 1992 Russia had agreed to build a nuclear reactor for Iran at Bushehr for a cost of between $800 million and $1 billion. The Russians finished the Bushehr nuclear reactor in October 2004. "We're done," was the statement of a spokesperson for Russia's Atomic Energy Agency (Rosatom). "All we need to do now is work out an agreement on sending spent fuel back to Russia."[18]

Bushehr is located in southern Iran, along the Persian Gulf, a location consistent with Iran's plan to decentralize its nuclear facilities. We need also remember that Russia is a member of the UN Security Council. Iran has counted on Russia's support, believing that Russia would resist sanctions against them should the US be able to bring Iran before the Security Council. (There are reasons for this that we will explore in chapters 5 and 7.)

But despite the "We're done" statement, at the end of 2005 the Bushehr reactor was still inoperable. Iran caused delays and complications by changing the plant's design specifications and operational requirements several times over, even after the plant was under construction. Moreover, even though the Iranians claim Bushehr was built for peaceful purposes, the linkage between the plant and Iran's civilian electrical power system remains unclear. A reasonable argument can be made that the plant was never intended to produce electricity. Sitting on vast reserves of petroleum and natural gas, it is not as if Iran even needs a nuclear plan to produce energy. Instead, the real goal may have been subterfuge. Iran could get permission if the world believed Bushehr were built to generate electricity. Meanwhile, the spent nuclear fuel could be diverted to make nuclear bombs. (Perhaps that is exactly why no agreement had yet been reached regarding sending it back to Russia.)

Iran has typically kept nuclear activities secret until details of those activities were reported by others. In May 2006, while the EU3, US, China, and Russia prepared for further talks with Iran, a former Pakistani general produced evidence of another kind of talk altogether, held between Iran and Pakistan. "They didn't want the technology," said General Mirza Aslam Beg of a 1990 Iranian visit to Islamabad. "They asked: 'Can we have a bomb?' My answer was by all means you can have it, but you must make it yourself. Nobody gave it to us."[19]

One group that has hounded Iran is the National Council for Resistance on Iran (NCRI), the political arm for the People's Mujahedin of Iran (also known as the Mujahadeen-e-Khalq, or the People's Mujahedin, the MEK). The US Department of State has placed the NCRI and the MEK on its list of terrorist organizations since 1997, maintaining that the MEK has been involved in attacks on US interests abroad, including several murders of US servicemen and civilians plus bombings of US businesses overseas.[20]

The MEK was formed in Tehran in 1965 as a far leftist, anti-imperialist organization dedicated to the overthrow of the Shah. But its communist sympathies never fit into Ayatollah Khomeini's view of radical Islam, so the mullahs forced the MEK to leave Iran, causing the organization to split up, with factions settling in the United States, in France, and in Iraq. Since its inception, the MEK has been characterized as a cult, shaped by the personalities of the husband-and-wife team of Maryam and Masoud Rajavi. Followers have been known to behave as a quasi-military organization, distinct for portraying women members in military uniforms brandishing weapons.

Even today, the NCRI doggedly attacks the Islamic Republic of Iran at every available opportunity. Many key aspects of Iran's secret push to develop nuclear weapons are known to the world because the NCRI held international press conferences to reveal information obtained by MEK members who remain active as underground operatives in Iran.

The nuclear facility at Natanz was clandestine until the NCRI revealed the site in a press conference held in Washington DC, in mid-August 2002. The NCRI press release was highly detailed, revealing for the first time that the Natanz site was being built to contain two large underground structures designed to house the centrifuges necessary to enrich uranium to weapons grade. Each of the underground structures was reportedly being buried twenty-five feet underground, protected by eight feet of concrete and surrounded by a protective shield to make the structure resistant to explosions.

The NCRI press release even disclosed the names of the construction companies that had been hired to start building the Natanz facilities. The press release made public how the Atomic Energy Organization of Iran had set up a front company through which the AEIO intended to pursue the project's needs for facilities and equipment, including such detail as the street address of the fronting company in Tehran.[21] None of this information was known to the International Atomic Energy Agency until the NCRI held the Washington press conference. Afterwards, the IAEA investigated and confirmed the accuracy of the NCRI report.

While Iran was supposedly halting its uranium processing, on 14 November 2004, the NCRI issued a press release disclosing a major nuclear site in Tehran that had been kept secret. According to the document, the Iranian Ministry of Defense had set up The Modern Defense Readiness and Technology Center (MDRTC) on a sixty-acre site previously occupied by three heavy transport battalions operating under the Ministry of Defense. The NCRI report listed the street addresses of the facilities entrances and described the buildings and installations on the site in detail. The report explained that "activities in nuclear and biological warfare" that had previously been performed elsewhere were moved to the MDRTC. The press release gave the names of commanders and described how the Iranians had deceived IAEA efforts to investigate.

This was an important report. For the first time, the NCRI gave a full explanation of how the Iranian government had assigned nuclear work to the military, calculating to keep the military operation secret even to Iran's own atomic energy agency.

The MD [Ministry of Defense] and the AEIO [Atomic Energy Organization of Iran] are the two bodies who are conducting Iran's nuclear activities in a parallel manner. The AEIO is pursuing the nuclear power stations and the fuel cycle whereas the MD is seeking to achieve nuclear bomb technology and keeps all its activities secret from the AEIO. For this reason, redoing of works is a major problem in Iran's nuclear project and many research and preparations are carried out repeatedly and in a parallel manner with huge expenses.[22]

The NCRI information was obviously obtained from its underground agents operating in Iran. Much of what was reported had been previously unknown by the IAEA, or by American intelligence units, including the CIA.

Regardless of the State Department designation of the NCRI as a terrorist organization, what is clear is that the MEK and NCRI hate the Iranian regime of the mullahs. One of the key weapons in their unrelenting attack has been information. The NCRI is determined to expose Iran's nuclear ambitions. NCRI reports have repeatedly revealed to the world the exact nature of the clandestine nuclear weapons activities going on in Iran. This does not mean that all aspects of the NCRI's reports are fully accurate. Still, the vast majority of what they expose ends up being subsequently verified by the IAEA or one of the major intelligence operations run by the United States or other governments around the world.

IAEA reports confirm a history of instances in which Iran failed to report material aspects of its nuclear program. Iran intentionally took steps to mislead IAEA inspectors. It is clear that Iran actively engaged in extensive concealment behavior.

On 2 September 2005, the IAEA Board of Governors issued

yet another report concluding that "Iran had failed in a number of instances over an extended period of time to meet its obligations under its Safeguards Agreement with respect to the reporting of nuclear material, its processing and its use, as well as the declaration of facilities where such material had been processed and stored."[23] The multi-page report listed violations that went back to 1991, when Iran had failed to disclose the import of uranium.

What the diplomatic language takes pains to gloss over is the embarrassment caused to the IAEA every time Iran's deception is revealed by someone else. Third party disclosures and international press reports are fed information leaked from within Iran by internal dissidents. These disclosures force IAEA inspectors to go back and look for what they had missed. Finally, the IAEA issues new, corrected reports. The embarrassment to the IAEA is immediate as the world realizes that the Iranians had fed the IAEA, half-truths, and outright deceptions.

It took the release of the truth by opposition groups such as the NCRI before Iran's clandestine nuclear activities were disclosed publicly by others. The obvious conclusion was that the IAEA could not be relied upon to do its job.

THE STATE DEPARTMENT'S SLIDE SHOW

In a rare move, the US State Department released a set of briefing slides on Iran that were presented to foreign diplomats in Vienna in September 2005.[24]

The purpose was to question whether Iran's pursuit of the nuclear fuel cycle was intended for peaceful uses, as Iran maintained, or for the creation of nuclear weapons, as the State Department contended. The slides were meant to make the argument that the way Iran had constructed their nuclear facilities was more consistent with the way a country would build a weapons program, not a peaceful program intended to generate electricity.

In the slides, the State Department "confirmed a record of hiding sensitive nuclear fuel activities from the IAEA," charging that "Iran's rationale for a 'peaceful' nuclear fuel cycle does not hold up under scrutiny." With Iran sitting on proven oil reserves of 125.8 million barrels, roughly 10 percent of the world's total, plus 940 trillion cubic feet of proven natural gas reserves, 15.5 percent of the world's total and the world's second largest supply in any country, the State Department doubted that Iran needed nuclear power in order to provide civilian electricity.

The State Department argued that instead of spending $6 billion to develop the seven new nuclear reactors Iran proposed to build, Iran could make the same dollar investments in the country's aging and neglected oil and natural gas infrastructures. This investment would permit Iran to build one or more new refineries, all designed to reduce Iran's domestic cost of energy and eliminate the need to import refined gasoline. The slides argued that: "If Iran were to invest $5.6 billion in a high gasoline yield Western-type refinery, it could eliminate its dependence on imported gasoline and increase its annual net oil-related revenue by approximately $982 million."

The slides also revealed satellite photographs of Iran's nuclear facilities. The photos taken over time showed how Iran had misrepresented the facilities, and constructed them so as to bury and hide key functions. Some facilities Iran had simply failed to disclose at all. With regard to the gas centrifuge uranium enrichment at Natanz, for instance, the State Department identified the site as "a covert facility in a remote location, which could be used to enrich uranium for weapons." Satellite and ground photographs showed dummy structures designed to prevent detection and identification, as well as facilities that were concealed underground, hardened and well-defended.

Significant progress constructing a heavy water reduction complex in the central-Iran city of Arak was shown for the time period of June 2004 through March 2005. These photos demonstrated that the reactor construction was progressing rapidly, despite IAEA Board requests to forgo construction altogether. The State Department dismissed Iran's claim that the Arak reactor was needed for medical and industrial isotopes, a capability that Iran already had inherent in their 10 megawatt Tehran research reactor.

The only reason Iran would need a heavy water facility is if the country were planning to build a plutonium bomb. The Russian-built reactor at Bushehr does not use heavy water. Heavy water is required to moderate the nuclear chain reaction needed to produce weapons-grade plutonium. Fission bombs requiring plutonium are more sophisticated to design and detonate than bombs using highly enriched uranium. But the explosive magnitude of plutonium bombs is many times greater.

The slides also documented the development of the uranium mine at Gachin, a uranium mine that was larger and more promising that the uranium mine at Saghand, the only mine Iranian reports had bothered to disclose prior to 2004.

The State Department concluded that Iran's nuclear program is "well-scaled for a nuclear weapons capability," especially when compared to the progress being made in the nuclear weapons facilities of North Korea. "When one also considers Iran's concealment and deception activities," a slide argued, "it is difficult to escape the conclusion that Iran is pursuing nuclear weapons." The State Department's analysis further argued that "Iran's uranium reserves cannot support planned nuclear power plants, but are well-scaled to give Iran a significant number of nuclear weapons."

Finally, so as to leave no doubt, one of the last slides drove home the point: "Iran's past history of concealment and deception and the nuclear fuel cycle infrastructure are *most consistent with an intent to acquire nuclear weapons.*" The last part of the sentence was underlined for emphasis in the original slide.

If Iran hadn't telegraphed its plan clearly enough, the following month, October 2005, Ahmadinejad placed the military in control of the nation's nuclear program.[25] This decision strongly undermined Iran's argument that the purpose of the country's nuclear program is entirely peaceful.

REVELATIONS OF IRAN'S PROGRESS

Whenever the subject of rogue nations sharing nuclear weapons secrets comes up, the name of A.Q. Khan is not far behind. In 2004, the father of Pakistan's nuclear weapons program went on Pakistani television and apologized to the nation for having sold Pakistan nuclear secrets to other countries. "It pains me to realize that my lifetime achievement could have been placed in jeopardy," he said with an emotion that looked like regret.[26] One of those nations was Iran, which had "received significant assistance" in the past from "the proliferation network headed by Pakistani scientist A.Q. Khan," according to a CIA report.[27]

Suspicion regarding Khan's secret nuclear black market was reinforced on 18 November 2005. On that date, the IAEA released a report disclosing a hand-written one-page document that constituted an offer made by Khan's network to Iran in 1987. The document, which had been voluntarily turned over to the IAEA by Iran, represented an offer to sell Iran nuclear components and equipment. Iran admitted that some components of one or two disassembled centrifuges, as well as supporting drawings and specifications, were delivered by Khan's procurement network and that other items referred to in the document were obtained from other suppliers.

Additional documents handed over by Iran relating to the 1987 offer included "detailed drawings of the P-1 centrifuge components and assemblies; technical specifications supporting component manufacture and centrifuge assembly; and technical documents relating to centrifuge operational performance."[28] Furthermore, the documents included schematic drawings showing a centrifuge layout for six cascades of 168 machines each and a small plant of 2,000 centrifuges arranged in the same hall.

Perhaps most alarming, the documents explained the procedural requirements for reduction of uranium hexafluoride gas to metal, an important step in making a nuclear warhead. The documents included precise technical discussions of how to cast machine-enriched uranium into hemispherical forms needed for warheads. Uranium metal is not useful in civilian nuclear power plants. Casting uranium metal into hemispherical forms is a discussion appropriately reserved for producing nuclear warheads. And there was more startling information coming to light.

Only a few days earlier, US intelligence agents had briefed IAEA officials privately regarding some 1,000 pages of information found on a laptop computer obtained from an unspecified source in Iran. The laptop evidently contained "computer simulations and accounts of experiments believed to be part of a long-term program to design a nuclear warhead compatible with Iran's Shahab missile and capable of reaching Israel and other Middle Eastern countries."[29]

Immediately, critics countered that the information on the laptop was intended for nonmilitary applications. David Albright, from the Institute for Science and International Security, a credible expert, objected that the laptop files were describing a re-entry vehicle for a missile, not the design of a nuclear warhead. The "black box" contained by the reentry vehicle may appear to be a nuclear warhead, but the laptop documents themselves did not specify a nuclear warhead. Conceivably, the documents could have been created by an Iranian missile team on its own, not as part of a nuclear warhead design project.[30]

Iranian Foreign Ministry spokesperson, Hamid Reza Asefi, called the US claims "worthless and naïve." He questioned the credibility of the entire laptop find, as well as the validity of any conclusion that the information on the laptop proved Iran had developed a deliverable nuclear warhead. "The baseless claim made us laugh. We do not use laptops to keep our classified documents. It is another fuss ahead of the IAEA board meeting to poison the board's atmosphere."[31]

The laptop controversy came just as the Bush administration was under intense attack from Democrats in the US Senate questioning whether the administration had misled Congress regarding weapons of mass destruction intelligence in the ramp-up to the 2003 war in Iraq. Was the US using similar unverified intelligence to stampede the IAEA into referring Iran to the Security Council?

Despite these questions, UN nuclear analysts studying the laptop documents evidently found them to be credible evidence of Iranian nuclear weapons progress. According to a *New York Times* report that broke the story to the public, several officials and nuclear weapons experts in Europe and the United States with detailed knowledge of the intelligence concluded that the laptop documents reflected a concerted Iranian effort to build a nuclear warhead.[32]

With nearly $200 million a day in windfall oil revenue after a 2005 spike in oil prices, Iran had ample revenue to purchase the international talent and technology needed to develop a nuclear weapons program. That the United States was pushing another pre-emptive case regarding Iran, just as the United States had pressed against Saddam Hussein, was also undeniable. No doubt, a much weakened President Bush was entering a second term defending the ongoing Iraqi war. Iran knew the relative weakness of the Bush administration was a strategic opportunity. The evidence looked bad, but Tehran now had additional latitude to raise doubts internationally. Meanwhile, the Iranians continued to press their argument that their only reason for pursuing nuclear capabilities was for peaceful uses, regardless of evidence or arguments to the contrary.

IRAN STARTS ENRICHMENT

Once enough uranium hexafluoride gas of adequate quality had been produced at Isfahan, the next logical step would be to ship it to Natanz. Producing highly enriched uranium in the centrifuges would then be a matter of months. And that meant crisis time.

"If they start enriching, this is a major issue and a serious concern for the international community," ElBaradei told the *Independent* (London). "I know they are trying to acquire the full fuel cycle. I know that acquiring the full fuel cycle means that a country is months away from nuclear weapons, and that applies to Iran and everyone else. If Tehran indeed resumes its uranium enrichment in other plants, as threatened, it will only take several months to make a bomb."[33] As of January 2006, there was no more *If*.

On Tuesday, 3 January 2006, Mohammad Saeedi announced from Tehran that Iran had informed the IAEA in writing that nuclear enrichment work at Natanz would soon resume. "Within the next few days we will start researching that field in cooperation and coordination with the IAEA," Saeedi said on Iran's state television.[34]

The announcement sent shocks around the world. There was no

cooperation with the IAEA in the works. Just the opposite was true. The IAEA had threatened to send the Iranian file to the UN for "noncompliance." Saeedi's announcement gave further indication that Iran was willing to openly defy the United States and the EU3.

The announcement was confirmed by Alaeddin Boroujerdi, head of the Majlis National Security and Policy Commission, who said openly that work at Natanz would be resumed soon: "Completion of the nuclear fuel process upon international regulations is a part of our policies and we are determined to make the Natanz project active after the Isfahan one."[35] Boroujerdi stressed that uranium enrichment in Iran could proceed with Russian technical assistance, so long as the enrichment process itself was conducted on Iranian territory. When the IAEA note was released, it disclosed 9 January as the date Iran intended to begin "R&D (research and development) on the peaceful nuclear energy program which was suspended."[36]

Only a day behind schedule, on 10 January, Iran resumed nuclear "research and development" at Natanz. Saeedi made the announcement in a way that suggested the IAEA had approved: "Nuclear research officially resumed at sites agreed upon with IAEA inspectors."[37]

Yes, IAEA inspectors had traveled to Natanz to remove the seals from the research installations at Natanz. But, no, the IAEA had not "approved" Iran's decision to resume uranium enrichment activities at Natanz, even if these activities were distinguished by Iran to be only "research and development," not full uranium enrichment. In reality, ElBaradei had asked Iran to agree voluntarily to keep Natanz closed, in order to build international confidence.

After asking Iran to clarify what was meant by "research and development," ElBaradei released a thirty-five-page report to the IAEA board revealing that Iran did intend to release uranium hexafluoride gas into the centrifuges but in "a small amount"—an attempt by Iran to distinguish these "research activities" from "full scale uranium enrichment."[38]

The pattern Iran was following for the resumption of uranium enrichment at Natanz paralleled the path it had followed when resuming uranium processing at Isfahan. Both plants had been closed voluntarily by Iran in November 2004, in a move Iran claimed was designed to comply with an IAEA requirement for negotiations to commence on Iran's nuclear program. Critics charged that Iran only agreed to close both plants because Iran's nuclear scientists and engineers were experiencing technical problems.

In August 2005, when Iran defied world diplomats by deciding unilaterally to resume uranium processing at Isfahan, the regime argued that "uranium processing" was not "uranium enrichment," in that uranium processing ends with uranium hexafluoride gas, not with actual enriched uranium. Then, virtually verifying that technical problems had been the real issue, Iran confirmed on 1 January 2006 that major advances had been made at Isfahan developing a "mixer-settler" process to separate yellowcake uranium from uranium ore.[39] In other words, Isfahan was reopened for full-scale uranium processing when Iran was ready to do so, after technical "research and development" problems had been solved, deciding to open the plant unilaterally, regardless of what the IAEA or world diplomats said in objection.

The regime was repeating the "news control" process at Natanz. Here, the research and development required was learning how to master the operation of the 164-centrifuge cascade needed to enrich uranium to relative low grades, overcoming the technical hurdles of uranium enrichment that can be transferred to the larger cascade structures required for the higher enrichment grades.[40]

By masking the regime's true intentions with disclosures that stress technical distinctions, the regime gives the impression that

Iran is being less than truthful about actual events. This is far from the "transparency" required by fully-disclosed nuclear activities subject to open inspection by the IAEA. Especially by deciding to proceed in defiance of strongly-expressed world diplomatic objection, the Iranian regime further fueled concerns that the true intent was for Iran's nuclear industry to master the production of weapons-grade uranium on Iranian soil.

WORTHLESS BRIBES

Since November 2004, the EU3 and the IAEA had bent over backwards offering Iran every imaginable concession, if only Iran would agree not to enrich uranium.

Iran claimed that national security concerns demanded that the government maintain a strong military, for defensive reasons only (even though its nuclear program had nothing to do with weapons development?). Yet, the EU3 and the IAEA even offered to negotiate with Iran a multinational security agreement, saying a nonaggression pact would be signed by any and all countries Iran felt were potentially threatening their national security. This was not enough.

Then the EU3 and the IAEA offered to promote Iran's entry into the World Trade Organization, under the premise that such a major economic incentive might tempt Iran to step away from any and all nuclear weapons ambitions. The added concession was still not good enough for Iran.

Russia's proposal to enrich uranium in Russia for Iran was still on the table. The Russian offer was designed to permit the Iranians to gain technical knowledge regarding uranium enrichment, while making sure the process remained under Russian control. The Russian-Iranian uranium enrichment joint venture promised to produce for Iran all the enriched uranium Iran could possibly need for peaceful civilian energy purposes. But even this was not enough for Iran. The Iranians were determined to complete the full nuclear fuel-cycle on their own soil.[41]

But not only did Iran reject the offers, in response to all these intense diplomatic overtures, Iran became even more belligerent. The Associated Press reported that Iran's Guardians Council had accepted a bill passed by the Majlis affirming that if the IAEA voted to refer Iran to the UN's Security Council, then the Iranian government would respond by blocking any further international inspection of its nuclear facilities. The new law's language was clear: "If Iran's nuclear file is referred or reported to the UN Security Council, the government will be required to cancel all voluntary measures it has taken and implement all scientific, research and executive programs to enable the rights of the nation under the Nuclear Non-Proliferation Treaty."[42]

This was nothing more than a threat: If Iran were taken to the Security Council for sanctions, any and all efforts to cooperate with continued IAEA inspections would be terminated.

The Iranians could afford to be belligerent. A report issued by the United States Institute of Peace at the close of 2005 suggested that Iran's windfall profits from the spike in energy profits gave the country enough economic strength to ride out any new sanctions the US and others might impose.[43] Israel came to the same conclusion. Speaking at Tel Aviv University the previous month, IDF chief of staff Lt. General Dan Halutz told the audience, "A state like Iran which has accumulated just in the past two years $150 billion beyond what it planned due to the rise in oil prices is not so sensitive to economic sanctions."[44]

Halutz despaired that a diplomatic solution would be found. "The fact that the Iranians are succeeding time after time to get away from the international pressure either under the IAEA Board of Governors or the UN Security Council is encouraging them with their nuclear project," he said in separate remarks. "I believe that the political means that are used by the European countries and the Americans to convince the Iranians to stop their project will not end in the stopping of the Iranian project."[45] These were hard words coming from the Israeli Army chief of staff.

CLOSING IN ON THE BOMB

On 11 April 2006, Ahmadinejad announced that Iran had joined the nuclear club, declaring on state television that, "I officially announce that Iran has joined the world's nuclear countries."[46]

Two days before, Iran had successfully enriched uranium to 3.5 percent. A ceremony was held in Mashad, one of Iran's holiest cities. Dancers in traditional Iranian costumes held up capsules of uranium hexafluoride gas. The celebration was on a raised stage, amidst a pageantry of banners and Iranian flags, in front of a festive blue backdrop with images of doves released into the air.

Then, on 3 May 2006, Iran's nuclear chief Gholamreza Aghazadeh announced that Iran had enriched uranium up to 4.8 percent purity, the upper end of spectrum needed for peaceful purposes, to power a nuclear plant intended to generate electricity.[47]

Subsequently, the IAEA confirmed that Iran's announcement was true. By pursuing a path of deception and defiance, Iran had reached a major milestone along the road to developing the bomb. Uranium was now being enriched on Iranian soil by Iranian nuclear scientists and technicians. The Pakistani general had told his Iranian visitors who asked for a bomb in 1990, "you must make it yourself." They were close. Iran now had everything necessary to make a nuclear weapon within their control.

Given that, the important question is, *How soon will they have it?*

ElBaradei told the *Independent* a bomb was possible in a few months once enrichment was underway. Israeli Prime Minister Ehud Olmert has echoed that. "The technological threshold" for Iran to make a nuclear weapon "is very close. It can be measured by months rather than years."[48]

But these views are not shared by all. In August 2005, the *Washington Post* published a report on a leaked classified document that claimed Iran was still ten years away from having enough enriched uranium to make a nuclear weapon. The previous intelligence estimate was five years.

The story supported Bush administration critics who had argued that the administration was "hyping" intelligence estimates to represent a nuclear weapons scare. Political critics charged that the administration was scaring us about Iran, just like the administration had used intelligence reports about weapons of mass destruction to justify going to war against Saddam Hussein in Iraq.[49]

This new report directly contradicted White House statements that Iran was close to developing a bomb:

> The carefully hedged assessments, which represent consensus among US intelligence agencies, contrast with forceful public statements by the White House. Administration officials have asserted, but have not offered proof, that Tehran is moving determinedly toward a nuclear arsenal. The new estimate could provide more time for diplomacy with Iran over its nuclear ambitions. President Bush has said that he wants the crisis resolved diplomatically but that "all options are on the table."[50]

Moreover, definitive proof was lacking that Iran was building a bomb. This uncertainty was crippling to any decision to take military action against Iran:

The new National Intelligence Estimate includes what the intelligence community views as credible indicators that Iran's military is conducting clandestine work. But the sources said there is no information linking those projects directly to a nuclear weapons program. What is clear is that Iran, mostly through its energy program, is acquiring and mastering technologies that could be diverted to bomb making.[51]

More than anything, the story affirmed the brilliance of the Iranian strategy. Without more precise intelligence, how could the United States design a clear response, either diplomatic or military?

Between the various players, estimates for a bomb were now all over the map: 2007, 2010, 2015.[52] Which estimate was correct?

With the administration under heavy pressure from the political left and the Democratic Party over the war in Iraq, President Bush was blocked from taking military action against Iran, even if that was the administration's first choice. Without reliable intelligence estimates, President Bush would look unreasonably aggressive if he were to pursue a military solution instead of a diplomatic solution. Despite evidence which suggested Iran's nuclear program was a weapons program, the argument was inferential and circumstantial at best. The administration lacked definitive proof that Iran was planning to build a bomb soon and that its likelihood of success was high.

All the mullahs had to do was keep pushing for a while longer—keep building and keep denying it. As long as they did that, we'd never know they were preparing for the apocalypse and the second coming of the Mahdi until it was too late.

3

THE PRESIDENT
AND THE MAHDI

*"In history, revolutions similar to Iran's revolution are
achieved only with the help of messengers of God."*

—AYATOLLAH KHOMEINI, 1981

On 25 June 2005, Mahmoud Ahmadinejad was elected president of Iran. He beat former president Akbar Hashemi Rafsanjani in a "run-off" election, winning a reported 60 percent of the vote.

Prior to the election, expatriate Iranians called for voters to boycott the 17 June election. The opposition coalition argued that any vote would be seen as a vote for the regime. Charging that the only candidates were those that the mullahs handpicked from among the "regime's Mafia families," opposition leaders wanted Iranians to stay home on Election Day. A boycott was seen as the best way to protest "the convoluted and despotic nature of the regime," in which "the power is controlled by non-elected mullahs, and the elections are used as a tool to create the perception of legitimacy for the regime."[1] In May 2005, the Guardians Council had rejected the applications of some 1,000 candidates who wanted to run for president, a decision which narrowed the list of candidates to seventeen mullah-approved hopefuls.[2]

From his prison cell, Akbar Ganji, one of Iran's leading investigative journalists and writers, whose prolonged hunger strike had more than once brought him to the point of death, joined his voice to those who were calling for an election boycott. "In a political system that forbids women and the Sunni Muslims from becoming president, where one man holds all the powers and is above the Constitution," Ganji argued, "there is no point for the people to go to the polls." He urged "civil disobedience" and "no collaboration" with the ruling ayatollahs as the "best way" to democratize Iran.[3]

Election Day street protests were ruled out as too risky. Opposition leaders feared that the protesting crowds would be attacked by the mullah-backed thugs of the Basij, the brutal civilian militia organized by the clerics to enforce their theocracy with officially-sanctioned violence. Cautiously, Ayatollah Khamenei, the Islamic republic's supreme leader, had issued a decree banning any kind of street demonstration until the morning after the vote.

In reality, Iranians accepted that the "winner" of the presidential election would be the candidate Khamenei wanted to win. By staying away from the poles, dissident Iranians hoped the world community would note their expression of disgust in a rigged election they saw as illegitimate. By rejecting civil disobedience, however, a quiet protest risked being unseen. A boycott would go unreported by the mullah-controlled press. But massive street demonstrations could attract the attention of the worldwide press, especially if they had turned violent.

By all reports, the boycott worked, but it was also underneath the media radar. Some 29.3 million votes were cast out of 46.7 million eligible voters, for a turnout of 62.7 percent.[4] But with an unseen protest, the mullahs proclaimed the election a huge success nonetheless. President Bush joined the critics, calling the election a "sham." He charged that the voting ignored "basic democratic standards" and asserted that the election farce was additional evidence of the Islamic Republic's "oppressive record."[5]

For all the controversy, there was still another problem—the vote produced no clear winner. A run-off election was scheduled for 25 June. In the days before the run-off, the government press billed the choice as a decision between former President Hashami Rafsanjani, a "reform" candidate, and the ultraconservative former mayor of Tehran, Mahmoud Ahmadinejad. The press presented Ahmadinejad as a "man of the people," every bit the "austere image of a God-fearing public servant." With his thin frame, modest clothes, and close-cropped black beard, Ahmadinejad appealed to Iranians suffering from years of unemployment, inflation, and corruption.[6]

The world was shocked when the relatively unknown Ahmadinejad was declared the winner. Only months before, he trailed in the polls with backing of only 1 percent. Insiders knew that Ahmadinejad's victory was a clear sign that the ruling powers in Iran had decided to move in an ultraconservative direction. It was also seen by Ahmadinejad as a sign of divine calling.

With Ahmadinejad's election, the signal was clear. The ruling mullahs were not prepared to tolerate internal dissent or civil disobedience. Instead, under Ahmadinejad, the regime planned to reinforce a strict Islamic moral code. Gone would be western-type freedoms such as the Internet or free speech. No longer would moral abuses be tolerated. Gone were the days when young lovers could hold hands in public. Women who did not properly cover their heads and faces with the traditional *hejab* veil would be accused of "indecent behavior" and punished.

In accepting the victory, Ahmadinejad gave a short, but important statement. He stressed his devotion to the late Ayatollah Khomeini and to the radical Islamic revolution which Khomeini had led. "Iran has high capacities and can promulgate Islamic civilization worldwide," he said.[7] These words were carefully chosen. Ahmadinejad's spiritual and moral roots are deeply embedded in Khomeini's revolution and its worldwide spread.

Moderates around the world reacted sharply. Almost immediately upon Ahmadinejad's election, six former US embassy hostages claimed that Ahmadinejad had been one of their captors. A photograph surfaced showing a blindfolded American hostage being displayed to the crowd outside the American embassy, being held by a radical whose appearance, including his neatly trimmed black beard, resembled Ahmadinejad.[8] Experts established that the person in the photo was someone other than Ahmadinejad. Still, former Iranian Prime Minister Bani-Sadr, who was living in exile after being deposed in 1981, claimed that Ahmadinejad was part of the circle of revolutionary youths close to Khomeini. Bani-Sadr claimed that Ahmadinejad "wasn't among the decision-makers but he was among those inside the Embassy."[9] Quickly, the world press stressed that Ahmadinejad was a prominent member of the Pasdaran, the Islamic Revolutionary Guards Corps, commonly known as simply the Revolutionary Guards. The group was created by Khomeini in May 1979 to defend the revolution against internal enemies.[10] With Ahmadinejad's election, Iran moved to the right, in a determined move to realize once and for all the victory of the revolution.

PEOPLE'S CHAMPION

Ahmadinejad was born in 1956, in Garmsar, a small town outside Tehran, the fourth of seven children. When he was one year old, his family moved to Tehran where his father, an ironworker (who is sometimes described as a "blacksmith"), had better chances of employment. In 1975, Ahmadinejah entered the University of Science and Technology where he studied civil engineering, but he put his studies on hold when the revolution began. In 1987, he received a doctorate, with a specialty in traffic management.

Following the 1979 revolution, he became a member of the Office of Strengthening Unity Between University and Technology

Seminaries. This group was founded by Ayatollah Mohammad Beheshti, a close associate of Khomeini. The purpose of this office was to organize radical Islamic students against the radical socialists Mujahedin-e-Khalq (MEK) who at that time were rivaling Khomeini.

With the start of the Iran-Iraq war in 1980, Ahmadinejad joined the Revolutionary Guards and rushed to the front. In the Revolutionary Guards, Ahmadinejad advanced to become a senior officer in the Special Brigade, stationed at Ramazan Garrison near Kermanshah in western Iran. This was the headquarters of the Guards' Extraterritorial Operations unit, which was organized to launch attacks to kidnap or kill Iranian expatriate dissidents. Ahmadinejad participated in these covert operations, notably around the Iraqi city of Kirkuk. When the Guards formed the Qods Force (Jerusalem Force), Ahmadinejad became a senior commander, directing assassinations in the Middle East and Europe.[11]

Before becoming mayor of Tehran in April 2003, Ahmadinejad had served as governor of Maku and Khoy, cities in the northwestern province of Kurdistan for two years. In 1993, he was appointed as governor general of the newly established northwestern province of Ardebil, although he was removed by the newly-formed "reform" administration of President Khatami. In 1997 he became a member of the scientific board of the Civil Engineering College of the University of Science and Technology.

As mayor of Tehran, Ahmadinejad reversed many policies of the previous reform mayors. He placed emphasis on a fundamentalist adherence to Islam, going so far as to transform the city's cultural centers into prayer halls during the Islamic holy month of Ramadan. He closed fast-food restaurants and required city male employees to grow beards and wear long sleeves. He instituted a policy of separating men and women in municipal offices. And he insisted that women in municipal work always adhere to strict Islamic codes regarding conservative dress and cosmetics.

Given Ahmadinejad's extensive background in education, civil engineering, and government, we would be mistaken to assume that he is inexperienced or naïve. On the contrary, he is fully aware of his political appeal to Iran's vast lower middle class and urban poor, as well as the country's still extensive rural communities. Ayatollah Khomeini came to power through this same economic and rural base, his way paved by many rural clerics who continue to struggle in relatively second-class and out-of-the-way mosques.

His experience in the Revolutionary Guards gives Ahmadinejad credentials that place him in the first ranks of today's middle-aged Iranian revolutionary leaders. Khatami and Rafsanjani dare not push themes of democracy and reform too openly today. Ahmadinejad has turned back the clock, reversing years of work by the reformists. In his first four months in office, Ahmadinejad completely destroyed the years of work done by Khatami and Rafsanjani to convince the world that Iran was not ruled by fanatics.

In running for election, Ahmadinejad presented himself as a commoner, a *mar domyar* ("man of the people").[12] His few suits were not foreign-tailored. His shirts were simple, open at the neck, not worn with gold cufflinks or closed at the neck with a golden pin. His message was that he came to bring justice for the poor who had suffered in Iran and that he was cut from the same cloth as the average Iranian who struggled to work and feed a family. Ahmadinejad powerfully invoked the name of "Allah the Merciful," and he ended his speeches with a plea to prepare the way for the Mahdi's return.

He drew great support from the Basij, the loosely-organized volunteer militia serving under the direction of the Revolutionary Guards. The Basij is Ahmadinejad's power base, his enforcers assigned to demand a strict adherence to Islamic law throughout Iran, reaching even into small towns and rural communities.[13]

Under the reform presidencies of Khatami and Rafsanjani, the religious piety and simple devotion displayed by Ahmadinejad were treated disparagingly and considered quaint. Under Ahmadinejad, orthodox religion serves as a direct connection to the vast Iranian underclass. Millions in Iran have never enjoyed the material advantages or the abundant lifestyles of the wealthy mullahs or the government officials who rose to the top in the reform years since the Ayatollah Khomeini died.

In Tehran, families crowd into apartments, with young adult children afraid to marry simply because low incomes make raising a family extremely taxing—not just for feeding children but even for paying for a separate apartment in which to live apart from parents. Lower level employees in Tehran's government bureaucracy miss meals or work second jobs as taxi drivers to put food on the table for the family.

The World Bank estimates that 67 percent of the urban population of Iran lives in poverty.[14] Moreover, Iran has undergone a rapid process of urbanization since the Revolution that has emptied many small villages and created a new urban underclass that lives in the grip of dire poverty, prostitution, and international crime. More than 1.3 million people in Iran earn less than a dollar a day.

The number of women engaged in prostitution in Iran is estimated at approximately 900,000 to 1 million; the number of hard drug addicts is estimated at about 2.5 million people. A growing sex slave trade in Iran is considered one of the country's most profitable businesses. Families may have no financial alternative but to sell a daughter into the sex trade. Parents know that their child may end up being passed around the Persian Gulf states to be abused. Other Iranian children sold into the sex trade end up being abused in one of the many sex slavery rings operating in Britain, France, and Germany.[15] But parents feel as if they have no choice. If one child is not sold, the others may not eat.

Universities graduate some 300,000 students a year, with 800,000 students entering the job market each year. With its troubled economy, the influx of new workers means an unemployment rate of 50 percent for those under the age of thirty-five.[16] Some 10,000 doctors in Iran have no jobs.

Not surprisingly, more than 150,000 Iranians emigrate each year.[17] The situation is particularly serious among Iran's best-educated young people. Over 80 percent of Iranians studying in foreign universities never return home, and as many as four out of five who win scientific awards do everything they can to emigrate. This rate of "brain drain" is one of the highest experienced by any country in the world and inflicts even more damage to the economy.

It's only worsened since Ahmadinejad's election. The Iranian stock market has dropped nearly 25 percent under his administration. Share prices have lost up to 60 percent of their value, reflecting a flight of capital and a concern that Ahmadinejad is leading the country toward war. In the last three months of 2005, approximately $100 billion of Iranian capital was invested in nearby Dubai. Another $100 million of Iranian capital fled to investments in Iraq and Kurdistan—not exactly safe or secure places to invest, reflecting the grim realities of Iran's markets by comparison. Still more capital has fled to Europe and Canada. When the stock market reached an all time low in October 2005, the Iranian regime was considering closing down the market altogether.[18]

Part of the problem is that Ahmadinejad seems clueless when it comes to basic economics. During his campaign, he described stock market investing as "a game of chance, contrary to Iranian principles."[19] In November 2005, he had Iran's most important bankers fired. His government then appointed a former Revolutionary Guard commander to run the central bank and appointed a young economics graduate who previously worked in the finance department of the Khomeini Foundation to run the stock market.[20] In a move that surely worries investors, the new director was hired for his aversion to free enterprise. Related appointments were much the same—marginal professional qualifications except undying loyalty to the president. Before the new appointments Ahmadinejad said, "[I]f it had been possible to hang a couple of people, the Tehran stock exchange would already have been put in order."[21]

The only sure winners are the mullahs themselves. In the quarter-century since the 1979 revolution, they have greatly enriched themselves. Today they are firmly in control of Iran's government-run businesses, including the oil industry. The top mullahs hide away millions in foreign bank accounts and foreign-controlled business ventures. In the past few years, they and their cronies have stashed nearly $400 billion in bank accounts in Dubai. Over 500,000 of these wealthy Iranians now make the United Arab Emirates their home, many with luxury high-rise apartments on Dubai's world-class beaches. Even Rafsanjani, emerging from near poverty in 1979, has become a billionaire. Then, he was a poor pistachio farmer in rural Iran. Today, he is probably one of Iran's wealthiest citizens.

As for the rest of the country, there is little chance of much improvement. Oil-rich Iran actually *imports* gasoline because the country's antiquated energy infrastructure cannot refine enough gasoline to meet domestic demand.[22] But rather than invest in this crucial infrastructure, Ahmadinejad's seems bent on directing Iran's scarce resources into the country's pursuit of nuclear technologies and supporting international terrorist organizations, like Hezbollah and Hamas. These are objectives central to his politically religious aims of destroying Israel and America. If the people have Islam, Ahmadinejad may well argue, why would they need more?

Besides, while Ahmadinejad has not been the economic savior the people voted for, he does offer another type of salvation that the people may consider even more compelling.

MYSTICAL MANIPULATION

Ahmadinejad's chief spiritual advisor is Ayatollah Mohammad Taqi Mesbah Yazdi, known as "the Crocodile" for his rugged facial features and his hard-line orthodox religious views. During the presidential election, Yazdi told believers that Ahmadinejad was the "chosen" of the Mahdi. Because Ahmadinejad is the person designated to prepare the way for the Twelfth Imam's second coming, Yazdi told followers they had a duty to vote for him.

Yazdi heads the Imam Khomeini Research and Learning Center in Qom, site of the sacred Jamkaran well, down which the Twelfth Imam supposedly disappeared as a child centuries ago. At the well there is a green "post office box" to permit devout Shi'ites to write prayer requests on small pieces of paper and to "mail" them to the Mahdi. The practice bears a resemblance to devout Jews writing prayer requests to Yahweh on small pieces of paper that are placed in the cracks of the Western Temple Wall in Jerusalem. It was at this site where the Ayatollah Khomeini lived prior to being forced to leave Iran in exile. Here, Khomeini led his opposition to the Shah. Unsurprisingly, when Ahmadinejad became president, he reportedly allocated $17 million to the Jamkaran Mosque for renovations.

Ayatollah Yazdi heads a particularly radical Mahdi sect called the Hojatieh. The Hojatieh believe that world suffering and poverty must reach a crisis point before the Mahdi returns. The Hojatieh are comfortable with allowing evil to spread, believing that tyranny and misery only hasten the Mahdi's return and the final triumph of Islam.[23] Reformist mullahs, such as Khatami and Rafsanjani, consider the sect the lunatic fringe. But Khatami and Rafsanjani are no longer in power, and Ahmadinejad has reportedly placed Hojatieh devotees in key government positions.[24]

The Iran Press Service operating out of Paris, France, documents how closely fundamentalist Shi'ites identify Ahmadinejad with the second coming.

> Iranian observers say that since the arrival to power of Mr. Ahmadinejad, there is an "escalation" of religious superstitions and add that "extremist personalities" around the president "unabatedly" tell him about the signs pointing to the resurrection of the Mahdi, going as far as "convincing" him that the controversial issue of Iranian nuclear activities is "in direct relation" with the appearance of the Imam of All Times.
>
> "In private and public meetings, these figures insist that Government must stand firm to international pressures over the legitimate and natural right of Iran to have nuclear technology for the question is one of the ways to prepare for the re-apparition of the Mahdi," one source close to the president told the Iran Press Service on condition of not being named.[25]

The Bright Future Institute in Qom, one of several centers dedicated to study of the Twelfth Imam, operates a telephone hotline and runs an Internet site dedicated to spreading the message of the Mahdi's imminent return. The most common question asked? "How will we know when the Mahdi is ready to return?" With 160 staff, workers at the center answer dozens of questions daily, responding to e-mails and writing letters. The institute has a growing reach in local schools, publishes chil-dren's and teen magazines, and produces books and films. The day the Mahdi returns is seen to be the beginning of a new age, where Islam is victorious worldwide and people live in peace and harmony.[26]

In this context, we should not be surprised that Ahmadinejad ended his 17 September 2005 speech at the United Nations with an invocation based on the doctrine of the Mahdi, whom he referred to as "a perfect human being."

> From the beginning of time, humanity has longed for the day when justice, peace, equality and compassion envelop the world. All of us can contribute to the establishment of such a world. When that day comes, the ultimate promise of Divine religions will be fulfilled with the emergence of a perfect human being who is heir to all prophets and pious men. He will lead the world to justice and absolute peace.[27]

Most of the world missed these references in Ahmadinejad's speech to the United Nations. Secular diplomats find it hard to believe that today the political leader of a nation would be driven by such religious views. This short-sightedness blinds many to Ahmadinejad's perception of his mission. Ahmadinejad has com-mitted his life to preparing for the second coming of the Mahdi. He believes the moment is imminent for the Twelfth Imam to come out of occultation.

As the nuclear crisis with Iran deepens, millions of Christians worldwide are consulting the Bible and praying to sort out how current world events fit into "last days" prophecies. Similarly, millions of Iranians are listening to their president and teachings of Ayatollah Yazdi to prepare for their own second coming.

While in Qom in January 2006, Ahmadinejad took the opportunity to stress his belief that the return was close at hand. "We must prepare ourselves to rule the world and the only way to do that is to put forth views on the basis of the Expectation of the Return. If we work on the basis of the Expectation of the Return of the Mahdi, all the affairs of our nation will be streamlined and the administration of this country will become easier."[28]

Clearly, for Ahmadinejad, politics and religion are inseparable. The goal of the theocracy remains the worldwide expansion of the Iranian revolution.

"Some politicians think we had a revolution so that some could hit others in the head and have one party ruling for some time and another party in opposition for some time," Ahmadinejad continued. "But we had a revolution to achieve a lofty goal, on the basis of the Expectation of the Return. Our interpretation is that the hand of the Almighty is putting every piece of the jigsaw puzzle of the future of the world in place, in line with the goals of Islam."

He ended by stressing the goal of eliminating the United States from the region: "The Global Oppressor [the United States] occupied these countries [Afghanistan and Iraq] with the aim of putting pressure on Iran, but God let the fruit of this fall on the lap of the Iranian nation."

For millions of Muslims, the defeat of the Soviet Union in Afghanistan was not viewed as a victory for the US, but rather a Muslim victory. Millions of Muslims worldwide also view Osama bin Laden as a hero, precisely because he has stood up against the US, the same way Afghanistan stood up against the Soviet Union. If Saudi Arabia were to have a democratic election, Osama bin Laden would be elected president. Muslims believe that Osama bin Laden was anointed by Allah to defeat the evil empires of both the Soviet Union and the United States. Ahmadinejad agreed.

Israel was a clear enemy, but there was only one evil empire left to defeat, and that was the United States.

Still, there is more to fulfilling the mission of the Mahdi than ridding the world of Israel and the United States. The faithful must be pure. As such, restoring the Iranian people to rigid Islamic orthodoxy is also part of the mission. When asked by the people of Iran what they can do to bring on the Mahdi's return, Ahmadinejad's simple admonition is "be pure and devout." All too often, purity and devotion are a product of coercion under Islamic governments.

CRACKDOWN

Ahmadinejad's election marked a determination by Ayatollah Khamenei and the mullahs at the top of the regime, specifically those on the Council of Elders, to move in a fundamentalist direction.

Systematically, Ahmadinejad has replaced reformers and democratically-oriented bureaucrats with his radically religious associates from the Revolutionary Guard. Student protests have been put down with renewed aggression, and dissidents have been hunted and silenced with a firmness not seen since the heyday of the 1979 revolution.

This new wave of internal repression is fundamental to Ahmadinejad and Ayatollah Khamenei's vision of how Iran's revolution must next be expanded. Fulfilling the predictions of Ayatollah Khomeini that Israel and the United States were both doomed to fall, Iran's leadership is determined to maintain tighter control at home as a precondition for expanding the revolution abroad.

In part, the decision by reform-minded dissidents to boycott the 2005 presidential elections cleared the way for the religious establishment to tighten its grip. Core supporters, including the nation's remaining rural peasants and ever-growing number of urban poor, voted strongly, while the more liberal-minded elite classes stayed home. Today, Iran under Ahmadinejad is positioned, perhaps better than ever, to spread its radical revolution abroad.

Analysts within Iran argue that Ahmadinejad's election was part of the planned "Second Islamic Revolution" organized by Ayatollah Khamenei to make sure fundamentalist religious conservatives control all aspects of government, including the military and the judiciary.[29]

In November 2005, President Ahmadinejad ordered Foreign Minister Mottaki to purge reformers out of the diplomatic corps. In response, Mottaki dismissed some forty ambassadors, including those to London, Paris, Berlin, Geneva, and Kuala Lumpur.[30] This dramatic shake-up effectively eliminated any ambassadors who might muddy diplomacy by suggesting Iran was willing to compromise on the nuclear program, when in reality Ahmadinejad was beyond compromise.

Then, in December 2005, Ahmadinejad issued a circular warning all ministers and state bodies that "no official may go abroad, or on a mission or for personal reasons, without prior authorization and without coordinating with the foreign ministry."

Reversing years of reforms and turning back the clock to the ultraconservative repression of the 1979 revolution, Ahmadinejad issued a directive on 19 December 2005 banning all Western and "indecent" music from state-run television and radio stations.[31] Whether Ahmadinejad could really take all Western music from Iran's youth was doubtful, though the ban on state-run television and radio showed the direction in which Ahmadinejad was headed.

Throughout Iran, the Basij are today ever-present and ready to suppress dissent. In towns throughout Iran, including the central cities of Shiraz and Isfahan where Iran's nuclear processing plant is located, hundreds of Basij militia have been deployed under the pretext of fighting hooligans or tracking down drug or alcohol smugglers.

The regime wanted to flex its muscle, in the process harassing women under the usual pretexts of "non-observance of Islamic tradition" or not wearing the mandatory *hejab* veil in public.[32] In the northeast city of Shahrood, two female students were reported injured by Basij who splashed acid to their faces, reacting against dress code violations, a further effort to re-impose the "Gender Apartheid Policy" initiated with the 1979 revolution.[33]

On 7 January 2006, an Iranian court sentenced a teenage rape victim to death by hanging after she confessed in tears that she had unintentionally killed a man who had attempted to rape her and her niece. The woman identified only as Nazanin, testified that she stabbed one of three men who had attacked her and her sixteen-year-old niece, Somayeh, while the two teenage girls were visiting with their boyfriends in a park west of Tehran. Nazanin, who was seventeen at the time of the incident, described how the three men had pushed her and her niece to the ground and tried to rape them. Nazanin took a knife from her pocket and stabbed one of the men in the hand. As the girls tried to escape, the men attacked them again. At this point, Nazanin stabbed one of the men in the chest. According to a report in the Iranian press, Nazanin broke down in tears, explaining to the court that she had no intention of killing the man; she was only trying to protect herself and her niece from rape.

The court still condemned her to death by hanging. Nazanin and Somayeh were held suspect simply because they dared to be in a public park with their boyfriends. Even though the stabbed boy was one of three who assaulted the girls with the intent to rape them, the strict application of Islamic law saw the girls as seducing the men by their indiscreet behavior with their boyfriends.[34]

The same day, Fatemeh Alia, a deputy in the Majlis and one of Ahmadinejad's closest allies, revealed a government plan to segregate Iran's pedestrian sidewalks on a gender basis. Alia revealed that as part of a government plan to "increase the *hejab* culture and female chastity," the Ministry of Housing and Urban Development received orders to construct separate sidewalks for men and women.

As Tehran's mayor, Ahmadinejad had ordered all city buildings to have separate elevators for men and women.[35] The Ministry of Roads and Transport was also being asked by the government to examine all walkways, roads, railways, and other transportation routes to eliminate any further reports of "mal-veiling," or innapropriate attire, being filed with government offices by offended citizens.

All these steps were designed to fulfill Ahmadinejad's promise when he first took office as president, that he would "return the Islamic Republic to the days of the 1979 revolution." The steps were important, especially in their clear confirmation that the reforms instituted under the previous presidencies of Rafsanjani and Khatami were terminated. Within Iran, the mullahs moved to tighten their grip.

Violations of human rights, imprisonments and torture, arrests of journalists and intellectuals, bans and excommunications in the name of religion all continue. But R. Nicholas Burns, undersecretary for political affairs at the State Department points to "a clear struggle . . . between the reactionary Iranian government and the moderate majority."[36] As these outrages enflame the fury of moderates in the country, some are pushing back.[37]

Farsi has become the fourth most widely-used language on the Internet. There are over a hundred thousand Iranian websites, most of which are operated by those who oppose the Iranian regime inside and outside Iran. Internet discussions have become a widespread phenomenon, supplementing illegal satellite radio and television broadcasts by the expatriate community. These serve as links to the outside, through which the Iranian people are able to find out what is happening in the world. Iranians found hiding illegal satellite receivers are subject to being arrested without notice, imprisoned without legal representation, and tortured or killed without notice to their families or friends.

In December 2005, a soccer riot broke out at Tehran's Azadi ("Freedom") Stadium. Youth attending the soccer match began attacking symbols of the regime, such as flags and posters. When the Basij militia moved in, a riot broke out. The violence spilled into the streets and surrounding residential neighborhoods, escalating to the point where the youth protesting began smashing windows of security patrol cars and collective buses. The clashes continued until late in the evening and resulted in a huge traffic jam; dozens of people were injured before the violence subsided.[38]

Around the same time, hundreds of students gathered in Tehran's College of Technology and began shouting freedom slogans critical of the regime. Again, Basij militia moved in, paying special attention to attack the female demonstrators. Members of Herrasat, a regime intelligence organization, took photographs of the students for later identification purposes.[39]

Scores of these incidents are reported out of Iran every month. Expatriate groups document the incidents, trying to build the case that internal dissent continues in the face of brutal regime suppression of protest. Still, study after study shows that the Iranian censorship on Internet websites is the most sophisticated and severe in the world. The Iranian regime uses sophisticated filtering systems, playing a "cat and mouse game between those who would speak freely and those who would stop them."[40] Bloggers writing in Farsi are today more likely to be blocked than those writing in virtually any other language, including Chinese.

Within Iran the rigid rule of the mullahs has been resisted since the death of Khomeini. Yet always, the regime's control of the apparatus of force and social control has suppressed potential rebellions while brutally pursuing outspoken dissidents, even if they flee Iran.

NUCLEAR PRIDE

Ahmadinejad is not a "nut" or a "loose cannon." He may be a fanatic and a religious zealot, but Ayatollah Khamenei and the Guardians Council approve his statements and actions. If they did not, he would be quickly advised to change course. Given the religious control maintained by the mullahs, Ahmadinejad and the rest of the Iranian government can only act with the approval of the supreme leader and the top mullahs and imams who advise him.

With Ayatollah Yazdi responsible both for elevating Khamenei to succeed Ayatollah Khomeini as supreme leader and for serving as Amadinejad's spiritual mentor, we have to assume that Yazdi wields a great deal of influence. The doctrine of the second coming of the Mahdi is driving the rebirth of Iran's revolution we are seeing right now, and Ayatollah Yazdi heads the radically messianic Hojaiteh sect.

Iran's goal seems to be to drive as fast as possible to be able to produce nuclear weapons on Iranian soil by Iranian nuclear scientists and engineers as soon as possible. With nuclear weapons in hand, the regime can bring about at any time the apocalypse seen as necessary for the return. Then a glorious new age can dawn in which Shi'ite Islam triumphs over all other religions and religious sects worldwide.

Despite this apocalyptic undercurrent, Ahmadinejad strives to present Iran's actions as reasonable—and any opposition as unreasonable. He has made this point repeatedly: "Our path is clear.

We are for dialogue, logic, and law, and we do not wish to escalate tension; however, we certainly do know how to defend our interests." Portrayed as the misunderstood underdog, Iran wants to be seen as a defender of rights, not an aggressor. No mention is made of Iran's support for Hezbollah or its ties to terrorist organizations including al-Qaeda and Hamas, all of whom are engaged in ongoing attacks on both Israel and America. Iranian officials always present Iran as innocent, the defender of democratic rights, even though active dissidents, including bloggers, are regularly imprisoned in Iran without consideration of legal rights.

As part of his goal of appearing reasonable and balanced, Ahmadinejad is quick to remind listeners that Israel has nuclear weapons and the world is not demanding Israel lay down their nuclear ambitions: "I ask under what pretext does the Qods [Jerusalem] occupying regime have 100 nuclear warheads? What power does it have when its very foundations are shaken by just one question? We have asked a question and they [the Zionist state of Israel] began to become insecure. Thought, ideology, and wisdom are getting to rule the world. Those investing in nuclear weapons are irrationally depleting the assets of their peoples."[41]

Iran continually maintains that their nuclear program is peaceful and that Israel has the aggressive intent. Israel is not a signatory to the Nuclear Non-Proliferation Treaty, and Israel's nuclear program has never been inspected by the International Atomic Energy Agency. Iran wants to present itself, in contrast, as fully in line with IAEA inspection requests. Iran even asked IAEA inspectors to be present when the seals were removed from the "research and development" uranium enrichment facilities at Natanz:

> The West should stop their political games. Iran asks the UN
> nuclear agency to install its cameras on the nuclear sites of the

Western states which have embarked on a propaganda campaign against the Iranian nuclear program. We know they will not allow the UN nuclear agency to do so. They don't believe in international conventions. The world public opinions know that they are making a mockery of themselves.[42]

In other words, the charge is that the United States, England, and France all have nuclear weapons. Still, the IAEA does not inspect nuclear sites in these states, so why would the IAEA single out Iran for special treatment? Iran feels this is especially unfair when Iran claims its goals are entirely peaceful.

The tactic is all about misdirection and blame, attacking others rather than defending oneself. In the Tehran press conference, Ahmadinejad used the tactic repeatedly. Here's how he answered a question about the possibility that the IAEA would vote to bring Iran before the Security Council:

The Middle Ages era is over and they should quit using the language of force and bullying. If you are in search of a role to play in global equations, you should avoid discrediting the international organizations. We have always called for negotiations but we advise them [the Europeans] to get to know the revolutionary nature of Iran and its government. You assume that by insulting others on your TV and confirming each other's words you will be able to get a right for yourselves in the world. Can you call your behavior a civilized one? Our nation is an independent nation which is taking action under international regulations and is to pursue its own path.[43]

Ahmadinejad portrayed revolutionary Iran as a country on a high spiritual plane, as compared to the aggressor countries, such as the United States, who resort to bullying and war to impose their will. "If sustainable peace and tranquility is to be secured in the world," he said, "this will not be materialized unless it is based upon 'justice' and 'spirituality.' A peace imposed through swords as well as nuclear, chemical, and biological weapons will not last long. A peace based upon looting, discriminatory decisions, and unjust progress does not make any sense."

Iranian rhetoric blasts a "double standard." Israel is allowed to have nuclear weapons, but not Iran. Iran disputes that Israel never started any of the Middle Eastern wars that threatened Israel's survival. Ahmadinejad is following the Nazi principle of propaganda: Tell a big lie and tell it often.

The only way today that Iran's push to make a deliverable nuclear weapon will be stopped is if some country or coalition of countries marshals enough courage to launch a preemptive strike. We may already be at the moment where Israel will have no choice but to act alone. Israel cannot afford to conclude that the existential moment has arrived when Iran can put at risk its survival.

If Ahmadinejad views an apocalypse as a precondition for the second coming of the Mahdi, then all bets are off. Calculations of mutually assured destruction no longer apply when Iran believes war is destined with a religious purpose. Ahmadinejad's extreme rhetoric is not accidental. Quite to the contrary, Ahmadinejad's extreme rhetoric is calculated to place Iran on a confrontational path with Israel and to let the world know that the confrontation is coming very soon.

4

WIPING ISRAEL FROM THE MAP

"We should be afraid when President Ahmadinejad declares that Israel should be wiped off the map. We shouldn't be surprised, but we should be very much put on alert."

—GENERAL MOSHE YA'ALON,
FORMER ISRAELI DEFENSE FORCE
CHIEF OF STAFF, 2006

"Israel cannot accept a situation where Iran has nuclear arms. The issue is clear to us and we are making all the necessary preparations to handle a situation of this kind."

—PRIME MINISTER ARIEL SHARON, 2005

"Death to Israel! . . . Death to America!"

—IRANIAN CHANT UNDER THE AYATOLLAHS

O n 26 October 2005, President Ahmadinejad spoke at a seminar in Tehran entitled "The World without Zionism." In the speech, Ahmadinejad called for the destruction of the state of Israel. "Our dear Imam [Ayatollah Khomeini] ordered that the occupying regime in Jerusalem must be wiped off the face of the earth," he said. "This was a very wise statement. The issue of Palestine is not one which we could compromise on."[1]

He saw the establishment of Israel as "a very grave move by the hegemonic and arrogant system [the West] against the Islamic world." His vision was that Islam was locked "in the process of a historic war between the World of Arrogance [the West] and the Islamic world, and this war has been going on for hundreds of years."[2]

Ahmadinejad lamented that for the past 300 years, "the Islamic world has been in retreat vis-à-vis the World of Arrogance." Key to the advancement of the West, in Ahmadinejad's view was the creation of Israel: "During the period of the last 100 years, the [wall of the] world of Islam was destroyed and the World of Arrogance turned the regime occupying Jerusalem into a bridge for its domination over the Islamic world."

He made clear that he could envision a "world without America," and he stood behind the slogan "Death to America." His vision derived from the prophetic words of Ayatollah Khomeini who envisioned the demise of the Shah, the fall of the

Soviet Union, and the demise of Saddam Hussein, all of which have come to pass. Ahmadinejad believes that all of Khomeini's prophecies will soon be fulfilled:

> When the dear Imam [Khomeini] said that [the Shah's] regime must go, and that we demand a world without dependent governments, many people who claimed to have political knowledge and other knowledge [asked], "Is it possible [that the Shah's regime can be toppled]?"
>
> That day, when [Khomeini] began his movement, all the powers supported [the Shah's] corrupt regime . . . and said it was not possible. However, our nation stood firm, and by now we have, for 27 years, been living with a government dependent on America. Imam [Khomeini] said: "The rule of the East [USSR] and of the West [US] should be ended." But the weak people who saw only the tiny world near them did not believe it.
>
> Nobody believed that we would one day witness the collapse of the Eastern Imperialism [i.e., the USSR], and said it was an iron regime. But in our short lifetime we have witnessed how this regime collapsed in such a way that we must look for it in libraries, and we can find no literature about it.
>
> Imam [Khomeini] said that Saddam [Hussein] must go, and that he would be humiliated in a way that was unprecedented. And what do you see today? A man who, ten years ago, spoke as proudly as if he would live for eternity is today chained by the feet, and is now being tried in his own country.[3]

Since these prophecies had come true, Ahmadinejad argued, so too Khomeini's prophecy that Israel and America would be destroyed.

Ahmadinejad spoke with conviction and zeal. His faith in

Khomeini was clearly the driving force motivating him to think that Islam would be victorious. "I do not doubt," he told the seminar, "that the new wave which has begun in our dear Palestine and which today we are also witnessing in the Islamic world is a wave of morality which has spread over the Islamic world." He encouraged resolve: "Very soon, this stain of disgrace [i.e., Israel] will be purged from the center of the Islamic world—and this is attainable."[4]

Behind him as he spoke was an image of a large hourglass projected on the wall. Through the neck of the hourglass fell what appeared like two glass balls. The first, a glass ball with the US flag coloring its surface had already landed and cracked. A fragment of the surface with the American flag image had broken off and separated as the ball crashed to the bottom of the hourglass. A second ball, with the image of the Star of David, was seen falling into the bottom half of the hourglass, on its way to a similar destruction.

The message was clear: "Death to America" and "Death to Israel." In the twenty-seven years since Khomeini's revolution began, the themes had not changed. Ahmadinejad's zeal was as fervent as ever. Only now, given the fall of the Shah, the fall of the Soviet Union, and the fall of Saddam Hussein, Ahmadinejad was certain that the day is drawing near for the foretold fall of America, the "Great Satan," and of Israel, the homeland of the hated Jews.

ANTI-SEMITISM UNLEASHED

Reaction was instantaneous. "Since the United Nations was established in 1945, there has never been a head of state that is a UN member state that publicly called for the elimination of another UN member state," said Israeli Vice President Shimon Peres the following day.[5] Peres called for Iran to be expelled from the UN. Predictably, the UN was unwilling to respond formally in defense of Israel. No motion of censure against Iran was seriously considered. Had an Israeli senior official similarly attacked Iran, the UN would undoubtedly have moved immediately to censure Israel in no uncertain terms.

Rhetoric in the Muslim world is known for anything but moderation and understatement. Not content that his earlier threat to "wipe Israel off the map" was sufficient, Iran's President Ahmadinejad issued yet another threat on Thursday, 8 December 2005, as international concern over the Iranian nuclear program was mounting. In an interview with Iran's Arabic-language satellite channel, *Al-Alan*, Ahmadinejad said that if Germany and Austria felt responsible for massacring Jews during World War II, then a state of Israel should be established on their soil. "Now that you believe the Jews were oppressed, why should the Palestinian Muslims have to pay the price? Why do you come to give a piece of Islamic land and the territory of the Palestinian people to them? You oppressed them, so give a part of Europe to the Zionist regime so they can establish any government they want. We would support it."[6]

Calling Israel a "tumor," Ahmadinejad was suggesting that Israel should be uplifted from the Middle East and moved to Europe. "So, Germany and Austria, come and give one, two, or any number of your provinces to the Zionist regime so they can create a country there which all of Europe will support and the problem will be solved at its root."[7] *Al-Alan* told its audience that Ahmadinejad was speaking from Mecca in Saudi Arabia, Islam's holiest city, where he was attending a meeting of the Organization of the Islamic Conference.

As if this were not sufficiently outrageous, Ahmadinejad decided to add his voice loudly to the voices of anti-Semites who have proclaimed the lie that the Holocaust never happened. "Is it not true that the European countries insist that they committed a Jewish genocide? They say that Hitler burned millions of Jews in furnaces. Then because the Jews have been oppressed during the Second World War, therefore the Europeans have to support the occupying regime of Qods [Jerusalem]. We do not accept this."

Then, even more specifically, Ahmadinejad added: "The Europeans believe in this [the Holocaust] so much and are so determined that any researcher who denies it with historical evidence is dealt with in a harsh way and sent to prison." This last comment was evidently a reference to outspoken British historian David Irving who was arrested in 2005 in Austria under a 1989 warrant, which charged him with violating Austrian laws making Holocaust denial a crime.

In Ahmadinejad's twisted logic, he has to make clear that he too denies the Holocaust ever happened. Yet, if the Europeans believe in the Holocaust enough to make Holocaust denial a crime, then in Ahmadinejad's way of thinking, the Europeans should be true to their beliefs and make a place for Israel in Europe. Ahmadinejad was objecting that Muslims in the Middle East were somehow being "forced" to pay the price of European guilt by giving up "Muslim land" to provide a Jewish state in Israel. This radio interview from Mecca left no doubt that Ahmadinejad meant every word of his previous speech calling for the destruction of Israel.

Immediately, Israeli Foreign Minister Silvan Shalom strongly expressed outrage at Ahmadinejad's hate-filled expression of aggression: "I think the statement that was made today by the Iranian president should be a wake-up call to all of us around the world. We should do everything we can to stop him, and to stop the Iranian effort to develop a nuclear bomb. This country [Iran] will do everything it can in order to destroy the state of Israel."

Speaking for President Bush, White House press secretary Scott McClellan said Ahmadinejad's interview "further underscores our concerns about the regime in Iran. It's all the more reason why it's so important that the regime not have the ability to develop nuclear weapons."[8] The world is reminded to take seriously the anti-Semitic threats issued by Ahmadinejad. History amply demonstrates that world leaders who start by public utterances that suggest war against Jews, all too often end up carrying out those threats in reality.

Neither Ahmadinejad's anti-Semitic attacks on Israel nor his Holocaust denials are unique to Iranian history. Iran's fascination with rabid anti-Semantic ideology goes back to World War II. Reza Shah Pahlavi changed the name of the country from "Persia" to "Iran" in 1935 because "Iran" in Farsi signifies "Aryan," referring to the proto-Indo-European lineage that Nazi racial theorists and Persian ethnologists both embraced.[9]

Nazi Germany reached out to include Iran in the Axis powers. During the pre-war years, Iran welcomed Gestapo agents, allowing the Nazis to use Tehran as a base for agitating against the British and the region's Jews. Berlin's envoy to the Middle East, Fritz Grobba, was often called the "German Lawrence" because he had promised to create a pan-Islamic state reaching from Casablanca to Tehran. The parallels are alarming to draw.

Hitler and Ahmadinejad share a belief in a fated mission of world domination that involved the elimination of Jews. Remarkably, that Iran played a role complicit in the Holocaust does not prevent Ahmadinejad from denying that the Holocaust happened. Maybe that complicit role is why he wants to deny the historic tragedy.

Since the revolution, these sorts of pronouncements have only increased in number and vitriol. Since 1979, the Iranian media, including government-controlled newspapers and television, have broadcast a steady stream of anti-Jewish hate. Their message has regularly denied the Holocaust. The Jews are accused of having stolen the land of Israel from the supposedly "rightful owners," the Palestinians. The statements Ahmadinejad has made against Israel have been fully intentional, with malice aforethought, part of a consistent pattern of attack on Israel that stretches back over generations.

On Wednesday, 14 December 2005, Ahmadinejad gave yet another speech, this time in Iran's southeastern city of Zahedan. The speech was rebroadcast on Iranian state television. Ahmadinejad repeated his attacks on Israel, in open defiance of the prominent international criticism. "They have fabricated a legend under the name 'Massacre of the Jews,'" Ahmadinejad told television viewers, "and they hold it higher than God himself, religion itself and the prophets themselves."

Ahmadinejad repeated his request that Israel be removed from "dear Palestine," to be relocated in Europe, America, or Canada. "If somebody in their country questions God, nobody says anything, but if somebody criticizes the myth of the massacre of the Jews, the Zionist loudspeakers and the governments in the pay of Zionism will start to scream." Ahmadinejad continued pounding the theme: "Our proposal is this: give a piece of your land in Europe, the United States, Canada, or Alaska, so the Jews can create their own state."[10] In other words, Iran does not believe the Holocaust ever happened. But, if America and Europe want to believe the Jews were massacred, then let the "guilty" provide the territory for the Jewish homeland.

Ahmadinejad's theme does not vary—Iran intends to wipe Israel from the map, at least from the map of the Middle East.

With these attacks, Ahmadinejad makes clear that he is a fervent religious ideologue. He sees himself as advancing the plan laid down in prophecy by Ayatollah Khomeini. The shared view is that the Iranian revolution is fated to expand and that Israel is fated for destruction.

According to the vision, once Israel is gone, the Iranian revolution will take its next fated expansion, expanding worldwide. Soon, the United States too will be wiped from the face of the earth. Iran defiantly pursues uranium processing and enrichment while these verbal assaults are being made by the country's president. This only reinforces the unfortunate conclusions that Iran has secretly planned all along to make atomic bombs. With each passing day the "point of no return" grows nearer. If left unchecked, Iran will soon have the weapons needed to fulfill Ayatollah Khomeini's dream.

ISRAEL'S SURVIVAL AND THE UNITED STATES

Since the formation of the State of Israel in 1948, the United States and Israel have been allies. The United States has viewed the survival of Israel as a matter of American national security. Historically, Israel has been the only true democracy in the Middle East.

Now, the United States is engaged in a great struggle, as part of the War on Terrorism declared by President Bush, to see if democracy can be established in Afghanistan and Iraq. The spread of democracy in the Middle East represents a fundamental threat to the revolutionary zeal of the Islamic Republic of Iran.

The Islamic republic was pursuing nuclear weapons in a thinly disguised, clandestine program. Ahmadinejad was signaling constantly that Iran was ready to expand its radical Islamic revolution, to the detriment of Israel. Coupled with strategic alliances Iran was making with other nations opposed to Israel, it was no small wonder that the outpost of Middle East democracy felt its survival was being seriously threatened.

Israel is already entangled with Iran in a life-or-death struggle because of Iran's involvement with terrorism. In December 2005, I spoke with the former chief of staff of the Israeli Defense Force, General Moshe Ya'alon. "Iran is the main generator today of terrorism against Israel," he said. "We continue to see Hezbollah attacks from Lebanon. Hezbollah is an Iranian-made organization supported by Iran. They get about $18 million annually. Iran armed Hezbollah for attacks against Israel, using Lebanon as a platform." In July 2006 Israel was rocked by a barrage of missiles, killing and wounding more than a hundred, as Hezbollah sent rockets raining down in Northern Israel, even hitting the country's third largest city, Haifa, for the first time ever.[11] And it's not just Hezbollah.

Hamas, which now heads the Palestinian government, started receiving funding by Iran through Hezbollah after its main source of funding, Saddam Hussein, was removed from the picture. "It is a new phenomenon, this connection with Hamas," said Ya'alon. "Hamas in the past refused to cooperate with Iran, because of [religious] differences. Iran is Shi'ite ideology, and Hamas has a conflict. According to the different ideologies, they agree that they should impose a new caliphate all over the world, but Iran believes it should be a Shi'ite caliphate; other Arabs believe it should be a Sunni caliphate. So, they argue about it; meanwhile, their common interest is to destroy the State of Israel."

Ya'alon said Iran also supports other organizations, including the Palestinian group Islamic Jihad. "They fully finance this organization. In the Palestinian Authority, Iran finances Fatah activists. They finance the families of those who commit bombing attacks. Families of suicide bombers get $25,000-$40,000 for suicide bombings. That's a lot of money in the Palestinian Authority."

Funding the ongoing terrorist attacks on Israel while pursuing a more "final solution" via nuclear weapons shows not only the complexity of Iran's strategy but also its determination to wipe Israel from the map. But extending the game metaphor introduced earlier, if the Persians designed the game of chess, then the Israelis are expert at another game, poker. Israel has been dealt an ace-high royal flush in the first five cards of a seven-card stud game. Sitting with the only nuclear arsenal in the Middle East, Israel is not at a point of annihilation. The only threat is that Iran might manage to develop one or more nuclear weapons in such total secrecy that the weapons can be launched on Israel before anyone knows.

Israel remains a one-bomb state—a single nuclear weapon, even one of relatively low grade, detonated successfully over Tel Aviv would destroy the modern Jewish state as we know it.

Israel has only two major cities, Tel Aviv and Jerusalem. At the height of any business day, Tel Aviv has a population of between two and three million people, in a nation with a population of about 6.3 million people. Tel Aviv is the business and finance center of Israel. It is the location of many important government offices, including the Ministry of Defense. The destruction of Tel Aviv would bring Israel to financial chaos, compounded by a telecommunications nightmare, to say nothing of the massive human suffering inflicted by the strike.

The Islamic Republic of Iran has repeatedly denied the Holocaust and broadcast countless television shows on state-run channels in which the fraudulent *Protocols of the Elders of Zion* is touted as authentic. As Iran's rhetoric has stepped up in intensity, Israel has no choice but to assume that the Iranian government has decided war. While its proxies wage terrorist battles from all fronts, Israel has repeatedly stated that a diplomatic solution was preferred in dealing with Iran. But the preparation for war was proceeding on a separate track.

In April 2005, the Pentagon's Defense Security Cooperation Agency proposed selling Israel one hundred laser-guided bunker busting bombs, valued at $30 million.[12] The GBU-28 (Guided Bomb Unit-28) ordinance is a 5,000 pound conventional weapon with a 4,400 pound warhead containing 630 pounds of high explosives.

The weapon is capable of penetrating through twenty feet of reinforced concrete or a hundred feet of earth. The GBU-28 was designed after the 1991 Gulf War began, to penetrate hardened Iraqi command centers located deep underground.[13] The bunker-buster bombs fit on the F-15 and F-16 fighter aircraft the US had previously sold to Israel. The weapons would serve well in attacking the underground nuclear facilities the IAEA knew Iran had built to harden nuclear installations from air attack.

Under US law, the bunker-buster bomb sale had to be presented to Congress, to give Congress thirty days in which to reject the deal. This required the Bush administration to reveal publicly the sale of the bunker-busting bombs to Israel, such that the deal was picked up in newspapers worldwide. By making the announcement, the US was telling the world that America would support Israel in a military confrontation with Iran.

Appearing on the Don Imus TV-radio show on Inauguration Day, 20 January 2005, Vice President Dick Cheney suggested that Israel might launch a preemptive attack against Iran, arguing that "if the Israelis became convinced the Iranians had significant nuclear capability, given the fact that Iran has a stated policy that their objective is the destruction of Israel, the Israelis might well decide to act first, and to let the rest of the world worry about cleaning up the diplomatic mess afterwards."[14]

These comments signaled that the Bush administration had calculated Israel might act in self-defense. The administration was previously on record suggesting that America would support Israel's right to do so. The vice president's comments almost suggested that the US government would prefer Israel to strike first, saving the US the political difficulty of launching a second preemptive war in the Middle East (something that we'll explore later).

In his second Inaugural Address later that day, Bush also spoke in a way that encouraged dissidents within Iran to oppose the regime. By proclaiming that US foreign policy would support the growth of democratic movements and institutions worldwide, President Bush spoke words that were heard in Tehran as a message of hope: "When you stand for your liberty, we will stand with you."[15]

Yet the situation quickly proved uncertain. How would the Bush administration support dissidents with Iran who might seek to overthrow the mullahs? How would the Bush administration support Israel if it launched a preemptive military strike against Iran?

As Bush entered his second term, the administration's foreign policy on the Middle East seemed to go soft. The first term had been marked by unilateralism and military power.[16] The second term, however, began with Secretary of State Condoleezza Rice and President Bush taking diplomatic trips to Europe.

Speaking in Brussels on 21 February 2005, President Bush still spoke harshly about Iran saying, "For the sake of peace, the Iranian regime must end its support for terrorism, and must not develop nuclear weapons. In safeguarding the security of free nations, no option can be taken permanently off the table." But in the very next sentence, the president suggested diplomacy would be the administration's first choice, just as diplomacy was the first choice argued by the Sharon government in Israel: "We're in the early stages of diplomacy. The United States is a member of the IAEA Board of Governors, which has taken the lead on this issue. We're working closely with Britain, France, and Germany as they oppose Iran's nuclear ambitions, and as they insist that Tehran comply with international law."[17]

This statement was made in the glow of good feelings that the EU3 and the IAEA were promoting. The Europeans had argued that the Iranian decision in November 2004 to stop uranium enrichment marked a change of heart. Maybe now the Iranians were willing to comply with the reasonable requests of international diplomacy regarding the development of its nuclear program. We know now that it was more a change of tactics than heart.

By agreeing that the EU3 and the IAEA should lead negotiations with Iran, the Bush administration chose to take a supportive role. Bush was abandoning the unilateral, military approach. He embraced instead a conclusion that what America seeks to achieve in the world "requires that America and Europe remain close partners." The Bush second term started on a conciliatory approach to Iran, despite the vice president's Inaugural Day suggestion of military force and the president's own Inaugural Address language in support of democracy. And it went downhill from there.

As 2005 progressed through December, the beleaguered Bush administration felt the need to make repeated national speeches trying to bolster the diminishing public support for America's continued military presence in Iraq. By the end of 2005, President Bush could not risk even suggesting that US military action might be needed to keep the threat of an Iranian secret nuclear program from progressing.

In 2006, Iran came to the conclusion that the United States is weak and unable to stop its advance. In the first year of his second term, President Bush has been under increasing attack from the Democrats in Congress that he lied when arguing that intelligence reports prior to the Iraq war justified the conclusion that Saddam Hussein possessed weapons of mass destruction.

A growing peace lobby from the political left has made clear their position that the preemptive war in Iraq was not sufficiently justified. Arguably, President Bush's political opponents would like to see him impeached for lying about weapons of mass destruction in Iraq and leading the US into an unnecessary war. How could President Bush possibly justify yet another preemptive war, this time in Iran? If President Bush seriously pressed for a military attack on Iran, he would most likely risk impeachment. That is the political reality in Congress.

The mullahs have watched very carefully the internal political criticism the president is facing over Iraq. Every argument that Iraq is another "Vietnam quagmire" convinces the mullahs that President Bush lacks the political strength to launch a military attack on Iran. As a consequence, Israel has been forced to realize reluctantly that possibly even the United States cannot be counted upon to come to Israel's defense.

Rapidly, Israel is approaching the point where only one alternative is left to assure the survival of the Jewish state. In 1981, Israel took out Iraq's nuclear reactor at Osirak with a military strike. Israeli officials were beginning to wonder openly if the military option once again would be the only way to stop Iran from building a bomb.

On 17 December 2005, Ahmadinejad addressed local officials in Tehran and called for Muslims around the world to increase their vigilance against Israel: "The Zionist regime [Israel] is today a threat to the whole Middle East region and therefore Moslems should increase their vigilance against this regime."[18]

How will Israel endure the menace posed by Iran? This is a question we can no longer avoid asking, not in the face of a growing nuclear threat. Day by day, Iran grows more determined, more emboldened, and more openly belligerent against Israel. A confrontation is building to the point where a crisis is inevitable.

THREE CONVERSATIONS

On a September evening in 1980 in Tel Aviv, I sat with Isser Harel, the founder of Mossad, Israel's intelligence agency renowned for its success against terrorism. "Do you think terrorism will come to America?" I asked.

"I fear terrorism will come to you in America," Harel replied. "America has the power, but not the will, to fight terrorism. The terrorists have the will, but not the power, to fight America. But all that could change with time. Arab oil money buys more than tents."

He predicted that Islamic terrorists would strike in New York City, the center of American capitalism. He foresaw that the attack would be on the city's tallest, most iconic buildings.

I objected, saying that I thought America might not be hit. I told Harel that America was dedicated to fighting terrorism.

He smiled and said, "In America, you kill a fly and you celebrate. In the Middle East, we live with flies daily. One dies and 100 flies come to the funeral." Twenty-one years later, the first part of Harel's prediction came true, on 11 September 2001.

Since 9/11, I have often thought back to that conversation with Isser Harel. He was right, and I had overestimated our resolve and our preparedness.

I have also given much thought to a conversation that happened two years later, in 1982. This time, I was summoned to New York by Reuven Hecht, who was then-aide to Prime Minister Menachem Begin. Israel had just invaded Lebanon to root out Arafat's terrorist infrastructure.

Hecht was in New York from Washington, where he had just met with then-secretary of state Alexander Haig. The conversation shook Hecht. Haig told him that America had changed its mind. After the terrorist bombing of the Marine barracks in Beirut, the Reagan administration had decided to pull out. America was no longer going to support Israel's war against terrorism in Lebanon. Hecht was in shock. How was he going to explain his conversation with Haig to Begin?

I did not know how to respond. I too was in shock. How were we going to defeat radical Islam, I wondered then, if we couldn't stay the course in Lebanon? Yes, the casualties in Lebanon were horrible, but the victims were Marines. Our Marines had suffered terrible losses many times before. My mind flashed to the staggering casualties our Marines took in the island warfare against Japan in World War II. Still, we continued, despite the fatalities, until we were victorious. Were we now going to abandon Israel in its fight against Hezbollah in Lebanon? Unfortunately, that is exactly what we did.

Today we stand at yet another crossroads, much like 1982. How strong is America's resolve? Will Israel endure if Iran does succeed in developing nuclear weapons? Iran is at the center of the terror network today. Will we and Israel have the resolve to stand up to the mullahs, or will we lack the determination to protect ourselves once again? These are questions we need to grapple with more seriously now than ever before.

When I spoke with Ya'alon in late 2005, he drove home the urgency of our current situation. "What we are facing today is not just the challenge of the Israeli-Palestinian conflict or the challenge of the Israeli-Arab conflict," he said. "It has become, in the last decade, a clash between civilizations—a conflict between Islam and the infidels." How else to view Ahmadinejad's apocalyptic visions of Islam sweeping the globe and ushering in the Mahdi?

"You have to listen to what Ahmadinejad is saying. He is talking about a nation of Islam all over the world, defeating the West, and on the way to defeating the West, Israel should be annihilated . . . wiped off the map."

He continued, "This is the challenge, not just to the State of Israel. We need a wake-up call in Israel, but we need a wake-up call everywhere, in Europe and in the United States, to understand the situation, not to ignore it, but to deal with it. And we are strong enough in the West to deal with it, either to prevent the Iranian nuclear capabilities, or at least, to demonstrate more determination by forcing Iran to pay the price. Yet if we don't isolate Iran or impose sanctions, the Iranians do not pay the price. They are sure that the West is afraid of them; this is the case. So, this is a challenge, not just for the State of Israel; this is a challenge for the Western world today."

Iran has a messianic mission to destroy Israel. But it doesn't stop there. The country's leaders are working behind the scenes with any nation they think can bolster their position—knowingly or not—to help bring an apocalypse upon the world.

5

STRATEGIC ALLIANCES

"Islam is politics or it is nothing."

—AYATOLLAH KHOMEINI

O n 4 January 2006, Ahmadinejad held a three-hour closed
door meeting with cabinet members and the Foreign Policy
and National Security Committee of Iran's parliament, the Majlis.
Here he made a series of statements openly criticizing the foreign
policy of his predecessors, presidents Mohammad Khatami and
Hashemi Rafsanjani. "In the past 16 years we implemented a policy of détente and tried to get closer to Europe and to trust them,"
Ahmadinejad noted, "but this policy has achieved nothing." He
noted that by the end of Khatami's second term in 2004, "we were
distanced from the goals of the 1979 Islamic revolution and our
activity in the Islamic world had been somewhat diminished."[1]

In the same meeting, Ahmadinejad insisted that his remarks
calling for Israel to be "wiped off the map" and describing the
Holocaust as a "myth" were a calculated policy to produce a "shock"
designed to waken Muslims who are living in a 'state of lethargy.'[2]
He argued that his chain of statements contained a logic that was
designed to unify the Islamic world, preparing for what he fully
anticipated would be the final elimination of Israel.

Ahmadinejad also spoke clearly to a group of students: "Some
in Iran and abroad thought we were making these statements
without a specific plan and policy, but we have been pursuing a
specific strategy in this regard. The wave that these speeches have
caused has a lot of supporters among young people in the Muslim

world and it will continue to move forward."[3] This logic was consistent with the teachings of Ayatollah Khomeini since before the fall of the Shah.

Ahmadinejad made clear to the students how the policy to attack Israel fit in the strategy of causing the United States to fall. "Those who defend today the crimes of the Zionists," he told the combined meeting of his cabinet with the Majlis committee, "must be held accountable and sentenced. Of course, they claim that they are very strong, but this is one of their big lies."[4]

In direct reference to the United States, Ahmadinejad said, "The revival of Islam is whipping the frail body of the Global Hegemon. This Global Hegemon will soon be toppled."

He rejected the authority of the United Nations mandate that created the state of Israel, emphasizing yet again, "You who claim that there was a Holocaust are today repeating such a thing in Palestine." He defied the international condemnation his remarks had drawn: "We do not fear their screams. The more they shout, the more they show their own weaknesses."[5]

These are not the ravings of a madman. They are the calculated statements of a zealous religious believer who is also the head of state. For us in the West who are used to the separation of church and state, we must combine the two spheres to comprehend Ahmadinejad. As Ayatollah Khomeini taught, in Shi'ite Islam, politics and religion are one.

As mentioned before, Khomeini predicted that the Shah would fall, that the Soviet Union would fall, and that Saddam Hussein would fall. All three events had happened. Now Ahmadinejad was telling his government, the time had come for Israel to fall. In defending Israel, America would take the steps necessary for America to fall. All this fit together, seen through the lens of Ayatollah Khomeini's predictions. Ahmadinejad was attacking Israel verbally because he was setting the stage for Israel to be attacked in reality, and that would bring the United States into jeopardy.

In the extreme religious views held by Ahmadinejad, all this was fated by God, such that no human intervention could change Iran's destiny, not as long as Iran remained true to Khomeini's 1979 revolution. Ultimately, Khomeini had prophesied that Shi'ite Islam would conquer the apostate Sunni version of Islam, all a prelude to Shi'ite Islam sweeping across the world. The final destiny of Islam would be realized under the personal direction of the Twelfth Imam, the Mahdi.

Ahmadinejad believes that he is destined to be the agent who will bring about the second coming of the Mahdi. Before the Mahdi returns, there must be chaos, world apocalypse. For all this to happen, Iran needs nuclear weapons to force the removal of Israel and the return of Palestine to Islamic control. And to achieve that goal, Iran needs help.

Iran has moved to form strategic alliances with nations that can help it economically, militarily, technologically, and in areas of diplomacy—partnerships with Russia, China, India, and others. All of these nations have their own reasons for dealing with Iran, and none of them include Islamic revolution. But in terms of the nuclear threat and Iran's revolutionary ambitions, we are misevaluating these partnerships if we fail to realize that Iran is attempting to use these alliances as chess pieces in its strategy to checkmate Israel and the United States.

STRATEGIC PARTNERSHIP WITH RUSSIA

When Iran defied the EU3 by resuming uranium processing at Isfahan in 2005, negotiations broke off. Curiously, it was Russia that surfaced to offer a solution. Iran could enrich uranium at a nuclear facility within Russia. This solution went counter to the desire of the Iranian regime to control "the full fuel cycle" within Iranian territory, but the offer showed Russia's desire to support Iran. Why?

US diplomacy pushed the EU3 and the IAEA to declare Iran noncompliant for its repeated refusal to run a transparent nuclear program. At the end of November 2005, the IAEA once again postponed referring Iran to the United Nations Security Council, this time choosing to give Iran more time to consider the Russian proposal and resume negotiations. Iran told the world that Russia's proposal was unacceptable, unless the Russians were willing to help them enrich uranium at nuclear facilities located in Iran. Still, as 2005 came to a close, few diplomats had any doubt that Russia was aligned with Iran.

To understand why Russia has been so willing to help Iran, a little history is needed. In the early 1980s, the Reagan administration saw that the price of oil could be used to inflict a body blow to the Soviet Union. Manipulating the price of oil would also hurt both Iraq and Iran, who were heavily dependent upon their oil revenue to continue financing the war against one other. It was a win-win-win situation for the US.

The strategy was first implemented in 1982 "to attack the fundamental economic weaknesses of the Soviet system."[6] Peter Schweizer, who details the scheme in his book *Victory*, based his argument on a review of national security decision directives of the time and on interviews he conducted with top Reagan administration aides, including Caspar Weinberger (Reagan's secretary of defense), George Schultz (secretary of state), and John Poindexter (national security advisor).

At the time, oil was the Soviet Union's most important export earner, accounting for more than half of the Soviet hard currency.[7] Reagan's advisors, with the assistance of a secret Treasury Department report, calculated that if oil could be taken from the 1983 price of $34 a barrel to approximately $20 a barrel, the US would benefit and the Soviet Union would lose. US energy costs would be lowered by approximately $71.5 billion, a transfer of income to American consumers amounting to 1 percent of gross national product. Oil prices that much lower would act basically like a tax cut, with the resultant positive stimulation of the US economy. Meanwhile, it would take a lot of wind out of the Soviet sails.

Part of the plan was to convince Saudi Arabia and other Middle Eastern oil-producing countries to increase output about 2.7 million barrels a day, to a total of 5.4 million a day. The increase of supply would create a 40 percent drop in the world oil price. Every $1 change in the price of oil resulted in a $500 million to $1 billion impact on hard currency holdings for the Kremlin. These calculations formed the basis for a deal which Reagan's aides hammered out with the Saudis. Thrown into the formula was America's willingness to extend national security guarantees to the Saudis.[8]

Early in 1985, the oil deal was finalized in meetings Saudi King Faud held with President Reagan in the White House. The Saudis increased their oil production from 2 million barrels a day to almost 9 million barrels a day, substantially greater than the needed increase. The results were powerful and nearly immediate.

"In November 1985, crude oil sold at $30 per barrel," says Schweizer; "barely five months later, oil stood at $12. For Moscow, over $10 billion in valuable hard currency evaporated overnight, almost half its earnings. And the Soviet economy began breathing even more heavily."[9]

Reagan dealt a mortal economic blow to the Soviets. The move also made clear the oil mismanagement of the Carter administration. Carter had been hamstrung by his inability to reverse high oil prices. The price of oil had been a drag on the US economy since the 1973 OPEC oil embargo and the painfully long gasoline lines of the Ford years. The Saudis, able to produce oil at a $1.50 cost per barrel, still made a handsome profit even at the lower price. Iran and Iraq protested the Saudi decision to increase oil production, to no avail. As a result, both countries came to appreciate how oil economics could be used as a political weapon.

Reagan wasn't done yet. The Soviets were fighting a difficult war in Afghanistan, so the Reagan administration decided to supply Stinger missiles to the Mujahadeen fighters. This tipped the military balance in favor of the Mujahadeen. Soviet helicopters were no match for Stinger missiles.

The Soviets were stretched economically by Reagan's oil manipulation. They were bleeding resources into the Afghanistan operation. Then Reagan insisted on pursuing the "star wars" SDI missile defense system. Already under significant economic strain, competition with "star wars" pushed the Soviets along a downward spiral from which they could not recover.

Now, as a new crisis engulfs the world, Russian President Vladimir Putin saw an opportunity to do to America what had been done to the Soviet Union, using the same weapon. In 2005, oil prices spiked to over $55 a barrel, providing both Russia and Iran with windfall profits amounting to several hundred millions of dollars a day. The US had conveniently removed Saddam Hussein from power in 2003, effectively winning for Iran their 1980s war with Iraq. Now it was America's turn to fight a costly war with insurgents, as money to fight the Iraq war bled from the US Treasury. The Russians calculated that if the price of oil were to go from $55 a barrel to a sustainable level of near $70 a barrel, the cost to America would be approximately $65.7 billion a year.

As had been the case with Russia fighting in Afghanistan, now with the United States fighting in Iraq, public opinion slipped at home and around the world. Moreover, this time US troops in Iraq would be cast into the uncomfortable role of Christian "Crusaders" occupying a Muslim land—a common trope now seemingly vindicated for the Muslim world. Vladimir Putin demonstrated that he had not lost the cunning he gained as a KGB officer. By turning the tables on America in Iraq, Putin behaved like a former communist who was still not happy that the Soviet Union lost the Cold War.

A close relationship with Iran gave Russia a substantial lock on world oil, mirroring the power and influence wielded by President Reagan in his close 1980s relationship with the Saudis. Moreover, the Iranian regime had never lost its nationalistic desire to increase influence in Iraq. Iran may have lost the 1980s war with Iraq, but many Iranians still savored the idea of seizing political control over Iraq, along with economic control over the huge oil and natural gas resources.

By the end of 2005, Russia and the United States had changed places. The United States was potentially overextended in Iraq, both politically and economically, as the Soviets had been in Afghanistan in the 1980s. Now, through Iran, the Russians were positioned to exert firmer influence in the Middle East, just as President Reagan had done in the 1980s.

And what did Iran get out of the deal? With Russia, Iran benefited indirectly from the damage done to the US economy and Bush's political standing—both hits that decreased somewhat the likelihood of interference with its nuclear program. As mentioned previously, getting support for an Iranian incursion may cost more political capital than Bush can afford.

In addition to helping it increase its nuclear know-how, Iran's partnership with Russia also provided security for Iran's nuclear program. On 2 December 2005, Russian newspapers announced an agreement with Iran under which Russia agreed to sell Iran $1 billion worth of the Russian TOR-M1 anti-missile defense system.[10]

Operating on a mobile platform, the TOR-M1 can track multiple targets and is capable of firing at two targets simultaneously. The TOR-M1 functions very effectively as an anti-aircraft missile system, operating much like a SAM system (Surface-to-Air-Missile). By deploying the TOR-M1 anti-missile batteries around nuclear facilities, Iran intends to harden these facilities against air attack by the United States or Israel.

Once the TOR-M1 systems are operational, loss estimates increase dramatically for aircraft involved in strikes on Iran. This agreement escalates the arms race in the Middle East. Now Israel has to be concerned about countermeasures. Are Israeli military aircraft capable of fighting the TOR-M1 system? Is a missile attack on Iran's nuclear facilities now the only viable alternative? Will Russian military be assigned in Iran to train Iranians to use the system, or will Russian military be permanently stationed in Iran as advisors regarding the systems operation? These are questions that will inevitably be asked in Israel's highest military circles.

Despite the international pressure following the Russian announcement, Russian Defense Minister Sergei Ivanov affirmed that the sale would go through. Among others, the United States had strongly objected to the sale, reminding Russia of various international agreements not to sell arms to any nation which openly supports terrorist organizations, directly referring to Iran's continued financial support for the Lebanon-based terrorist organization Hezbollah. The technology transfer continues to undermine the claim that Iran's nuclear program is peaceful.

Iran benefits in other ways as well. In October 2005, Russia launched Iran's first-ever satellite into space, aboard a Kosmos-3M rocket. The satellite, named Sina-1, was described by Iran as intended to be used in space only to monitor natural disasters in the earthquake-prone country and to improve telecommunications, the type of "peaceful uses only" that Iran continually asserts for its nuclear program.[11] Many credible international observers disagreed, arguing that the Sina-1 was designed to spy on Israel. Russia also confirmed plans to launch a second satellite, a move which allows Iran to get satellites without diverting time or money to make their Shahab missiles capable of delivering their satellites into orbit.

The Russian rocket which launched the Iranian satellite also carried into orbit a satellite for China. This suggested that both Russia and China had plans to make Iran a strategic ally, to counter American presence in the Middle East. Russia would like nothing better than for the US to lose its influence around the globe because as US influence decreases, Russian influence can increase.

A Russian and Chinese alliance with Iran would make more difficult any American move to confront the Iranian regime regarding its sponsorship of terror or the development of its nuclear and missile programs.[12] Recognizing this balance of power realignment and realizing that both Russia and China are members of the UN Security Council, we can see why the United Nations is unlikely to be able to stop Iran. Because of their economic and geopolitical interests in Iran, Russia and China are likely to veto or mitigate the severity of any additional sanctions the US might impose.

STRATEGIC PARTNERSHIP WITH CHINA

China is the sleeping giant of the world's future economy. Just now, China is emerging from a predominately rural population. Great pains are being taken to ease the restrictions imposed by communist central planning. China has been plagued by the inefficiencies and resource mismanagement typical of all government bureaucracies that try to control economic growth and development. Still, with over 1.3 billion people and a staggering 2004 increase of 9.5 percent growth in real gross domestic product (GDP), China is an economic powerhouse.

China is responsible for 40 percent of the growth in demand for oil worldwide since 2000. Today, China consumes 6.5 million barrels of oil per day, a number the Energy Information Administration of the US Department of Energy expects to hit 14.2 million barrels of oil per day by 2025.[13] These numbers are certain to increase.

By American standards, China's use of oil is still relatively small. Worldwide, approximately 85 million barrels of oil are consumed daily. The United States uses some 20 million barrels a day, roughly 25 percent of total world consumption. Yet, in 2003, China surpassed Japan for the first time, becoming the world's second largest consumer of oil.

Like the US, China imports most of its crude oil. In the US, we import approximately 60 percent of the oil we consume. This reflects our growing oil dependence on foreign countries. America's oil fortune has suffered a dramatic reversal from World War II, when US domestic production was depended upon to fuel the war machine of the Allied nations.

China is expected to continue importing 75 percent of its oil through year 2025. So, like the United States, China must establish trading relations with other countries to get the oil the country needs for continued economic growth at home.

Iran is the top choice on China's list as a potential partner from which to import oil. "Iran is currently China's biggest oil supplier and Iran wants to be China's long-term partner," said Iranian Oil Minister Bijan Zanganeh in Beijing, October 2004.[14] Such a partnership is a boon for Iran. China is willing to invest generously in the development of Iran's oil fields. This is an important concession given Iran's lack of capital to invest in developing their ample reserves of oil and natural gas.

Iran's oil industry has suffered under the mullah's regime. Under the Shah, oil production reached 6 million barrels of crude oil a day in 1974.[15] Since the 1979 revolution, crude oil production in Iran has never exceeded 3.9 million barrels a day on an annual basis.

The oil fields are hampered by an aging infrastructure, plagued by dilapidated equipment and inadequate investment. Moreover, during the 1980s war with Iraq, Iran is believed to have strained production out of its oil fields. Trying to get every possible dollar out of oil to use for weapons against Iraq, it may have permanently damaged the oil fields themselves.

In the past two years, Iran has made renewed oil exploration efforts. As a result, its oil ministry currently estimates that Iran has 132 billion barrels of proven reserves, a number slightly higher than the US Energy Administration's estimate of 125.8 billion, roughly 10 percent of the world's total. These numbers have increased almost by one-third, from the 2003 estimate that Iran held 90 billion barrels of proven reserves.

Iran's economy remains heavily dependent upon oil export revenues. Fully 80 to 90 percent of Iran's total export earnings come from oil. Those oil earnings add up to as much as half of the government's annual budget.

With oil at $50 a barrel on world markets and Iran exporting nearly 4 million barrels a day, Iran realizes some $200 million a day in gross oil revenue. As the crisis with Iran developed in 2006, oil began to spike on world markets at prices in excess of $70 a barrel. Oil windfall profits flow largely into the government budget, diverted to keep the Iranian mullahs and their cronies wealthy, as well as to support terrorism and develop the Iranian nuclear program. Meanwhile, millions of people in Iran continue to live on less than a dollar a day.

In October 2004, Iran and China announced that China's second largest oil firm, Sinopac Group, had agreed to invest $70 billion in Iran. This investment would buy a 50 percent share to develop the oil and natural gas resources of the newly discovered Yadavaran field in southwestern Iran.[16] Iran currently supplies about 13 percent of China's oil, a percentage expected to rise dramatically once production in the new Yadavaran field begins.[17]

Sinopac is a Chinese state-owned oil company. In October 2000, Sinopac sold a minority 15 percent interest in an international $3.5 billion Initial Public Offering on the New York and Hong Kong stock exchanges. About $2 billion of the Sinopac IPO was purchased by ExxonMobil, BP, and Shell.

The American oil companies made their investment in Sinopac before the Iran-China oil deals were proposed. The Iran Libya Sanctions Act of 1996, passed under the Clinton administration, places Iran under sanctions and threatens penalties for any large international oil companies making deals with Iran. Still, when the Sinopac deal was made with Iran for the Yadavaran oil fields, the Bush administration threatened no penalties against Sinopac, or their minority US owner, ExxonMobil.

The complexity of ExxonMobil owning a minority interest in Sinopac reveals how intertwined the international oil business is. Through ExxonMobil's ownership interest in Sinopac, America will be indirectly involved in developing Iran's oil economy, despite US sanctions currently in place against Iran. The unwillingness of the Bush administration to impose penalties on ExxonMobil raises questions about whether our economic oil self-interest complicates our policy on Iran.

The hard-line theocrats controlling Iran see this as typical US capitalist hypocrisy. The mullahs believe that oil economics are at the core of Washington's opposition to the regime, as well as the reason America invaded Iraq. Nor was Washington able to exert pressure on Beijing to not seal the oil deal with Iran, despite the US being China's leading trade partner and primary export market. How can we impose strong sanctions on Iran over its nuclear policy when we take a hands-off approach to the Iranian oil deal with China?

BUILDING THE REVOLUTION ON OIL

When the Yadavaran field was discovered, Iranian Oil Minister Zanganeh announced that the discovery held an estimated 328.3 billion cubic yards of recoverable natural gas, plus an estimated 442 million barrels of liquid natural gas, in addition to 17 billion barrels of crude oil.[18] These estimates immediately shot the Yadavaran field to the top of the list, making it Iran's largest oil and natural gas field.

Zanganeh claimed that this new discovery put Iran in the "Number 2" world position in global crude oil reserves. That statement might be disputed by Saudi Arabia and Russia. Still, the continued discovery of enormous energy resources in Iran left no doubt that Iran continues to hold strategically valuable reserves of oil and natural gas, despite the possible depletion of older oil fields.

Without its abundant energy resources, Iran would have no economic strength on which to advance its radical revolution regionally or worldwide. Iran's oil revenue is the ultimate source of the funding which finds its way to Hezbollah and other terrorist organizations, such as the Islamic Jihad and Hamas, which Iran directs as surrogates in their war against Israel.

This Sinopac deal also shows Iran's awareness that the country's newly discovered energy resources can be capitalized for immediate revenue. Hungry for cash, the mullahs wasted no time turning the newly found oil field into ready money for themselves, in total disregard for the indigenous owners of the land in Iran.

The Yadavaran oil fields in the Khuzestan region of southwest Iran are on the ancestral land of the indigenous Ahwazi Arabs. Some four to five million Ahwazi Arabs live here, in a region they have traditionally called al-Ahwaz, or Arabistan.

When the Iranian regime realized that the Iranian Oil Engineering and Development Company had found some 17 billion barrels of oil there, the regime in Tehran quickly expropriated the land and gave the oil field a Persian name. Yadavaran, the renamed oil field, was assigned to the government-owned and operated Iranian Oil Engineering and Development Company, a part of the National Iranian Oil Company, operated under the Ministry of Petroleum.[19]

Though Muslim, the Iranians are ethnically and culturally Persian and regard ethnic Arabs as inferior, and felt justified taking the land without compensation. Moreover, the regime planned to pay no compensation to the tribal landowners for oil and natural gas production taken from the field.

Almost immediately, the regime in Tehran began negotiating with major international oil companies from France, Russia, Norway, and China, to see who would commit the most capital to develop the field.[20] The memorandum of understanding signed with China at the end of 2004 proved China had paid the top amount. The rightful tribal owners of the oil field including the Kaab, Adris, Albo-Nassar, Zergan, Bawi, and Bani-toroof—all Arabs—were left high and dry.

Iran has absorbed and internalized the Arab-originated religion of Islam, and it would also absorb and internalize the Arabs' money.

In January 2005, Iran's National Iranian Oil Company sold a minority 20 percent share of the Yadavaran oil field to India's

ONGC Videsh Ltd. (OVL) in a deal valued at $40 billion. The deal also involved a fixed-price formula that set a ceiling on the price India would be charged for the oil developed.[21]

Ownership in the Yadvaran oil field ended up being 50 percent China, 20 percent India, and 30 percent Iran. The Iranian deal with India resembled Iran's deal with China; in both cases, Iran received much needed capital, while China and India made long term investments guaranteeing reliable future access to a large quantity of energy at relatively fixed prices.

All this should trouble America. India and China are increasingly looking to Iran and Russia for strategic alliances. Iran and Russia have oil. India and China need oil. The deals being made are expected to tie the countries together over the next twenty-five years, and all of these nations stand to prosper if America comes down a few rungs on the superpower ladder.

When the Indian deal to invest in the Yadavaran oil field was announced, Russia also let out word that China's Sinopec and India's ONGC had each been invited to invest $2 billion for a stake in Yuganskneftegaz, the main production unit of Yukos. Yukos is Russia's second-largest oil company and one of the largest non-state oil companies in the world, having been privatized by Russia in the late 1990s.[22] Yukos holds the largest proven reserves of oil and natural gas in Western Siberia, responsible for nearly 20 percent of Russia's total oil production in 2003.[23]

In 2004 and 2005, a series of top-level meetings were held by government leaders and energy ministers among Russia, China, India, Pakistan, and Iran. A framework of economic cooperation agreements was signed. Its purpose was for Russia and Iran to provide oil to India and China. Pakistan was willing to see oil pipelines built across Pakistani territory to transport Iranian oil to India and China.

When Indian Petroleum Minister Mani Shankar Aiyar met in

Moscow in October 2004 for energy discussions with Russian government officials, he proposed Indo-Russian cooperation in the security field. "In the first-half century of Indian independence, Russia has guaranteed our territorial integrity," Aiyar noted in Moscow, "in the second half it may be to guarantee our energy security. What I am talking about is the strategic alliance with Russia in energy security, which is becoming for India as important as national security."[24]

Subsequently, when Russian President Vladimir Putin visited India, the two countries signed a memorandum of understanding for joint exploration and development of Iranian oil and natural gas from the Caspian basin. Included in the agreement was a proposal for building underground natural gas storage facilities in India and transferring Russian energy technology to India.

India and Pakistan even agreed to start work by 2007 on a 1,750 mile, $4 billion pipeline to transport oil from Iran to India via Pakistan by 2010.[25] The agreement, reached over the objections of the United States, was viewed as a breakthrough. Suddenly the nuclear states of Pakistan and India, who have traditionally been enemies, were cooperating. The pipeline was proposed originally in 1996, but never got off the ground because of Indian concerns over the security of the pipeline in Pakistan.

PARTNERSHIPS IN POWER

In 2004, China's Premier Wen Jiabao and Russia's President Vladimir Putin exchanged visits. The joint statement issued at the conclusion of Putin's October 2004 state visit to China repudiated the Bush administration's policy of pursuing a unilateral war on terrorism in defense of US national security interests.

In a reference that easily applies to Iran, China and Russia declared together that "it is urgently needed to compose international disputes under the chairing of the UN and resolve crises on the basis of universally recognized principles of international law. Any coercive action should only be taken with the approval of the UN Security Council and enforced under its supervision."[26] With China and Russia both members of the Security Council, the joint statement reinforced the conclusion that any US-initiated resolution to place sanctions on Iran for non compliance with IAEA nuclear inspections would be blocked.

A Tehran-Moscow-Beijing axis looked like it might be forming to protect Iran from US or Israeli preemptive military actions.

Today, Iran is working in close proximity with Russia, China, India, and Pakistan on energy issues. With careful maneuvering, Iran has used its ample oil and natural gas resources to leverage a working alliance with four members of the world's small club of nuclear-armed nations. Why Iran as a sovereign state should not be allowed to pursue nuclear technology unimpeded, on an equal basis with its energy partners Russia, China, India, and Pakistan, is a question Iran is asking the world.

On 26 December 2005, Iran's Foreign Minister Manouchehr Mottaki told a news conference in a visit to the Afghan capital of Kabul that Iran did not need anyone's permission to pursue nuclear technology. "We do not accept global nuclear 'apartheid' and 'scientific apartheid,'" Mottaki told the news conference. "We are not waiting for any country's permission for the right of the Iranian nation and the Islamic republic to enjoy nuclear technology."[27]

It's a question of apparent double standards. Evidently, the United States has no problem that Israel possesses nuclear weapons, but Iran is considered unworthy to have the same nuclear privileges. Iran charges that the United States and Israel are the true aggressor nations. Iran claims that America's real goal is to establish American hegemony in the Middle East so we can hold on to cheap access to Middle Eastern oil.

Ultimately, Iran resolves to continue terrorism, as long as the US continues to occupy Middle Eastern countries and as long as Israel continues to exist. Ultimately, Russia, China, and Iran fear American hegemony. Iran predicts America will be defeated as other imperialist nations have been defeated when they over-reached in colonialist ambitions.[28]

Moscow and Beijing continue to pursue their own nationalistic objectives as well. Russia and China see advantages in leveraging for their benefit Tehran's radical revolutionary zeal. Russia and China both want to counterbalance the military and economic power of Washington.

Iran dismisses Washington's argument that we are in Iraq and Afghanistan to establish democratic reform as "a thinly disguised method for the US to militarily dispose of unfriendly regimes in order to ensure the country's primacy as the world's sole super-power."[29] Iran charges that Bush launched a war of choice against Iraq, not to combat terrorism, but to transform the Middle East. Israel is then seen as a client state of the United States, established to impose the Western principle of democracy on the Middle East, a region where Iran wants to establish rigid Islamic theocracies.

With Iran taking the lead against the US on the question of Israel, Russia and China can stay in the background, prepared to defend Iran if Iran should be attacked while still achieving their geopolitical goals. Ahmadinejad's radical statements against Israel and the US serve their purposes, keeping the expansion of US power in check.

THE TURKEY FACTOR

As 2005 wound to a close, CIA Director Porter Goss visited Ankara, Turkey, following a visit there by FBI Director Robert Mueller. Reports circulated that Goss warned Turkish officials to anticipate US air strikes against Iran and Syria. Immediately, Iranian Foreign Ministry spokesperson Hamid Reza Asafi warned Ankara, "We ask our Turkish friends to be careful."[30]

Turkey is a member of NATO, but with many complicated ties to Iran. Since the 1979 revolution, scores of Iranian dissidents have escaped that regime by walking out of the country's largely rural northwestern section into Turkey. Many of these dissidents fled after being imprisoned and tortured by the Iranian regime. Many required medical treatment for their injuries; many others died in the attempt to reach freedom. Rare for a Muslim nation, Turkey also has had excellent relations with Israel; for many Israelis, Turkey is a vacation destination where they do not experience the anti-Semitism typically found in the Middle East.

According to newspaper reports, Goss took with him to Turkey two important portfolios: One was aimed at showing Turkish officials US intelligence reports that Iran was pursuing a clandestine nuclear weapons program, the other was aimed at proving to Ankara that Tehran was continuing to support the terrorist PKK group in Turkey, promoting from Tehran the PKK's close relationship with al-Qaeda.[31]

Partiya Karkeren Kurdistan (PKK) is the Kurdistan Worker's Party, whose goal is to establish an independent Kurdistan embracing the Kurdish minorities across the region, including those in Turkey, northern Iran, and northern Iraq, in the region where the three nations' borders converge. The Kurds, some 30 million in number, are the largest ethnic minority in the Middle East without a state, despite the claims of the Palestinians to the contrary.

The PKK was formed in 1978 as a Marxist-Leninist insurgent group, composed primarily of Turkish Kurds.[32] In the 1980s and 1990s, violence between the PKK and the Turkish army reached the point of being virtually a war, with some 35,000 deaths estimated to have occurred on both sides together. Today, the PKK is estimated to number around 4,000 to 5,000 active members. The group continues to attack Turkish security forces and bomb tourist destinations in an attempt to press its cause. In 1991, Turkey dropped a ban on speaking the Kurdish language, and the PKK began shifting energies into winning electoral votes to advance its cause. Goss's portfolio on the PKK was particularly relevant given the pickup in violence that was experienced in Turkey in 2005.[33]

Turkey's Iranian terror problem didn't stop with the PKK. In December 2005, a Turkish court explained the convictions the previous July of nine Turkish Islamist militants in a long-running case involving the 1990s murders of four prominent pro-secular Turkish intellectuals. Turkey had accused Iran's Qods Force (Jerusalem Force) of training and funding these militants.

Qods Force is a major terrorist agency Tehran has created. It combines intelligence agencies and foreign operatives, estimated to number some 21,000 personnel, into an operation that is headquartered in the former site of the US embassy in Tehran. The organization was designed to train and fund terrorist operations in Muslim states that are considered too secular, such as Turkey.

Reportedly, Qods Force has trained operatives in a wide range of countries, including Iran, Afghanistan, Pakistan, India, Turkey, Morocco, and Lebanon. Its operations have reportedly branched from the Persian Gulf to reach as far as Central Asia, North Africa,

Europe, and North America.[34] Reports such as these reinforce the impression that Iran wants to destabilize any Islamic states it believes not to be on the right course. Iran is a suspect whenever terrorism erupts, even in the Islamic world. Since the US invasion of Iraq in 2003, Iran has been suspected of fueling the insurgency that has threatened to destabilize the US push to establish a stable democracy in Iraq. Saudi Arabia, a country dominated by Sunni Muslims, would feel threatened the moment Shi'ite Iran had a deliverable nuclear weapon. Armed with nuclear weapons, Iran would be able to engage in nuclear blackmail throughout the world, against obvious enemies such as Israel and the United States, as well as against supposed friends, including Gulf State Islamic neighbors, such as Egypt, that it considers "too soft" in their Islamist commitment.

On the diplomatic front, Iran has been openly courting favor with Turkey. Iran wants to quiet Turkey's concerns that the real agenda is to expand Iran's revolution into Turkey. At the end of 2005, former Iranian President Hashemi Rafsanjani, in his new capacity as Chairman of the Iranian Expedience Council, met with Turkish diplomat, Halit Bozkurk Aran. The meeting was prompted by Aran's retirement after a twenty-three-year career as Turkey's ambassador in Tehran. At the meeting, Rafsanjani promoted the theme of positive bilateral relations: "The two countries should make their efforts not to let their ties be affected by negative points," Rafsanjani said. "Efforts to establish stability and tranquility in Iraq can serve the interests of the regional states." Despite funding terrorism in the region, Iran still maintains that its goal is to end terrorism and establish stability. Rafsanjani urged trilateral cooperation among Iran, Turkey, and Syria, Iran's closest ally in the region.[35]

Cutting through the diplomatic niceties of the meeting, Iran's underlying agenda is to solidify its diplomatic position in the region. Iran would like to be seen as a responsible international player. Still, the regime will not renounce Ahmadinejad's extreme statements attacking Israel, nor will Tehran abandon its support for terrorism, or its direct funding of terrorist groups such as Hezbollah and PKK. Iran comfortably maintains a public face proclaiming that its theocracy aims for stability and economic growth. Meanwhile, it quietly advances the dark underside of terrorism and secretly pursues nuclear weapons.

On a visit to Egypt when the reports about CIA Director Goss's visit to Turkey broke on international wire services, Turkish Deputy Premier and Foreign Minister Abdullah Gul was asked at a press conference if Turkey had agreed to support the United States' supposedly planned air strikes against Iran and Syria. Gul responded that any reports that the US had pressed Turkey to support military action against Iran and Syria were not true: "The ministry received no demand of support from the United States on the issue of intervention."[36]

Examined closely, Gul's statement did not constitute a denial that Goss had visited Ankara to brief Turkish officials about a planned military strike. His statement only denied that the US had pressed Turkey to support military action against Iran and Syria. In the same press conference, reporters questioned Gul about Turkey's continued close relations to Israel. Again, Gul spoke carefully, noting only that Israel enjoys good relations with many countries, in addition to Turkey.[37]

Turkey has continued to rely on NATO and the US nuclear guarantee to protect itself against a nuclear Russia to the north. The Turks have been wary of Russian geopolitical objectives since the end of World War II.

Turkey's relationship with its Islamic neighbors in the Middle

East has been influenced by the history of the Ottoman Empire, which was closely identified with the Turkish Republic. Since the collapse of the Ottoman Empire, Turkey has sought to maintain stable relations in the region, including with Iran, which has no history of direct conflict with the Ottoman Empire or the Turkish Republic.

Israel has played a major role in modernizing the Turkish military, including supplying Turkey with both military equipment and training. This relationship is an ever-present undercurrent creating tensions in any discussions Turkey has with either Iran or Syria. As long as Turkey continues to enjoy a strong relationship with the United States and NATO, the threat from revolutionary Iran remains ever-present.

When Iran develops nuclear weapons, Turkey's security concerns will intensify. Ian Lesser, a Senior Scholar at the Woodrow Wilson International Center writes of the danger:

> Could Turkey act more radically, outside multilateral arrangements, to meet risks posed by a nuclear-ready Iran? The short answer is yes, but it is not very likely. Could Turkey "go nuclear"? Again, the answer is yes, but it is not very likely. The key in both cases would be a sharp deterioration in the quality of Turkish defense cooperation with the West, and a sense that Turkey was being left to go it alone in a dangerous geo-strategic setting. Overall, the existence of a nuclear-ready Iran poses some direct risks to Turkish security—and many indirect but highly consequential ones. Implications for US and Western policy abound.[38]

Clearly, the continued involvement of the United States in the Middle East will be a factor determining whether a nuclear Iran will lead to a regional nuclear arms race. Should US presence weaken in the Middle East, a nuclear arms race becomes a likely possibility as countries such as Turkey take steps to protect themselves from Russia and Iran.

6

THE SHOWDOWN APPROACHES

*"Iran does its utmost to undermine Middle East Peace
diplomacy."*

—HENRY KISSINGER, 2001

*"Pressures by several Western states will not succeed in forcing
us to abandon our [nuclear] rights."*

—MAHMOUD AHMADINEJAD,
2 JUNE 2006

Under Presidents Rafsanjani and Khatami, the West increasingly felt Iran could be moved by pragmatic political considerations, such that compromise and national self-interest were reasonable appeals to move Iranian foreign policy.

President Ahmadinejad clearly has embraced principles of expanding a messianic vision of the Iranian revolution, perhaps even more radical than the principles advocated by Ayatollah Khomeini himself. In dealing with a mystical politician of Ahmadinejad's conviction, the West has lost its compass. With a mystic as head of state, ordinary calculations of power politics no longer apply with the same pragmatic force.[1]

Particularly disturbing about Ahmadinejad is the belief that an apocalypse must occur before the Mahdi returns. An international nuclear war triggered by an Iranian attack on Israel could well be the apocalypse he believes he has a divine mission to start, regardless of the suicidal nature of the decision. There is no higher status than martyr in the Iranian version of Shi'ite Islam. A religious fascination with suicide fundamentally changes the definition of rational behavior that rests at the center of all calculations that the risk of "mutually assured destruction" will deter a head of state from initiating a nuclear war. Ironically, a suicidal leader motivated by religious mysticism might actually be attracted to a nuclear war.

So far, defiance and deception are the only sort of behavior we can count on. Ahmadinejad's radical mystical vision is consistent with using the arts of falsehood and duplicity in pursuing international political goals. His justification derives from his understanding of Shi'ite Islam itself, not from a calculation of Iran's national interests. Ayatollah Khomeini counseled as much:

> We know of no absolute values besides total submission to the will of the Almighty. People say: "Don't lie!" But the principle is different when we serve the will of Allah. He taught man to lie so that we can save ourselves at moments of difficulty and confuse our enemies. Should we remain truthful at the cost of defeat and danger to the Faith? We say not. People say: "Don't kill!" But the Almighty Himself taught us how to kill. Without such a skill man would have been wiped out long ago by the beasts. So shall we not kill when it is necessary for the triumph of the Faith? . . . Deceit, trickery, conspiracy, cheating, stealing and killing are nothing but means. On their own they are neither good nor bad. For no deed is either good or bad, isolated from the intentions that motivated it.[2]

So, the regime's lying about the true intention of Iran's nuclear program could easily be justified by following Khomeini's doctrine on the advancement of Islam. Lying even to the people of Iran would then be justified, so long as the lying was calculated to advance Islam along the fated path.

These considerations further caution that additional sanctions may do little to deter the Iranian regime from proceeding defiantly with the advancement of their nuclear program. Iran's revenue from energy sales will proceed strongly from the investment placed in the energy sector by countries such as India and China, whether or not the United States ever buys any Iranian oil or natural gas.

Khomeini fought an eight-year war with Iraq in the 1980s that virtually destroyed five of Iran's twenty-three provinces, left millions homeless, and killed or maimed an entire generation of Iranian males. Wave after wave of Iran's children were sent into battle ahead of the soldiers, often without weapons, simply to clear the mine fields, knowing they were rushing to their deaths. Khomeini advised his people in response: "Islam is a tree that needs the blood of martyrs to grow."[3] These are not the expected calculations of power politics or the pragmatic politics of national interest. These are the politics of a religious zealot who believes religion and politics must be joined such that religion drives the politics, not the other way around.

With Ahmadinejad openly expressing his mission to prepare the way for the Mahdi's return, we can expect that he will follow the same path. As was the case with the Nazis, Hitler could not be controlled by the international diplomacy of the British or the French, not even with the backing of the Americans, not because he didn't listen, but because he considered international diplomacy to be corrupt at its core, inherently opposed to his goal of advancing Nazism to world domination.

The Iranian revolution under Ayatollah Khomeini and today under Ayatollah Yazdi, Ahmadinejad's spiritual mentor, gives messianic Shi'ite Islam the same religious-political force for those under its sway as Nazism did for those persuaded by Hitler.

On 9 January 2006, Iran's state-run television aired a rally of Iranian pilgrims in Mecca. A speaker addressed a crowd, standing in front of a backdrop that showed the World Trade Center and an American flag in flames. The crowd was encouraged to chant the familiar "Death to Israel! ... Death to America!" Here is part of the broadcast dialogue:

We the pilgrims who have come to the house of God, strongly condemn the aggressive measures of "the global arrogance," led by the idol and center of evil, the criminal America. We condemn it for its aggression, warmongering, its murder, plundering, torture, espionage, its abductions, and its secret jails. We strongly condemn it.

We emphasize that the occupation forces must leave the lands of Islam. We express our hatred and our disgust at the mother of all corruption of this century, the Great Satan, and at its illegitimate offspring, the plundering Israel.[4]

"Allah Akbar!" cries the crowd in response. *"Allah Akbar! Allah Akbar!"*

Can we rule out that Ahmadinejad would not use nuclear weapons against Israel and America if the weapons were available to use, even if the consequences were suicidal to Iran? Most likely, we cannot, not when the divine is seen to tip the balance of the power equation in favor of the eternal.

Remember, the political culture of the Islamic Shi'ites gave birth to the modern concept of "suicide bombers," a culture which has been absorbed by terrorist organizations such as Hezbollah and Hamas, with the tactic aggressively used against Israel. The former chief of staff of Iran's army, Major General Ali Shahbazi, has commented on Iran's radical view of religious martyrdom, raising a disturbing point: "The United States or some country incited by it may be able to begin a military conflict . . . it will not be strong enough to end it." This is because only Muslims believe that "whether we kill or are killed, we are the victors. Others do not think this way."[5]

Iran exhibited this martyrdom complex during the 1980s Iran-Iraq war. Michael Eisenstadt, a senior fellow and director of the Military and Security Studies Program at the Washington Institute for Near East Policy, commented that the charisma of Ayatollah Khomeini was a major reason Iran exhibited suicidal zeal in the war against Iraq, saying that his influence led to an abnormal ability or willingness to absorb staggering costs.[6]

Ahmadinejad has sought to bring Iran back to the revolutionary zeal of Ayatollah Khomeini. Ahmadinejad is under the spiritual leadership of Ayatollah Yazdi, the major supporter in the Council of Elders responsible for promoting Ayatollah Khamenei to succeed the visionary Khomeini. With Ahmadinejad in power, the messianic vision of the Mahdi is a primary motivator behind the small group of zealots currently controlling Iran. Even if many of the mullahs may prefer a more conservative path, such as Iran took under the presidencies of Rafsanjani and Khatami, reformists in a zealot-controlled regime are pushed into the backseat. Moderates in a radicalized Iran are unable to find grounds within the religion with which to temper the zealots' determination. Moderates who push reform politics in a radical theocracy such as Iran risk being accused themselves of being traitors to the cause.

Rather than being deterred by the logic of mutually assured destruction, an extremist such as Ahmadinejad may be attracted by nuclear suicide, as long as Israel is destroyed in the process.

IRAN PLAYS THE NEGOTIATIONS GAME

Prolonging negotiations without achieving any material result is a game the Iranian regime has mastered. Most talks devolve into mere talks about future talks, while the Iranians press forward with processing and enriching uranium. Assuming ongoing talks are much the same, attention should turn to the effectiveness of sanctions. After all, hadn't worldwide sanctions against South Africa brought down apartheid in the 1990s?

The idea is tantalizing, but unfortunately there are important differences between South Africa's situation in the 1990s and the Islamic Republic of Iran today. For starters, South Africa may have had ample diamonds, but South Africa has virtually no oil. Iran's abundant oil and natural gas resources do more than produce a large and continually flowing income for the mullahs. Iran's energy resources give the mullahs important leverage with energy poor nations, including China and India.

In 2005, both China and India finalized major energy infra-structures investment agreements with Iran, which offered the mul-lahs billions of investment capital to develop Iran's oil and natural gas industries into the future. Even more important, by signing these deals with China and India, Iran bought two powerful supporters. With China a permanent member of the Security Council, the mul-lahs secured a possible veto, even if the Russians were to hesitate.

Another key difference is that in the 1990s, South Africa was on the politically incorrect side of the equation, while today Iran is on the politically correct side. Since the Supreme Court decision *Brown v. Board of Education* in 1954, the political left has opposed racial discrimination with the charge that white racism is the cause of racial inequality. Nothing proved this point better for the polit-ical left than South Africa. Under apartheid, a system of legal racial separation, South Africa's white, largely European population jeal-ously held all power and economic advantages. The black popula-tion clearly suffered poverty and oppression.

In the past four decades, the Palestinians have spent billions of dollars, many of which were funded to them by the United Nations, on a massive worldwide public relations campaign. As a direct consequence, the Palestinians have been assisted by some of the world's top legal, political, and media experts under contract. Israel, once a cause of the political left, has lost the front seat to the

Palestinians. Today, the left sees the Palestinians as oppressed second-class orphans of the Middle East, who rightfully deserve to
have a country of their own.

Ironically, Israel, by winning multiple wars against their Islamic
enemies and by siding with the United States, has lost much favor
with the left. Nor has American military support for Israel been
embraced by the left. American military power, almost by definition,
is never considered politically correct by today's mainstream media.

Because opposing apartheid was politically correct, the worldwide diplomatic effort against South Africa in the 1990s received
not only strong international support, but also the support of many
anti-American countries of the UN. Opposing apartheid became
virtually an extension of the American civil rights movement with
the same enemy, white racism.

Today, the political left worldwide leans toward Iran, despite
Iran's push for nuclear weapons. This tone is evident in the remarks
former president Hashemi Rafsanjani made in a prayer sermon at
the Tehran University Campus on 11 January 2006. Wondering
why the Western nations opposed Iran's push for nuclear weapons,
Rafsanjani surmised that "the root cause of these assaults lies in the
colonialist nature and policies of the West whose plan is to keep
countries backward."[7]

That rhetoric was perfectly formed for capturing the political
left. Rafsanjani—who, remember, was a reformer and something
of a moderate—skillfully placed Iran's move for nuclear technology
in the context of the continuing fight against colonialism. Rather
than seeing Iran as a terror-exporting aggressor, Rafsanjani con-
jured up an image of Iran as the proverbial underdog.

Rafsanjani continued, calling up the vision of how Saddam
Hussein had used chemical weapons, gassing Iranian troops, in the
1980s Iran-Iraq war: "Under the worst conditions when our country

was chemically bombarded by the enemy, we refused to go beyond humanitarian limits and avoided using inhumane weapons." This is a masterful statement, twisting the picture to the point where Iran is seen as the victim.

With speeches such as these, Rafsanjani provides a different perspective, inviting us to forget the aggression Ahmadinejad exhibits when he threatens to wipe Israel off the map. Even more brilliantly, Rafsanjani actually repositions Ahmadinejad's statements. Again, Iran is portrayed as the victim, not as the oppressor.

Another important difference with South Africa in the 1990s is that despite years of sanctions, Iran is not truly isolated. Scores of European countries have continued to work with Iran despite the American sanctions imposed during the Clinton administration. Sanctions are easily circumvented by Iran's extensive ties in Europe and Asia, as well as with rogue countries such as North Korea, and dozens of allied nations in the Islamic world.

Following Iranian newspapers or news services for any period of time, one quickly realizes how frequently Iranian officials travel the world for diplomatic meetings with other nations, as well as how many nations travel to Tehran for official government visits. Unless the United Nations were to restrict the ability of Iranian diplomats to travel worldwide, Iran is unlikely ever to reach the isolation South Africa endured before apartheid was abandoned. In the early 1990s, South Africa's Apartheid had become so unpopular with the political left that international diplomats or governments were reluctant to admit they had discussions with South African government officials or diplomats, let alone public governmental-level meetings. Even the United States granted President Ahmadinejad the right to enter the country so he could address the United Nations General Assembly in September 2005, despite strong protests from Iranian democracy advocates worldwide.

So the South African model isn't a good one to follow in Iran. Still, new and vigorous sanctions might put a crimp in Iran's plans. In 2006, Israel put forward a list of recommendations that, taken together, might prove effective.

- The US government could press for public disclosure of all corporations around the world who are doing business with Iran's nuclear industries, to see if any US corporations have ties that would violate applicable laws. Given its oil venture with China in Iran, ExxonMobil might be a good place to start.

- Despite having no diplomatic relations with the United States, Iran operates a mission in New York as part of its United Nations membership. Why not order Iran to close their New York mission? How about a motion to expel Iran from the United Nations if it refuses to comply with IAEA inspection requirements?

- The mullahs and various Iranian government officials might be denied travel permits. Iranian airplanes could be denied landing rights.

- International credit cards held by the mullahs or regime officials could be revoked, including their Visa, MasterCard, or American Express privileges.

- Iranian sports teams could be denied access to international competitions, including all world events and the Olympics.

- Photographs of the mullahs could be published, along with their involvement in the multiple human rights violations that international organizations have amply documented over the past twenty-six years.

Granted, these would be tough to impose across the board, especially considering the apparent timidity and weakness of American politicians. Consider how hard Senator Rick Santorum of Pennsylvania had to fight to get Congress to take action against Iran.

SANTORUM'S RESOLUTION

On Friday, 16 December 2005, the US Senate passed a resolution introduced by Senator Santorum condemning the anti-Semitic statements of President Ahmadinejad and demanding an apology for those statements of hate toward all the Jewish people of the world.[8]

The story here was the opposition from Democratic Party senators to the original wording of the resolution as submitted by Senator Santorum. The initial language supported the people of Iran's desire to exercise self-determination over their form of government. The resolution called for Iran to hold a national referendum with international observers to certify the fairness and integrity of the vote.

The referendum was aimed at exposing the fraudulent presidential election which Ahmadinejad supposedly won. Santorum was being responsive to opposing Iranians who charged that the election had been rigged by the mullahs. Over the past few years, the goal of the referendum movement in Iran has been to get an "up or down" vote on continuing the theocracy under the rule of the mullahs. Proponents of the referendum widely believe that the Iranian regime is so unpopular in Iran that the ruling clerics would lose any such clear vote on whether they should remain in power.

Democratic senators wanted the language of Senator Santorum's resolution watered down. Several prominent Democrats argued that the United States needed to accept the result of Iran's election as legitimate. While not going on the record directly in the Senate discussion, the discussion in the halls of the Senate was that the United States should not interfere in Iran's internal electoral process.

On every front, the most liberal Democratic Senators were pressing the Bush administration. Over and over, the charge was repeated that since the intelligence in Iraq had been faulty, why was it reliable now? These liberal Senators believed that the Bush administration had used the faulty intelligence intentionally, planning to mislead the US into war. They argued that President Bush had overstepped his authority under the Patriot Act to authorize "illegally" wiretaps against US citizens without obtaining a court order to do so. If the US could not win the war in Iraq, the liberal Senators pressed, how did we know we would win a war in Iran? Where was the administration's plan for withdrawing troops from Iraq? Would we really contemplate sending troops to invade Iran?

Ultimately, Senator Santorum's Iran resolution was watered down to demand an apology from President Ahmadinejad, not to criticize the electoral process which had put him in office.

Viewing the outcome of Senator Santorum's resolution, the Israelis could rightly conclude there was no majority in the US Senate in favor of getting tough with Iran. If the US Senate could not even pass the originally worded resolution, how would the Senate resolve to protect Israel from Iran?

The mood in the Senate strongly suggested that President Bush would risk impeachment if he decided to engage in a second preemptive war in the Middle East. Was the Senate willing to take any measure to stop Iran from developing nuclear weapons? What consequences would the Bush administration suffer if a decision were made to support an Israeli strike against Iran? Even if the support amounted only to granting Israel air rights to pass over Iraq on its way to attacking Iran's nuclear facilities, the Senate might react angrily.

To top it off, the Santorum resolution on Iran received almost no coverage in the American mainstream media.

On a much more positive note, around the same time, the United States imposed sanctions on nine companies for selling materials to Iran that can be used in the production of missiles and weapons of mass destruction, including atomic bombs. Six of the companies were Chinese. The State Department announced that the sanctions were based on "credible information" that the companies transferred equipment or technology in violation of the Iran Nonproliferation Act that was signed into law in March 2000, at the end of the Clinton administration.

According to State Department spokesperson Adam Ereli, the sanctions were more than a symbolic gesture; the Bush administration intended for the sanctions to "have an impact," alerting the governments involved "to activity taking place in their countries and instituting measures or taking actions to prevent those kinds of activities."[9]

This action marked a ratcheting up of the diplomatic seriousness with which the Bush administration was pursuing its case that Iran was secretly pursuing nuclear weapons. By singling out six of the nine sanctioned companies as Chinese, the Bush administration was clearly notifying China of the concern that it was aiding the rogue state of Iran in the push to acquire nuclear weapons.

If the case against Iran were effectively developed with the IAEA leading the argument, could effective sanctions against Iran be specified? The answer is yes. Information is readily available on international companies doing business with Iran. Each year in April, Iran's Ministry of Petroleum holds an Annual International Oil, Gas, and Petrochemicals Exhibition (IOGPE) in Tehran; the IOGPE website lists the hundreds of international companies who attend the conference in Iran.[10]

Pressure could be placed on the EU3, as well as other members of the UN Security Council, to prohibit energy industry companies headquartered in their nations from conducting further work with Iran's energy industry. Since Iran is so heavily dependent upon oil revenue, any blow to the efficient functioning of its energy industries would be severely felt in Tehran and throughout the country.

The Israelis worry that the negotiations currently underway with Iran are destined to become a textbook case. Unfortunately, the case will demonstrate how a relatively weak state in the Middle East has been able to lead the whole international community, including the world's only superpower, down the garden path.

By taking a defiant path and making no concessions whatsoever, Iran has managed to buy time. The EU3 has been reduced to virtually begging Iran just "to talk about more talks." Meanwhile, Iran has been given the leeway to threaten Israel directly, while the world stands by and watches. Every day, the Iranian nuclear program advances closer to weapons capability.

Before Iran gets nuclear weapons, and while Iran is yet weak, increased diplomatic pressure could drive concessions from the Iranian mullahs. But sanctions would have to be harsh, aimed at threatening the mullahs' personal wealth and inconveniencing their travel plans. When Iranian soccer teams compete freely in international competitions, the Israelis know the mullahs are feeling no pain. We should all worry that Israel will begin to conclude that the diplomatic support needed to ensure its survival is lacking. The crisis with Iran has reached a very dangerous point.

In 1938, Europe and America did not want to see a war emerging with Nazi Germany. Today, most Americans feel the same about Iran.

Still, Iran is planning a confrontation with Israel and the United States, but on Iran's time and in Iran's way. Right now,

President Ahmadinejad and Ayatollah Khamenei are happy just to win the game of nuclear chess. Iran's plan is to checkmate the world the moment it actually has deliverable nuclear weapons. Unfortunately, Iran's nuclear clock is ticking and that day of showdown is rapidly approaching.

AMERICA INCREASES DIPLOMATIC PRESSURE

On 12 January 2006, the *Washington Post* reported that Russian Foreign Minister Sergei Lavrov, in a phone call with US Secretary of State Rice, had confirmed that Russia would not block US efforts to call an emergency meeting of the IAEA to present the Iranian portfolio to the UN Security Council.[11] According to the paper, Lavrov told Rice that Russia would abstain on the IAEA vote, rather than vote against the United States. This was an important development, signaling that the US had been pressuring Russia, as well as China, behind the scenes.

Let's assume that the Bush administration has planned countermeasures to pressure even Russia and China into going along with Security Council action against Iran. Let's also assume that the Bush administration has given considerable thought to the Security Council's prior inaction, with dozens of resolutions having been ignored by Saddam Hussein despite United Nations' sanctions. What could the Bush administration be calculating as a strategy aimed at getting a different result this time?

We assume that President Bush fully appreciated the barriers in the United Nations and has resolved that a vote in the IAEA to bring Iran to the Security Council for noncompliance is not a waste of time. What different steps could be taken by the United States to get effective Security Council action against Iran now?

We want to make the argument as convincingly as possible,

even though we consider effective Security Council action unlikely. Here, we want to pause to examine a strategy the United States could calculate to give effective Security Council action the highest probability of actually happening.

The decision in December 2005 to single out six of the nine sanctioned companies to be Chinese suggests the Bush administration understands that our leverage with the Chinese is greater than with the Russians. Today America is China's major international trade partner.

In 2005, China negotiated several major contracts with Iran for oil and natural gas rights. The Chinese energy contracts with Iran were for the future; the quantities of US goods being manufactured in China are a reality today. Could China sustain trade import restrictions being placed on Chinese goods by a Bush administration determined to turn up the heat?

In the first weeks of the first Bush administration, the two countries squared off when a US military reconnaissance aircraft was forced down in China by Chinese military fighters.[12] What the Bush administration learned then was that China had backed down in the face of strong American protests. By sanctioning Chinese companies in December 2005, the US put China on notice that helping to develop nuclear weapons would not be ignored by the US. Was China willing to risk further US ire by stonewalling on Iran at the United Nations?

In the 20 April 2006 meeting at the White House between President Bush and Chinese President Hu, Iran was discussed. In response to questions from reporters at the end of their meeting President Bush commented:

> The first goal of any dialogue with a partner with whom we're trying to create peace is to have a common objective, a stated

goal. And we have a common goal, and that is that Iran should not have the nuclear weapon, the capacity to make a nuclear weapon, or the know-how to make a nuclear weapon.

And the second goal is to be in a position where we can work on tactics. And one of the tactics that I've been talking to the President about is the use of the United Nations Security Council Chapter 7 to send a common message to the Iranians that China and the United States and EU3 countries all deeply are concerned about the Iranian ambition.[13]

Although he had a chance to respond to the reporter's question, President Hu did not comment on Iran.

Russia may have had an awakening regarding Iran. When the Iranians rejected the Russian proposal to enrich uranium for Iran at a facility on Russian soil, the Russians realized that despite Tehran's growing closeness to Moscow, Russia still did not control Iran as a traditional "client state" of the Cold War era. The Iranian regime expressed that Russia made the offer as a "friend" but that the offer was rejected because Iran wanted to control its own nuclear destiny. Iran wanted no possibility that any foreign nation could have control over any aspect of its nuclear program.

Iran was determined to develop and control "the full fuel cycle" on Iranian soil under the direction of fully capable Iranian nuclear scientists and engineers. Even after Russia had agreed to sell Iran an advanced TOR-M1 surface-to-air anti-missile defense system to protect Iran's nuclear facilities, Iran remained determined to be independent of Russian control. The United States undoubtedly reminded Russia of this detail when expressing US determination to press for an IAEA noncompliance vote to refer Iran to the Security Council in January 2006.

The US needs Russia's help now more than ever. The truth is

that Iran does not have the native capability to build a nuclear program. Virtually their entire program is being built through Russian scientists and technology. Over 3,000 scientists are working on the primary reactor at Bushehr alone. The solution to the mystery of the Holy Grail is quite simple: Shut off the supplier and Iran's nuclear ambitions end.

A key to decisive, concerted action by the United States and Russia may be found in an agreement reached by former US president Bill Clinton and former Russian leader Boris Yeltsin at their seventh summit meeting on 2 September 1998 in Moscow. In their "Joint Statement on Common Security Challenges at the Threshold of the Twenty-First Century," the two presidents heralded the role both countries would play in "promoting prosperity and strengthening security throughout the world. In this connection, we reaffirm that the United States of America and the Russian Federation are natural partners in advancing international peace and stability.

"We understand that the most serious and pressing danger is the proliferation of nuclear, biological, chemical, and other types of weapons of mass destruction, the technologies for their production, and their means of delivery," says the statement. "We reaffirm the determination of the US and Russia to cooperate actively and closely with each other, as well as with all other interested countries, to avert and reduce this threat by taking new steps, seeking new forms of collaboration, and strengthening generally recognized international norms."

This is "a moment of truth for Russia," when it will choose whether to throw its lot with the West or keep the US and its allies at arm's length, Radzhab Safarov, director of the Iranian Studies Center in Moscow, told the *Los Angeles Times* (4 May 2006). Safarov confirmed that moving back toward the center of the world stage is a prime goal for Russia, and it can do so by acting as the world's broker on Iran, rather than trying to relive the Soviet days of client states.

The steps the US can take to induce Russia to play a more positive and active role over Iran's nuclear program range from political inducements based on Russia's desire to regain an international leadership role, to economic incentives, to the negative warning of the consequences of military action to remove Iran's nuclear threat. A combination of steps could induce the Kremlin to use its leverage over Iran to slow or halt its nuclear weapons program.

- Using the leverage of the US-Russia 1998 "Joint Statement," the US can induce Russia to refuse to complete the Bushehr reactor and supply it with fuel. Instead of being portrayed as Iran's nuclear arms provider, Russia could act as a bridge between the Islamic Republic and the West and thereby defuse the nuclear crisis. Keep Safarov's analysis in mind. Washington would offer Moscow a payoff of prestige in exchange for Russian influence over Iran.

- The US could change its approach and encourage nonproliferation assistance to Russia, including Russian imports of Western spent nuclear fuel for potentially lucrative storage contracts with foreign governments.

- The US should stress that it is in Russia's own strategic interest to prevent Iran from building nuclear weapons or abandoning the Nuclear Non-Proliferation Treaty. This would mean shifting the US approach to Russia from the economic realm to seeking ways to help Russia, and ultimately the IAEA, to deal with Iran.

- The US should act to change the way its policy on Iran is perceived in Russia; i.e., as not being against Iran's nuclear proliferation so much as being opposed to the Iranian regime and favoring regime change, as in Iraq. The US should reinforce Russia's own clear opposition to Iran acquiring nuclear weapons.

- The US could induce Russia to join a demand for Iran to immediately cease its enrichment activities by acknowledging that by doing so, it would be following its own economic and security interests, and be taking a world leadership role on nonproliferation. By doing so, Russia would avoid the UN sanctions and US military action it opposes, and at the same time, protect its economic and political interests with Iran.

The US and Russia have already agreed on what needs to be done. Will Russia support taking the necessary action?

While the United States will press Russia and China to vote additional sanctions in the Security Council, the strategy will be to accept a decision by both countries to abstain.

Iran's goal will be to confuse the debate before the Security Council such that no meaningful sanctions against it are passed. Iran's gambit may be to agree to half-measures, such as increased openness to IAEA inspections, whether or not Iran sincerely intends to honor the pledges made.

The Bush administration cannot be expected to have infinite patience. If the Security Council deliberations fail to achieve an adequate restraining impact on Iran, the US military may well move into position to a ready status for a military strike. Overcoming Russian and Chinese objections to sanctions on Iran will take masterful negotiating by the United States at the UN.

We can also assume that the closer we get to possible military action, the more likely the Bush administration will be to conclude that America must be involved. The United States will be implicated in the military action, even if Israel decides to launch the preemptive strike unilaterally. After all, the US at a minimum will have to grant air rights over Iraq to permit the Israeli Air Force to reach Iran.

To avoid the military option, the US will have to persuade the Security Council to take tough steps against Iran. A failure to impose meaningful sanctions in the Security Council will mark the diplomatic dead end. Already, Iran has defiantly boasted that no sanctions will stop the regime from pursuing nuclear technology. If Iran wins at the United Nations, or if it holds to its stated resolve despite sanctions being imposed, then the US and Israel will have no option left except military action.

THE UNITED STATES AGREES TO TALK

After months of failing to get Russia and China to agree to a tough Security Council resolution pressing for sanctions, the Bush administration changed direction. At the beginning of June 2006, the United States, together with the five permanent members of the Security Council plus Germany, offered to Iran a package of incentives, provided Iran would agree to stop enriching uranium. The United States even reversed course, offering to participate directly with the EU3 and the IAEA in resumed negotiations with Iran. Again, the precondition for US participation in direct talks with Iran was that Iran would agree to a new uranium enrichment moratorium.

On 31 May 2006, Secretary of State Condoleezza Rice announced that after three decades of a hard-line stance against Iran, the US and the European Union offered a package of "incentives" to Iran. Included among the "carrots" in the package were:

- Iran would get help building new nuclear power plants, specifically light water reactors that cannot be used to make weapons-grade nuclear fuel.

- Iran would get a new facility to hold a five-year supply of nuclear fuel.

- The deal would also open the door to "guarantees for [Iran's] territorial integrity"—words meant to assure Iran there would be no invasion by the United States.

- A package of economic incentives so Iran can purchase a new fleet of American and European aircraft, something that it is now forbidden to do. Its aging airline fleet has become a safety threat.

The incentives offered by the US and the EU3 were all contingent on Iran agreeing to stop enriching uranium—making fuel that can be used for bombs or nuclear power.

The proposal also said that Iran could be allowed to resume uranium enrichment in the future if it could convince the United Nations Security Council that the uranium was for peaceful purposes only.

The new incentives package included offering Iran nuclear fuel for peaceful purposes, a wide range of economic benefits, and security guarantees. Secretary of State Condoleezza Rice traveled to Vienna to finalize the offer, carefully avoiding any mention of sanctions or military options, so as to win the agreement of Russia and China.[14]

Immediately, Iran denounced the proposal as "propaganda." Cleverly, Iranian Foreign Minister Manouchehr Mottaki welcomed the opportunity to engage in direct discussions with the United States but rejected the requirement that Iran first stop uranium enrichment. "We won't negotiate about the Iranian nation's natural nuclear rights, but we are prepared, within a defined, just framework, and without discrimination, to hold dialogue about our common concerns," he told the world press.[15] Iran was ready for "unconditional" talks, not for making concessions.

Iran's response suggested the regime realized the prestige that enriching uranium had bestowed on the government. Acting as if Iran held the position of power, the regime was demanding "open talks" that would bring the US to the table as an equal, conveying to the world that the US was prepared to accept Iran's right to pursue the "full nuclear fuel cycle." If concessions could be gained from the Security Council's permanent members plus Germany, then Iran would emerge a true winner—as long as Iran was conceded the right to enrich some fuel on its own soil. With this result, Iran could claim the world community was accepting Iran's premise that their nuclear program was successful and that Iran was being rewarded for having succeeded with uranium enrichment.

Finally, the United States pushed a deadline of 12 July 2006 for Iran to give a response to the incentives package. A coalition that became known as the "Five + 1," the five permanent members of the Security Council plus Germany, held firm to the original offer: there would be no talks until Iran re-imposed upon itself a moratorium to enrich uranium. But, predictably the July deadline came and went, without any final response from Tehran. Instead, Tehran set a new deadline for itself, saying the regime would need until 22 August 2006 to prepare a meaningful response.

Had all this negotiation not been so deadly serious, Iran's response would almost be comic. Clearly, the regime was buying time. What would be different by 22 August that could not be expressed on 12 July?

In the interim, war broke out. Israel grew tired of the increasing rocket attacks from Hezbollah in southern Lebanon and from Hamas in the recently returned Gaza. When two Israeli soldiers were taken hostage by Hezbollah, Israel went to war, striking both Hezbollah and Hamas with air attacks against the terrorists and their strongholds. What the US and Israel argued was that Iran was at the center of the violence, encouraging Hezbollah and Hamas to step up their rocket attacks against Israel. Certainly, the timing of the rocket attacks supported Israel's contention. Once the shooting began, the world's attention drifted from demanding an Iranian response to the UN incentives package that had been proposed by the "Five + 1."

The entire drama of attempting to negotiate a settlement with Iran over its nuclear program reinforced the argument that Iran remains the major source of trouble for Israel and for the US in the Middle East. The likelihood is that the Middle East will remain in turmoil as long as the current Iranian regime remains in power. Ahmadinejad and the ultraconservative clerics who back him will continue to push to develop nuclear weapons and to lie to the world about their efforts. We have no reason to expect that the UN will piece together any meaningful sanctions against Iran, especially since Russia and China are permanent members of the Security Council.

The true enemy of Israel and the US is not Hezbollah or Hamas—the true enemy has been and will continue to be Iran, as long as the Islamic Republic of Iran remains the regime in Tehran.

NUCLEAR ENDGAME

Predictably, Iran has stalled the endgame of negotiations by refusing to give up the right to enrich uranium on its own soil. This, in the final analysis, is the sticking point. The United States and Israel know that if Iran wins the right to enrich uranium, cheating is inevitable. Whether it takes Iran only months to build a bomb or a year or more, the outcome is certain. If the world community allows Iran to enrich uranium, it is only a matter of time before Iran has nuclear weapons.

On 25 April 2006, Israel launched a new Eros-B spy satellite.[16] The Eros-B is one of the most sophisticated spy satellites available, capable of spotting objects on the ground as small as 27 inches.[17] The following day, Yitzhak Ben Yisrael, the head of the Israeli space agency, gave an interview on Reshet Bet Radio.[18] Mr. Ben Yisrael explained how the satellite would help Israel follow Iran's progress with uranium enrichment at Natanz:

Mr. Ben Yisrael: If today we take the famous example of the known centrifuges in Iran, how is the construction progressing? Are they building under the surface? Is it above the surface? How much have they done already? How much haven't they done? All these things. Is there concrete? How thick is it? It is possible, of course to know all kinds of things such as these with such a satellite.

Question: But you are saying, are they building under the surface, and there is, after all, news regarding the fact that Iran has a secret plan, a "Plan-B" for the building of nuclear power, and that plan is probably being carried out in underground facilities and there we will not be able to know what is really happening there.

Mr. Ben Yisrael: That too, is not precise. For even when you dig a tunnel to the depths, you see it in a photograph. You cannot know what is happening under the ground, but you can see where the location is, where it is, and even finer things, according to the dirt which is being taken out. You can even know how deep it runs. All kinds of things of this kind.

Iran took four months from opening Isfahan to being able to produce uranium hexafluoride gas, much more quickly than most intelligence experts estimated. Iran opened Natanz in January, and again, it took Iran four months to produce highly-enriched uranium. We believe it will only take Iran a matter of months to produce weapons-grade highly-enriched uranium. By the end of 2006 or the beginning of 2007, Iran could well be on the verge of having a deliverable nuclear weapon.

Israel plans to watch Natanz carefully to determine when and how many centrifuges are installed in the uranium enrichment facility. When the number of advanced centrifuges reaches about 3,000, Iran will hit a milestone. That number should be sufficient to produce weapons-grade uranium. The only remaining question will be how long it takes Iran to work through the final technical problems in making the 3,000-centrifuge cascade operational.

Today reminds many of the world in the 1930s, when Hitler's Germany won sympathy for having been unjustly punished after World War I. Bankers worldwide financed Hitler's Nazi government, allowing themselves to believe that his fascist regime was pursuing modernization for the economic benefit of the German people. Hitler's racist rants against the Jews were largely written off as not being of serious intent, just as his persistent steps to re-arm Germany were considered a sovereign right of self-defense.

Those who saw the coming Nazi threat in the 1930s were likely to be written off as alarmists, at least until Hitler invaded Poland and turned his armies toward France.

Stopping Hitler in the 1940s cost the world an estimated 60 million deaths in scores of countries across the globe. Will stopping an atomic Iran cost 600 million deaths in an international nuclear war? Time will only tell.

Yet today the international diplomatic resolve to bring Iran's nuclear program within genuinely "transparent" IAEA inspection seems lacking. As clearly as world diplomats preferred appeasement in the 1930s, today world diplomats continue to believe that strong admonitions will have a deterrent effect upon the religious zealots who control Iran's radical Islamic regime.

Ahmadinejad thinks differently. He believes the moment is imminent for the return of the Mahdi, ushering in the ultimate triumph of Islam. Is he right? Do the Jews once again have a cause for legitimate concern as they did under Hitler?

7

THE PROSPECT OF WAR

"Although we have the strongest army in the region, the strongest air force, and the strongest navy, there are many parties in our region who still underestimate Israel. Many are still reluctant to recognize Israel, and many are still active to annihilate the State of Israel."

—General Moshe Ya'alon, 2006

"Regarding Iran, Israel will take whatever action is necessary to protect itself."

—Former Prime Minister
Benjamin Netanyahu, 2006

"I made it clear, and I'll make it clear again, that we will use military might to protect our ally Israel."

—President George W. Bush,
20 March 2006

B oth Israel and the United States have stated repeatedly that Iran armed with nuclear weapons is unacceptable. If this point had been debatable before Ahmadinejad's tirades against Israel, by the summer of 2006 the risk looked unacceptably severe.

In the shooting war that broke out between Hezbollah and Israel in July 2006, the world once again moved to the brink of full-scale war in the Middle East. With Iran prompting Hezbollah and Hamas as their proxy terrorist organizations to intensify rocket attacks against Israel, a retaliatory response from Israel could be counted upon. Syria, Iran's client state, had done everything possible to maintain Hezbollah's position in the Lebanese government after Syria withdrew its troops from Lebanon. The regime in Iran knew that world attention from their continued nuclear program would be diverted the moment a shooting war began. Israel's only alternative was to turn the other cheek. But ignoring provocations became impossible when Hezbollah resolved to resume its old tricks of holding hostages. Israel could not stand by while Hezbollah held Israeli soldiers hostage, threatening to send them back to Iran.

Clearly Iran has continued playing chess with the world community. How Iran handled the negotiations over its uranium enrichment and processing is a good case in point. The diplomatic maneuvering successfully bought Iran much needed time, though the patience of the international diplomatic community was sorely tested. The EU3 throughout 2004 and 2005 had made abundantly clear its preference to resolve questions of Iran's nuclear program diplomatically. Yet, was Iran equally willing to work in a serious fashion with the diplomats assigned to the case?

On key points, Iran was increasingly unwilling to negotiate. Iran had openly insisted that pursuing the "full nuclear fuel cycle" was within Iran's sovereign rights. Iran insisted that uranium enrichment would be pursued on its own soil, regardless of what world diplomats said. Without concessions by Iran, how was diplomacy to succeed? Iran has acted as if the mullahs had concluded that eventually the Europeans and the IAEA would give in, abandoning the United States and Israel when it came to imposing tough sanctions.

If Iran wanted to assure the world community that the regime's nuclear purposes were entirely peaceful, establishing transparency to the Iranian nuclear program should not be difficult. The IAEA is more than willing to convey to Iran the type of inspection activities that could put even the United States and Israel at ease. Yet, rather than complying, Iran stonewalled the negotiations, refusing to make concessions.

For the United States and Israel to accept a nuclear-armed Iran, both countries would need to see meaningful confirmation that Iran had accepted Israel's legitimate right to exist. Iran would have to drop demands that the Jewish state should disappear in the Middle East, perhaps relocating to Europe. In addition, the United States and Israel would also require proof that Iran had stopped funding and supporting anti-Israel and anti-American terrorist groups including Hezbollah, Hamas, and the Islamic Jihad. Nothing in the current posture of the Islamic Republic of Iran gives any reason to believe that Iran is ready to make these necessary concessions. It not only runs counter to its revolutionary position; it also negates the firmly held belief in the Mahdi's return.

What the United States and Israel are increasingly unwilling to do is to give Iran more latitude within which to conceal a covert nuclear weapons program. Thus, the United States and Israel have moved toward bright-line tests. If Iran continues uranium processing and enrichment at both Isfahan and Natanz, then sanctions will be sought against Iran and the risk of a preemptive military strike escalates. The US and Israel have clearly asked Iran to resume its voluntary moratorium on uranium enrichment. So far, Iran continues to refuse. At this point, negotiations with Iran are finished.

Without international resolve or the ability to stop Iran diplomatically, military action is the only recourse to change Iran's nuclear direction. Conceivably, this dance could go on until Iran has a nuclear weapon ready to deliver. Then the game could shift to whether or not Iran could be deterred from using the weapon.

Israel has survived since 1948 by being aware of the reality of politics in a hostile world. For some fifty-eight years since achieving statehood, Israel has lived constantly on the edge, always ready to face the ultimate existential threat that a hostile Islamic neighbor might actually some day succeed in wiping the Jewish state off the map.

If Ahmadinejad were to succeed in eliminating Israel, it would be a major step to removing American presence from the Middle East. But, in the final analysis, for the Iranians to out maneuver the world's diplomats, Iran would also have to out maneuver Israel diplomatically. And that is unlikely to happen. What is much more likely is that Israel's patience will run out. At that point, history predicts Israel will launch a preemptive war against Iran, regardless of what the consequences may be. Israel knows that to strike first offers the best chance of victory.

In this game of nuclear chicken, Israel cannot afford to wait too long, not when the outcome may be that Iran secretly does develop nuclear weapons and decides this time to be the one who strikes first.

The remainder of this chapter will explore the shape and strategies possible in a military solution to the Iran crisis—first, if Israel attacks; second, if America does.

IF ISRAEL ATTACKS

Israel has maintained secrecy about its nuclear weapons program. Officially, the Israeli government had maintained a policy of "deliberate ambiguity," saying only that Israel will not be the first country to introduce nuclear weapons into a Middle Eastern war. This carefully worded statement was designed to avoid having to deny that Israel actually possesses nuclear weapons.

Still, along with India and Pakistan, Israel is one of the three sovereign states possessing nuclear weapons that has not signed the Nuclear Non-Proliferation Treaty (NPT). Israel made this decision simply to avoid lying about the nuclear program the world knows it has.

The existence of the Israeli nuclear weapons program was first disclosed by Mordechai Vanunu in the London-based *Sunday Times*, on 5 October 1986.[1] At that time, Vanunu was a thirty-one-year-old Israeli who had worked for ten years in a top secret underground bunker at Dimona in the Negev Desert, the site of Israel's nuclear reactor and the country's nuclear research establishment.

Vanunu published a series of photographs in the *Sunday Times*, which permitted international nuclear weapons experts to determine that Israel possessed a sophisticated nuclear arsenal, estimated to rank as the sixth most powerful in the world, behind America, Russia, Britain, France, and China, but ahead of India and Pakistan.

Since the 1950s, the United States had refused requests from Israel to help build the country's nuclear capabilities. Israel got the assistance required from France, which built the Dimona reactor and supplied Israel with the plutonium-extracting technology which was required to transform the Dimona reactor from civilian purposes into nuclear weapons capability.[2]

Studying Vanunu's photographs, nuclear experts in 1986 estimated that Israel might have as many as 100 to 200 nuclear weapons of varying capacities. This was more than ten times what experts had estimated prior to Vanunu's revelations. For smuggling a camera into the Dimona secret facility and taking more than sixty photographs, Vanunu was convicted of treason. In April 2004, Vanunu was finally released, after serving eighteen years in prison, including eleven years in solitary confinement. Estimates in 1997 placed the number of Israeli nuclear weapons at some 400 thermonuclear and nuclear weapons.[3]

Before her death in 1978, Prime Minister Golda Meir told friends that suicidal thoughts had plagued her during the Yom Kippur War. Yom Kippur is the Day of Atonement for the Jewish people. It is the year's holiest day. Prime Minister Meir referred to the surprise attack by Egypt and Syria. The initial forays by Israel's two enemies were disastrous. Moshe Dayan, the Minister of Defense, is said to have called for nuclear bombs to be put aboard fighter planes and nuclear warheads placed on Israel's Jericho missiles. He wanted to be ready should the attacking Arab states reach the point-of-no-return in endangering the State of Israel.

Dayan was gravely fearful that the attack would result in the destruction of what he referred to as the "third Commonwealth." The first had been destroyed by the Babylonians and the second by the Romans.

US Secretary of State Henry Kissinger prevailed on President Richard Nixon to assist the Israelis by providing weapons and ammunition in the most massive airlift since the Berlin Airlift following World War II.

Israel's nuclear weapons have always been considered the core of what has commonly been known as the *Samson Option*. The strategy is named after the biblical story of Samson using his great strength to bring down a temple, killing a great number of enemy Philistines, as well as himself, in the process. Israel has sworn "never again" in relation to the possibility of another Holocaust. Given this determination, the *Samson Option* postulates that Israel would be willing to use extreme measures if the country's survival were at stake.

In the crisis with Iran, the *Samson Option* has been used to mean that Israel would attack Iran in a preemptive war and would be willing to use nuclear weapons. Iran's possession of nuclear weapons is seen as a threat to Israel's continued existence. In other words, Israel would be willing to attack Iran even if the result of an Israeli preemptive strike ended up being retaliation by Iran that ended up with Israel's destruction. The Israelis judge that destruction in a military conflict with an aggressor like Iran would still be better than doing nothing and waiting to be destroyed. Passivity in the face of aggression has always been judged to be a mistake the European Jews made against Hitler. In extreme situations, Israel can be expected to attack, rather than to delay too long. This is why Israel's patience for negotiations with the mullahs can be expected to run out. Israel knows the mullahs are trying to buy time and that time in this crisis works against Israel.

Analysts argue that Israel's current nuclear arsenal opens up many strategic possibilities short of the *Samson Option*.

Israel has the type of relatively low-yield tactical nuclear weapons that can be selectively fired to eliminate specific targets. Low-yield "tactical nukes" could be used to hit the type of hardened underground centrifuge farm which Iran has built at Natanz to enrich uranium.

Israel's larger nuclear warheads have been adapted for the Jericho series of missiles. Israel first began developing these missiles with French assistance in the 1960s. The Jericho II is a solid fuel, two-stage missile that Israel has test fired into the Mediterranean Sea at ranges estimated at around 1,300 kilometers (800 miles). Reportedly, Israel has had a multi-stage Jericho III under development, more truly an intercontinental ballistic missile with a range of around 4,800 kilometers (3,000 miles).

Israel also has cruise missiles which can be adapted with nuclear warheads, such as the Popeye Turbo which is designed to be air-launched from Israel's F-15 and F-16 fighter jets.[4] The Popeye Turbo can also be launched from the three Dolphin-class submarines the Germans built for Israel.[5]

While details of the Israeli nuclear arsenal remain highly classified, analysts believe Israel can launch relatively low-yield tactical nuclear weapons from the air and sea via Israel's fighter aircraft and submarines. Conceivably, Israel could mix tactical nuclear weapons delivered via fighter aircraft with cruise missiles fired from sea. Higher-yield nuclear warheads deliverable by Israel's Jericho II missiles would most likely be held in reserve, waiting to see what retaliatory responses Iran launched and how the war escalated from the initial attack.

HOW MIGHT ISRAEL ATTACK IRAN?

The Iranian nuclear facilities were constructed in the anticipation that at some point Israel or the United States might launch a preemptive strike.

As covered in chapter 2, the mullahs learned from the Israeli attack in 1981 on Iraq's nuclear reactor at Osirak. Iraq's Osirak facilities had been geographically compact, hence relatively easy to hit with a targeted military strike. In contrast, Iran's nuclear facilities are geographically dispersed, with several important research facilities embedded in population areas.

Still, Israel could target five or six major facilities, such as the uranium processing plant at Isfahan, the uranium enrichment plant at Natanz, the heavy water facility at Arak, and the Russian-built reactor at Bushehr.

Yet military experience as far back as the massive allied strategic bombing campaign against the Nazis in World War II demonstrates how quickly bombed machinery can be recovered, with operations almost restored. At best, an Israeli attack would slow down the progress of the Iranian nuclear weapons program. At worst, adverse world reaction against Israel might backfire.

In the face of an Israeli attack, Iran might easily win world agreement that now Iran had a clear case justifying the pursuit of nuclear weapons for self-defense. European countries now trying to contain Iran's nuclear efforts might reverse their position. Besides, the Europeans would inevitably see opportunities to seize lucrative Iranian nuclear technology contracts. Iran might rebuild relatively quickly with better or newer models whatever nuclear facilities an Israeli preemptive military strike managed to destroy.

Important lessons can be derived from Israel's 1982 war with Syria at the onset of Israel's invasion into Lebanon.

From the 6th through the 11th of June 1982, Israel's Air Force "scored one of the most impressive military achievements in the history of modern warfare" against Syria.[6] Within a matter of hours, the Israeli Air Force destroyed Syria's Soviet-built surface-to-air missile defense system in the Bakaa Valley. Then Israel downed twenty-five Syrian fighter planes, most of them Russian-supplied MIG-23s, again attesting to Russia's support for Middle Eastern client-states.

Over the next few days, Israel virtually wiped out the Syrian

Air Force by shooting down what amounted to approximately eighty more Syrian fighter planes in dogfights. Remarkably, Israel did not suffer the loss of a single fighter plane in the course of the entire war. With this stunning air war victory, Israel effectively controlled the skies.

Neither Syria nor Lebanon wanted to confront Israel in a conventional ground war. Instead, with the assistance of Iran, a guerilla war broke out. Various Lebanese Shi'ite militias joined forces with the Lebanese Islamic Jihad, the Palestine Liberation Army, and Hezbollah. Together, they attacked Israeli forces and bombed the US Marine barracks in Beirut.

Finally, President Reagan ordered the withdrawal of US forces from Lebanon in response to the bombing of the Marine barracks in Beirut on 23 October 1983. Later, in 2000, the Israeli Defense Force also left Lebanon, unable to contain what amounted to a radical Islamic insurrection. In the end, all that was left was a small Israeli security zone created along the border in southern Lebanon.

What began as a great air victory for Israel ended up being a great victory for radical Islam. Terrorism tactics, including the type of signature suicide bombings developed by Hezbollah with the assistance of Iran, were highly effective.

Throughout the Muslim world, the war in Lebanon was ultimately seen as a major defeat for the United States and Israel. The defeat encouraged radical Islamic terrorists to continue a war against Israel. Iran provided additional funding for the Islamic radicals fighting in Lebanon. The alliance between Iran and Syria grew closer.

When Israel finally pulled out of Lebanon, Syrian troops and intelligence agents moved in. As a result, Lebanon became a client-state of Syria. Instead of removing the risk of rocket attacks on Israel from Lebanon, the risk has increased. In 2006, some 15,000 rockets, largely Iranian-supplied, were available to Hezbollah and positioned for launch against Israel.

Israel needs to consider the Lebanon War carefully before attacking Iran. Even should Israel succeed in scoring major damage on Iran's nuclear facilities by launching a surprise, preemptive air attack, Israel might ultimately lose. This was the experience of the 1982 Lebanon War, an experience Israel would not want to repeat.

In retaliation for a military strike on Iran, Hezbollah would undoubtedly launch rocket attacks on Israel from Lebanon. Hamas would probably launch rocket attacks from the Gaza. We might even see a resumption of the suicide bombings that marked recent Palestinian *intifadas* under Arafat.

US troops in the region could also expect retaliation, even if Israel struck alone. Militant groups within Iraq would be doubly motivated, attacking now to revenge the Israeli assault on Iran.

Even nationalistic groups such as the Mahdi Army of Moqtada al-Sadr would most likely support their Shi'ite brethren in Iran by launching renewed attacks in Iraq. An Israeli attack on Iran can be counted on to energize every radical Islamic terrorist organization in the region to renewed attacks, including al-Qaeda groups affiliated with the late Abu Musab al-Zarqawi.

As the Iraq war grinds onward, the American public grows increasingly restless with the inability to control terrorist attacks in Iraq. An Israeli attack on Iran would flame the fires of terrorism and worsen the situation in Iraq, causing the Bush administration a severe public opinion setback. This would make it more difficult for President Bush to hold positive American public opinion for the war long enough to establish in Iraq a democracy with a reasonable chance of succeeding.

Even if the United States did not directly participate in an

Israeli air strike on Iran, we would have to allow Israeli jets airspace rights over Iraq. This would be enough to argue that America was "complicit" in an Israeli air attack on Iran. Moreover, the fighter planes Israel would use would be F-15s and F-16s sold to Israel by the United States. Again, this would be seen as an argument that America was involved.

The US might also have to refuel Israeli jets involved in an air strike on Iran. The newest fighters in Israel's attack force are the Lockheed-Martin manufactured F-16I Soufa ("Storm") fighters. The second mainstay of the Israeli Air Force is the 1990s Boeing-built (originally McDonnell Douglas) F-15I Ra'am ("Eagle") fighter planes. Both aircraft have a strike radius that should extend to targets in Iran without having to be refueled. But the distances involved would not leave much room for error.[7]

Iran's military is no match for the United States or for Israel, not in any type of a conventional war. The Iranian military is still recovering from the 1980-1988 war with Iraq.[8] The ease with which the US military defeated Saddam Hussein is a good indication of Iran's conventional military strength. Iran was not able to beat Iraq in a conventional war in the 1980s. Today, the US military could easily defeat Iran's military in the field, though a land invasion would be costly to the US and extremely unpopular.

The Iranians would most likely retaliate with missile attacks which could be quite harmful both to the United States and Israel. Shahab-3 missiles, even conventionally armed, could cause considerable casualties on US military bases in Iraq and throughout the Gulf Region. All of Israel's cities, as well as Israel's nuclear facilities at Dimona in the Negev Desert, are within range of Iran's Shahab-3.

Joint military exercises were held in March 2005 between the Israeli Defense Force and the US Army stationed in Europe. Code-named "Operation Juniper Cobra," these exercises demonstrated

157

that a Shahab-3 missile could be intercepted by the combination of the Israeli Arrow anti-missile defense system working together with the US Patriot anti-missile system and backed up by the US Navy's Aegis anti-missile system. But while these anti-missile defenses might be effective in stopping one Shahab-3 attack, the defense system would have trouble taking down multiple missiles.

Should Iran fire a barrage attack of multiple Shahab-3 missiles at the same target, one or more missiles would most likely get through to hit the target. Russia, as we have noted, has already agreed to supply Iran with $1 billion worth of new TOR-M1 anti-missile SAM defense systems. Once these are in place, an Israeli attack on Iran's nuclear facilities would be much harder. Moreover, after an Israeli strike on Iran, Russia could decide to enter the conflict on the side of Iran. As Israel's ally, this would pit the United States and Russia head-to-head for the first time since the end of the Cold War.

Iran could also retaliate against the United States by attacking oil tankers in the Gulf. Iran maintains a key geographical position on the northern coast of the Straits of Hormuz, positioning Iran to easily attack oil shipments passing through the Gulf.

The US Energy Information Agency (EIA) clearly explains the strategic importance of the Straits of Hormuz flow of oil in the Gulf:

> In 2003, the vast majority (about 90 percent) of oil exported from the Persian Gulf transited by tanker through the Straits of Hormuz, located between Oman and Iran. The Straits consist of 2-mile-wide channels for inbound and outbound tanker traffic, as well as a two-mile-wide buffer zone. Oil flows through the Straits of Hormuz account for roughly two-fifths of all world traded oil, and closure of the Straits of Hormuz would require use of longer alternative routes (if available) at increased transportation costs.[9]

In May 2004, Mohsen Rezai, the secretary of the Iranian Expediency Council, directly threatened that if the US attacked Iran, then Iran would retaliate against Middle East oil exports. "An attack on Iran," Rezai said, "would be tantamount to endangering Saudi Arabia, Kuwait, and 'in a word' the entire Middle East oil."[10]

Iran could cripple oil flow worldwide by attacking shipping in the Straits of Hormuz. This would be a perfect example of "asymmetric warfare," wherein disproportionate damage is inflicted by a weaker enemy using minimal force at a strategic point of attack.

Iran currently operates four anti-ship missile systems acquired from China. One of these, the CS-801K, is an air-launched missile that Iran has test fired from its airforce F-4E fighters.[11]

Iran reportedly has also purchased eight Russian-built "Sunburn" anti-ship missiles (SS-N-22) from the Ukraine and has deployed them for use around the Straits of Hormuz. The Sunburn missile represents a significant increase in the threat level, in that it accelerates to a speed of Mach 2.2 (1,520 mph, over twice the speed of sound) in 30 seconds. The Sunburn missile has a sophisticated guidance system and can carry a 200 kiloton nuclear warhead or a 750-pound conventional warhead.[12]

For the purposes of a tanker war, a Sunburn missile with a conventional warhead traveling at Mach 2.2 would completely destroy any tanker the missile hit. The tankers are slow-moving targets with no defenses against missiles. Truthfully, there is enough kinetic energy in a cruise missile traveling at Mach 2 to destroy a tanker, even without an explosive warhead.

IS ISRAEL LIKELY TO ATTACK?

The key insight in evaluating *Samson Option* thinking is that Israel remains a one-bomb state. As Iran advances to develop an atomic bomb covertly, Israel may have no recourse but to attack. The point of the *Samson Option* is that Israel must be willing to use desperate tactics if there is no other way to stop an enemy set on the destruction of the Jewish state.

Israel could destroy Iran's most important nuclear facilities by launching a massive air strike designed to last a few days at most. If Iran retaliated in a massive way, Israel could expand the attack on Iran with tactical nuclear weapons, suggesting Israel's willingness to escalate the conflict if necessary.

A ground invasion of Iran by Israel is out of the question. Such a scenario would mobilize the entire Islamic world. It would produce a tactical dilemma for Israel even to get into the country. No Arab country would cooperate in any way and would, in fact, do everything in its power to obstruct an attempted invasion by Israeli forces. If Israel did decide to launch a preemptive air strike on Iran, the *Samson Option* would be exercised, and Israel would be on nuclear alert. Iran would most certainly retaliate with missiles from Lebanon and terrorist attacks on Jews worldwide. The most chilling scenario of all is the fear that Iran may possess one of the Soviet's suitcase nuclear bombs and would attempt to smuggle one into Tel Aviv.

While speaking with my long-time friend, Israeli Prime Minister Ehud Olmert, he offered this summation of Israel's position regarding a first-strike against Iran:

As the one who has to make the decision, I can tell you that I genuinely don't think Israel should be on the forefront of this war. I don't know why people think this is first and foremost a war for Israel. It's a problem for every civilized country. Iran is a major threat to the well-being of Europe and America just as much as it is for the state of Israel. I don't think America can tolerate the idea of a leader of a nation of 30 million people who can openly speak of the liquidation of another country. And therefore it is incumbent upon America and Europeans to form a strategy and implement it to remove this danger of unconventional weapons in Iran. To assume that Israel would be the first to go into a military confrontation with Iran represents a misunderstanding of this issue.

Over and over again, my Israeli friends stressed that Iran was not an Israeli problem. "Iran is a world problem," I was told again and again. "This is a clash of civilizations," was a constant theme of my discussions, regardless of whom I spoke with in Israel. "You in America are the 'Great Satan' to the radical zealots in Iran," I was reminded, over and over again. "We in Israel are only the 'Little Satan.'"

So what's the "Great Satan" to do?

IF AMERICA ATTACKS

As the debate before the Security Council proceeds, the United States could take some preparatory steps to move military resources into the region, in case a preemptive strike against Iran became necessary. Moving more military forces to the region would signal to Iran the seriousness of the United States to stand by President Bush's repeated statement that Iran would not be permitted to have nuclear weapons.

At the same time, Bush administration officials, including the president himself, would be expected to repeat that no military strike was planned, right up until the last moment. Until that point, the administration's goal would be to use every diplomatic measure possible to make clear that the goal is to get Iran to become compliant with IAEA inspection requirements.

Currently, regime change is not the policy of the administration toward Iran. Should the Security Council discussions begin to drift without imposing additional sanctions on Iran, the United States State Department could announce that US foreign policy toward Iran has been changed, such that regime change is now our goal. This would be a strong message to dissidents inside Iran as well as to the expatriate Iranian freedom-fighting community worldwide.

The State Department could back up the announcement by making financial resources available under current legislation to support non-governmental organizations in the United States with the capabilities of supporting dissidents in Iran. In Congress, involved senators including Brownback and Santorum, both Republicans, could advance new legislation, even more strongly worded than their previous attempts, with the aim of providing even more funding for the State Department to disperse to responsible organizations capable of effecting regime change in Iran.

All these efforts could be put in place short of going to war. As Iran saw that the US government was moving toward regime change, the additional pressure would warn Iran not to continue in a defiant path. Should President Bush decide that taking military action against Iran would require additional authorizing legislation, a new resolution could be prepared and submitted by the administration to Congress. Such preparations already seem underway.

In January 2006, the *Washington Times* reported that an entire F-16 wing, estimated at over 70 aircraft in total, of the Air National Guard's 122nd Fighter Wing based in Fort Wayne, Indiana, left for an undisclosed base in southwest Asia.[13] The report also indicated that a squadron of twelve F-16s and support personnel from the 4th Fighter Squadron of the 388th Fighter Wing based at Hill Air Force Base in Utah left for deployment in Iraq. The clear implication was that the United States military was positioning for a possible air strike against Iran's nuclear facilities.

What additional resources could the US Navy make available for a military strike on Iran? Here are the types of military preparedness steps we and other observers will be carefully watching to detect any moves the US makes toward going to war against Iran:

Aircraft Carriers in the Region
- In June 2006, the Nimitz-class aircraft carrier USS *Ronald Reagan* was in the Pacific Ocean in her maiden deployment in support of the global war on terrorism and maritime security operations. Carrier Air Wing One Four (CVW-14) was assigned to the USS *Ronald Reagan.*

- The Nimitz-class aircraft carrier USS *Abraham Lincoln* was deployed in the Pacific on a scheduled deployment.

- The USS *Kitty Hawk* was already on war-time readiness status in the Pacific.

- On 18 June 2006, in the Philippine Sea, the USS *Ronald Reagan*, the USS *Abraham Lincoln*, and the USS *Kitty Hawk*, sailed as part of a fifteen-ship formation. Navy and Marine Corps aircrafts participated in exercise Valiant Shield demonstrating integrated US military tactics.

- If the United States were to move two of these three carrier task forces into the Persian Gulf region, a clear signal would be given to Tehran of sufficient US firepower in the region available to launch a major sea-based air strike.

Submarine Mobilization
- In June 2006, the USS *Ohio* was in Bangor, Washington, preparing to return to service. The USS *Ohio* is the first ballistic missile submarine to undergo complete conversion to a new class of guided missile submarines. With guided missile capability, this new class of submarine is

being reconfigured to support Special Forces capabilities on the ground. Three other submarines are undergoing the same conversion process, including the USS *Michigan*, the USS *Florida*, and the USS *Georgia*. The US Navy could deploy the USS *Ohio* to the Persian Gulf region to support any Special Forces operations that might be involved in a strike on Iran.

Cruise Missiles

- Additionally, the US Navy could announce any task force assignments that would deploy additional Tomahawk cruise missile resources in the Persian Gulf. Knowing that the US Navy was deploying additional military resources to the region would clearly signal an attack on Iran; US military forces deployed in Iraq are currently scheduled for force-reduction, a trend which should continue as more Iraqi forces come on line prepared to take over the defense of their country.

Ground Forces

- There are several US military bases that observers will watch closely for activity that might signal an attack on Iran.[14] Fort Rucker, Alabama, is where the Army has consolidated air support operations, including the Apache attack helicopter, the Blackhawk, and the Kiowa that are used in reconnaissance as well as target acquisition/designation missions.

- The 16th Special Operations Wing (SOW) is stationed at Hulburt Field in Florida. The 16th SOW is the largest Air Force unit assigned to US Special Operations Command. The 16th SOW is uniquely equipped to undertake missions in enemy-controlled area or with politically sensitive objectives, such as Iran's nuclear facilities. Rather than launch a full-scale invasion of Iran, the 16th SOW could hit designated targets. The 16th SOW's motto is "Any Time, Any Place." The unit was responsible for the capture of Manuel Noriega in Panama and Operation Uphold Democracy in Haiti.

- A third key base is Twenty-Nine Palms, the Marine Corps Air Ground Combat Center near Palm Springs, California. Twenty-Nine Palms is located in a mountainous desert area that would be ideal for training in a physical terrain that resembles the sites of several key nuclear installations in Iran. Units from these three bases would be ideal to support a limited military incursion that could accompany a US air strike on Iran.

We should also expect that CIA Director Michael Hayden, appointed in May 2006, and Secretary of State Condoleezza Rice might make trips to confer with NATO allies prior to any US preemptive strike on Iran. The point is that prior to actually launching an attack, the ramp-up to an attack could be used as an additional, final opportunity to increase pressure on the regime in Iran to come within IAEA inspection requirements.

Our assumption in the remainder of the chapter is that the UN discussions will fail as clearly as the EU3 negotiations seem to have reached a dead end with Iran. The Bush administration has stated multiple times that Iran will not be permitted to have nuclear weapons. If the UN Security Council is totally ineffective, the case will shift to military preparedness.

We can expect a reasonably short period will precede the attack, to issue a final ultimatum to Iran and to prepare the American public for yet another preemptive war in the Middle East, just as the Bush administration did when preparing to attack Iraq. Even in this final stage, when the US military is positioning for attack, Iran still will have a last opportunity to see the serious-ness of the situation and recant.

The probability of Iran reversing course after Security Council action fails is small. If anything, Iran may become even more defi-ant. Ahmadinejad could be expected to argue that now Iran has no choice but to develop nuclear weapons as fast as possible, since the United States has taken military steps to prepare for an attack.

As we have repeatedly noted, ruling Iranians believe war and destruction are a necessary precondition for the second coming of the Mahdi. Moreover, the hard-liners in the Iranian regime believe that the United States will over extend by attacking Iran, believing that Iran is destined to defeat the United States in a Middle East war. The zealots ruling Iran may see a war with the United States as the beginning of the fulfillment of Ayatollah Khomeini's prediction that Israel and the United States will fall, just as he had predicted the Shah, the Soviet Union, and Saddam Hussein would fall.

A BATTLE PLAN

The US attack on Iraq involved a military invasion with the inten-tion to move on Baghdad and depose the regime of Saddam Hussein. We are going to assume here, at least initially, that the US strike on Iran would be more limited, consisting primarily of an air attack combined with Special Forces Operations on the ground. A move to a full-scale invasion could only follow an official US re-determination that regime change has become official US foreign policy with regard to Iran.

The goal in a more limited military attack would be to knock out Iran's major nuclear facilities, causing a major setback in Iran's ability to make nuclear weapons.

President Bush's decision to attack Iran would involve applying the "Bush Doctrine," such that the preemptive attack would be launched to protect US national security interests. The concern would be that Iran's ability to produce a nuclear weapon would constitute a threat that Iran might supply an Improvised Nuclear Device (IND) to a terrorist group that would try to smuggle the device into the United States—a very real threat given the porous state of our borders. The Bush administration most probably would also argue a US national security interest in protecting our ally Israel against a preemptive nuclear attack from Iran.

If the US decided to lead the attack, Israel could easily play a supportive role. But that would not change the overall tactics of the attack. Israel could be assigned certain military objectives as part of a coalition effort. Still, even with a limited coalition in place, the attack would be led by the United States, possibly even with Israel sitting on the sidelines.

The following Iranian nuclear facilities are likely primary targets:

- Arak, Iran's heavy water plant, about 154 miles southwest of Tehran
- Bushehr, Iran's nuclear reactor, located along the Persian Gulf, approximately 250 miles south of Tehran
- Isfahan, Iran's nuclear processing plant
- Natanz, Iran's nuclear enrichment plant
- Saghand, Iran's uranium mine[15]

About a dozen smaller facilities devoted to Iran's nuclear efforts would also be targeted, some of which are isolated within cities and will require precision bombs. While several hundred facilities may play some role contributing to Iran's nuclear technologies, the goal would be to target the major facilities which would need to be destroyed to stop Iran's progress toward enriching uranium and pursuing nuclear weapons technology.

Iran's missile facilities have also been systematically catalogued and studied by US military intelligence. Fairly comprehensive surveys are publicly available on the Internet. The National Threat Initiative, for instance, lists twenty-nine Iranian missile production facilities by name, location, and function.[16]

Iran's military air bases, including army, navy, and airforce, are also well known to US intelligence services; again, Internet resources make available many detailed descriptions of Iran's military forces and their base locations.[17] Iran's Shahab missiles are launched from mobile carriers; a satellite intelligence effort will have to be made in the days immediately prior to an attack to see if their current locations can be identified.

Secondary targets would include government buildings, including military buildings; Iran's media and telecommunications infrastructure, including radio and television stations; telephone switching facilities; government buildings; conventional power plants; bridges and highways; rail lines; and port facilities.

Hardened facilities, such as the underground centrifuge plants at Natanz, might be attacked with tactical nuclear weapons, either on ship-launched Tomahawk cruise missiles, or launched via air strike. Otherwise, the munitions utilized would be conventional, largely precision-guided bombs, such as were used in the 2003 attack on Iraq. Most likely, tactical nuclear weapons would not be used, so as to keep the weapons threshold conventional only.

The argument for using tactical weapons is that they are perfectly suited for piercing deep underground bunkers; the argument against them is that upon impact they shower radioactive dirt and debris around the blast zones, many of which would be located near civilians thanks to Iran's decentralized program.

When analyzing a more limited attack, we can still gain important insight from studying how the US successfully began the war on Iraq in 2003. As with Iraq, the war would start with a focused one-to-three day "shock and awe" attack that would see multiple waves of air strikes and cruise missile attacks. In a noted book about John Boyd, the fighter pilot whose ideas on air combat fundamentally changed the tactics of air warfare, author Robert Coram notes that air combat is a blood sport:

> Many civilians and those who have never looked through the gun sight—then called a pipper—at an enemy aircraft have a romantic perception, no doubt influenced by books and movies about World War I, that pilots are knights of the air, chivalrous men who salute their opponents before engaging in a fight that always is fair. They believe that elaborate rules of aerial courtesy prevail and that battle in the clear pure upper regions somehow is different, more glorified and rarefied, than battle in the mud. This is arrant nonsense. Aerial combat, according to those who have participated, is a basic and primitive form of battle that happens to take place in the air. Fighter pilots—that is, the ones who survive air combat—are not gentlemen; they are backstabbing assassins. They come out of the sun and attack an enemy when he is blind. They sneak up behind or underneath or "bounce" the enemy from above or flop into position on his tail—his six-o'clock position—and "tap" him before he knows they are there.[18]

Coram comments that effective aerial combat is a "knife in the dark." The same principle that makes one-on-one dog-fighting effective applies to massive air attacks. The goal is to apply massive air power to destroy key targets as rapidly as possible; catching the enemy unprepared, even surprised, is most effective in what amounts to a modern application of Nazi Germany's World War II *blitzkrieg* tactic.

When the "shock and awe" was launched against Iraq on 21 March 2003, the strategy was to end the war quickly by decapitating the government, including the destruction of key government and military illustrations, even though many were embedded in Baghdad, a city with a population of 5.5 million people.

The attack involved submarine- and ship-launched Tomahawk cruise missiles, B-2 stealth bombers, and F-117 stealth fighters, using precision-guided bombs and bunker-busters.[19] The Pentagon aimed to send 1,500 bombs and missiles over Iraq in the first twenty-four hours.[20] The same type of massive airpower could be launched against Iran, with a focus on Iran's nuclear facilities and military bases.

If the goal was not regime-change, the attacks on the government infrastructure could be aimed at reducing its ability to communicate internally or organize an effective counter-attack. The air attack could occur over the span of a few days, with no plan to launch a ground invasion, unless Iranian counterattack measures required an expanded war effort. While the air attack most likely would not eliminate Iran's ability to produce nuclear weapons permanently, the program could be significantly set back, perhaps to a point where recovery would be extremely costly, requiring several years to reach a pre-attack status.

Helicopter-delivered Special Operations attacks on the ground could supplement the air attacks by going after installations embedded in population areas or hardened targets that might be better destroyed by troops on the ground. The Special Operations attacks would most likely be defined as hit-and-destroy missions where there was no anticipation of a sustained campaign.

The overall design of a "shock and awe" offensive would be to inflict a hard blow over a limited time, with no expectation of launching a sustained invasion aimed at regime change. Our goal would be to destroy as much of Iran's nuclear technology as possible so that we could set back any nuclear weapons program and gain more time to deal with the government in Tehran.

IRAN RETALIATES

On 26 January 2006, Davoud Danesh-Jafari, Iran's economy minister, said that the country's role as the world's fourth-largest producer of oil gave Iran a position of power in the world oil economy. "Any possible sanctions from the west," he warned, "could possibly, by disturbing Iran's political and economic situation, raise oil prices beyond levels the west expects."[21]

This thinly-veiled threat at oil retaliation was intended to put the United States, the EU3, and the IAEA on notice. If this is Iran's response to possible Security Council review, how much more severe would the regime's response be to a military strike aimed at Iran's nuclear facilities?

Inflicting major damage on Iran's nuclear facilities could be accomplished by the US military launching a "shock and awe" air attack. Unless Iran's military capabilities were destroyed in the first few hours, however, a military and political counterattack could be costly.

Many, if not the majority of the mobile Shahab missile launchers may survive air strikes and be ready to hit selected targets, including the many US military bases we have in surrounding nations, including those in Iraq, Kuwait, Qatar, Azerbaijan, and Oman. Thousands of US military personnel could be killed in a missile attack which Iran could organize in the days and weeks after a US air attack.

Additionally, Hezbollah terrorists in Lebanon as well as Hamas and the Islamic Jihad in Gaza would most likely launch retaliatory missile strikes on Israel. Iran as well could launch conventionally-armed Shahab missiles against Israel's major cities, with the likelihood of inflicting thousands of human casualties and causing substantial infrastructure damage.

If any Iranian military fighter planes survived, a missile war could be supplemented by Iranian fighter sorties against US bases in the area and against Israel. A missile war, even a conventional missile war, would cost thousands of lives on all sides and would draw both Iraq and Israel into the conflict, even if the United States tried to position the war as a US preemptive strike.

I described the scenario in the fictional prologue with Iranian martyrs attacking the United States. Reuters reported on 16 April 2006 that some 200 Iranians had volunteered to carry out martyrdom missions against the US and British interests if Iran were attacked over its nuclear program. They signed a document called "registration form for martyrdom-seeking operations" and pledged to defend the Islamic republic's interests. Reuters went on to describe that the Committee for the Commemoration of Martyrs of the Global Islamic Campaign was formed in 2004. "Since then, some 52,000 people have signed up to be involved in possible attacks. The *Sunday Times* in London, quoting unnamed Iranian officials, reported that Iran had 40,000 trained suicide bombers prepared to strike western targets if Iran is attacked."[22]

Wherever terrorist sleeper cells had operational capabilities, a US military attack against Iran would provide an occasion for renewed attacks. Even if the attacks were only limited to the type of rail transportation and subway bombs we saw in Spain and London, terrorists could cause havoc by launching attacks in several Western countries simultaneously.

The United States would be blamed by those in the West predisposed to have sympathy with Iran's contention that the regime's only goals with their nuclear program were peaceful. As the world's only remaining superpower, the United States is cast in the role of being an international aggressor.

Even if we characterize our war against Iran as a war of self-defense for ourselves and Israel, worldwide public opinion will most likely be against the United States. A preemptive attack on Iran, especially following our war against the Taliban in Afghanistan and our preemptive attack against Saddam Hussein, would bear heavy political consequences for the United States, not only in the Islamic world, but also among many traditional allies as well. In the extreme, an attack against Iran could backfire, causing an anti-America rise of Islamic unity across the globe—starting in Iran and cascading outward.

In reaction to a US attack, we might stir up Iranian nationalism, even among the nation's dissidents. Following a US military attack, internal support for the Iranian regime might actually intensify. Iranians could oppose what would be portrayed as US aggression against Iran, with the regime certainly arguing that the attack was completely unjustified.

The Shi'ite minority in Iraq cannot ordinarily be considered supporters of the Shi'ites in Iran. During the Iran-Iraq war, Iraqi Shi'ites fought bitterly against Iranian Shi'ites. Even after the fall of Saddam Hussein, the Shi'ites in Iraq maintained their primary allegiance to Iraq, working to maintain their position in the newly formed Iraqi democracy, not allying with their religious brethren in Iran. Still, a US preemptive attack on Iran might be the trigger to move Iraq's Shi'ites closer to Shi'ite Iran.

If America were seen as opposing Islam, not simply going after Iran's nuclear facilities, a region-wide Islamic uprising might unify in support of Iran, regardless of whether the Muslims involved were Shi'ite or Sunni. Right now many of Iran's Muslim neighbors, including Turkey, are concerned about their own national security as Iran pursues nuclear technology aggressively. Even Saudi Arabia has taken a position opposing Iran's defiant pursuit of nuclear technology.

Following a US preemptive strike against Iran, many Islamic nations, including even Sunni Saudi Arabia, might reverse their policy, to express sympathy with Iran, if not outright support. By launching a preemptive attack against Iran, the US could well intensify anti-American sentiment throughout the Islamic world.

The aftermath of a preemptive military strike against Iran would be risky for the United States, even if the attack achieved the objective of knocking out Iran's nuclear capabilities, at least for the moment. As we learned from the 1982 military strike by Israel against Syria's airforce at the beginning of the Lebanon war, initial military success, even spectacular initial military success, is not always predictive of ultimate victory.

Any extended action could be disastrous, given the potential to stir up Islamic anti-American terrorism and insurgencies in the aftermath.

The United States has learned in Afghanistan and Iraq that a rapid military victory may only be the first chapter in managing a successful peace. In Iraq, continued terrorism has delayed the American military withdrawal and endangered the fragile movement toward democracy.

The final chapter on the Iraq 2003 war remains to be written, with the future of democracy in Iraq yet hanging in the balance. A

US preemptive strike against Iran could stir up terrorism and internal dissent in both Iraq and Afghanistan, further endangering the democratic process.

Ironically, attacking Iran may cost the US all the gains realized today in the hard-fought struggles to establish democratic governments in both Iraq and Afghanistan. Rather than stabilizing the Middle East, an attack on Iran might further destabilize the Middle East, such that Israel's ultimate survival is even more at risk than before the attack.

Should the Palestinians unite behind Hamas and Islamic Jihad in reaction to a US preemptive strike on Iran, we might well see intensified political pressure against Israel for further concessions. In the extreme, the US attack might occasion a new wave of terrorist attacks launched against Israel, with a new *intifada* declared.

THE REGIME CHANGE OPTION

Thinking through the scenarios of a limited "shock and awe" preemptive strike, the Bush administration may conclude that military action should aim at regime change in Iran, even if that option necessitates a land invasion. The following reasons argue for the regime-change solution:

- If Ayatollah Khamenei and President Ahmadinejad remain in power after a US preemptive military strike, the current regime structure can be expected to move toward declaring war on the United States. The military strike may have brought Iran's nuclear program to a halt, but that halt is only "for now." The radical regime under Ahmadinejad's direction will move to reconstitute its nuclear program immediately. Moreover, those countries who feel the US attack was unjustified may provide even more technical and financial support to Iran than before.

- A US military attack on Iran undoubtedly will cause world oil prices to spike, with the resulting increases reflected in US gasoline and heating oil costs. Conceivably, oil could increase to $100 a barrel, pushing US gasoline costs toward $4.00 a gallon or more. If the Iranian regime withstands a US military preemptive attack, we can expect retaliation to involve an oil war. At a minimum, Iran will urge OPEC to restrict supplies. The tanker war that ensued in the 1980s Iran-Iraq war may only be a small prelude to the chaos Iran could cause with oil transportation through the Persian Gulf region. Approximately 40 percent of the world's oil supply passes through the Straits of Hormuz, a narrow area Iran might seek to close down to all oil traffic, regardless of the nationality of ship transport.

- Former President George H. W. Bush decided to stop the Gulf War short of attacking Baghdad and removing Saddam Hussein from power. In retrospect, leaving Saddam Hussein in place only postponed the need to solve the problem. Hussein proved recalcitrant in the face of United Nations sanctions. Ultimately, the current Bush administration justified the need for the Iraq war of 2003 on the premise that Saddam Hussein needed to be deposed. President George W. Bush would not want to repeat the mistake his father made in Iraq. The decision to depose the current Iranian government would avoid leaving in place a regime who would declare the United States an enemy to be destroyed at all costs.

- Once rebuilt, Iran's nuclear program would be harder to control a second time. Withdrawing from the Nuclear

Non-Proliferation Treaty, Iran could immediately begin rebuilding its nuclear facilities, this time with the resolve to develop weapons. Having once defied the world community, Iran would not hesitate a second time to present the world with the choice of deposing the regime or facing the prospect of an atomic Iran armed with nuclear weapons. Having survived one attack, the Iranian regime would resolve to build a coalition of international allies into what could amount to a mutual security pact, where the allies would declare that any further attacks will be considered an attack on Iran's allies.

- Terrorist organizations would use the US preemptive attack as the justification for their open declaration to obtain nuclear weapons. Intensified terrorism in support of Iran would be aimed at further destabilizing the Middle East, Europe, and America. The goal would be to support Iran in the regime's determination to rebuild its nuclear program and obtain nuclear weapons as quickly as possible.

The Iranian regime would have to rebuild the physical facilities destroyed in the attack. The human talent, however, of Iran's nuclear scientists and engineers would remain in place, unless a large percentage of Iran's nuclear experts were killed at facilities which the attack damaged or destroyed.

The second construction of the facilities would be easier than the first. Conceivably, the second time, better facilities might be reconstructed faster, cheaper, better, and more secure from further attack. Ironically, Iran's nuclear infrastructure might emerge superior to what was destroyed. The result could produce superior nuclear facilities that were better built because they were built from scratch, rather than in an evolutionary fashion.

In rebuilding its nuclear infrastructure, Iran could go immediately to advanced-generation nuclear technologies. Many new, rebuilt nuclear structures could end up being superior to what had been in place prior to the attack. Ironically, in the longer run, we might have done Iran a favor to eliminate its old and experimental nuclear facilities so the regime could rebuild its nuclear program with new, state-of-the-art technologies. Within a short time, Iran's nuclear program could be back, fully functioning, possibly even more advanced than it had been before the attack.

The Bush administration clearly realizes that a preemptive strike aimed at taking out Iran's nuclear facilities involves attacking the symptoms, not solving the problem. If this realization can be communicated to the political left, especially to key Democratic party senators, and to the American people, an attack aimed at creating regime change in Iran offers a more realistic chance that the nuclear threat presented by Iran can be removed altogether, not just postponed.

Ironically, the political repercussions on the United States from a full-scale invasion of Iran might be less than we would realize from a more limited preemptive attack. With the Iranian regime left in place, the mullahs and their supporters would have a continuing podium from which to project their anti-American grievances.

Still, Iraq without Saddam Hussein has created a power vacuum which the United States has been struggling to stabilize. Similar problems would be realized in Iran if the regime of the mullahs was brought down.

Dissidents within Iran, as well as expatriate opponents of the regime worldwide, will have to come forward to reorganize what could hopefully emerge as a more democratic Iran. This would be consistent with the direction of change the United States is attempting to institute in Iraq and Afghanistan. Again, the United

States would need to demonstrate a desire to withdraw from Iran once a new Iranian government had been installed, exactly as we have announced for both Iraq and Afghanistan. This is the same model the United States followed at the end of World War II, where our goal was to establish democratic governments in Germany and Japan, as a pre-condition for the US withdrawing.

There is possibly one more major upside. The current regime in Iran is a central instigator of terrorism worldwide. As we have noted repeatedly, Hezbollah, Hamas, and the Islamic Jihad virtually owe their financial survival to the mullahs in Iran. Al-Qaeda operatives work actively with the Iranian government to further mutually-held aims.

By eliminating the Iranian regime of the mullahs, a central part of the War on Terrorism would be won. Without support from the mullahs in Tehran, Syria would have a much more difficult time dominating Lebanon. Without the constant encouragement from Tehran that Israel might one day be eliminated from the Middle East, the Palestinian Authority might have an easier time resolving a final agreement with Israel to implement a "two-state" solution, involving a compromise on the status of Jerusalem that would be acceptable to both the Israelis and the Palestinians.

The regime of the mullahs in Tehran has been a roadblock to Middle East peace since the 1979 revolution. As long as the regime in Tehran remains in power, we cannot expect terrorism to end. With the regime of the mullahs gone, however, substantial sums from Iran's abundant oil profits would no longer be available to fund terrorism. With interference from Tehran removed from the scene, the War on Terrorism might take important strides to a successful conclusion.

Tehran's funding and operatives stir up anti-American sentiments throughout the Islamic world. America has taken great strides since the 1980s, reconciling with a wide range of Middle Eastern countries, including Egypt, Jordan, and Lebanon, as well as Saudi Arabia. With the regime of the mullahs removed, gains America has made moving Iraq and Afghanistan toward democracy would become instantly more secure. Even Syria would have to re-evaluate its anti-American policies, as Libya did when Saddam Hussein fell.

Eliminating the regime of the mullahs would represent an important movement toward freedom and democracy in the Middle East, as well as the potential for a more complete reconciliation of Islamic peoples worldwide with America and the West.

Looked at from this perspective, the United States might well calculate that rather than launch a limited strike on Iran's nuclear facilities, we might suffer less by going after the regime itself. In other words, President Bush would make the decision not to postpone the ultimate problem of dealing with the radical regime in Tehran to a future president, as his father had calculated with Saddam Hussein in 1991.

NO EASY CHOICES

In some ways, the tactical complications of launching a land invasion against Iran are reduced because we have troops currently stationed around Iran, in the neighboring countries of Iraq, Afghanistan, and Azerbaijan. Again, the tactics of how the 2003 war against Iraq were launched would suggest how a comparable invasion of Iran would be stationed. The war most likely would be started by virtually the same "shock and awe" air strike described above. The first objectives would be to destroy key Iranian nuclear facilities, while simultaneously destroying Iran's military capabilities and decapitating the Iranian government.

The objectives of the "shock and awe" air strike would be expanded to include additional government targets, since our goal now would be to topple the government of the mullahs.

Iran would undoubtedly retaliate, as we described above, but the Iranian military forces would most likely be no more effective than Saddam Hussein's military had been in stopping the United States' military invasion. A war focused on Tehran would probably last no longer than a few weeks, following the same hard-charge strategy as the drive on Baghdad.

Solving the Iranian nuclear crisis involves no easy choices. All options have negative consequences. The choice then is to find the best among admittedly undesirable choices.

Winning a military invasion of Iran should be easier than winning the peace against Iran, and removing the oppressive regime of Iran might set in motion positive forces throughout the Middle East.

Russia and China, while opposed to any US invasion of Iran, would likely stand aside, deciding not to provide direct military assistance to the save the regime of the mullahs, just as they decided to stand by when the United States invaded Iraq to remove Saddam Hussein from power.

Skeptics within the United States as well as worldwide will argue that an invasion of Iran would overstretch the US military and prove too costly to undertake. Yet, with US military force levels being reduced currently in Iraq, redeployment to Iran is more achievable now, possibly even less costly than it would be should forces deployed from Iraq be fully repositioned at home.

Clearly, a military invasion of Iran will not be the option first considered by the Bush administration. At first, removing the regime in Iran will seem as too extensive an objective, one not fully demanded by the threat. Yet, after a serious attempt is made to deal with the Iranian regime on a more limited basis of engagement, the Bush administration may come to the regime-change invasion as the only option that truly makes sense. If our goal is to solve the problem, we might find ourselves frustrated by the Iranian regime's resistance to diplomatic pressure and its ability to absorb an attack on its nuclear facilities without permanently dislodging its nuclear weapons ambition.

It would be wise for the Bush administration not to start with the regime-change military option as first choice. All other options should be explored first. Still, after months of pursuing more limited objectives and tactical methodologies, the administration may face a fundamental choice: remove the regime of the mullahs once and for all, or accept the reality that sooner or later the mullahs will end up with nuclear weapons.

Ironically, in the final analysis, what might end up making the most sense is the same solution that we put off with Iraq for over ten years. After trying everything we could think of short of regime-changing invasion to rein in Saddam Hussein, we ended up invading simply because we could identify no other solution that had any real hope of long-term success. The same analysis applied to Iran could lead to the same conclusion. The only difference is that with Iran's determined push to develop nuclear weapons, we may not have a decade to explore alternatives.

The only easy choice in this situation belongs to Iran. If Iran's only intent with its nuclear program is peaceful, then all it has to do is to comply with the IAEA's request for verifiable inspections in conducting a "transparent" nuclear power program aimed 100 percent at civilian purposes.

Perhaps Iran would have to accept Russia's invitation to form a joint venture company under which uranium for Iran could be enriched on Russian soil. Again, if Iran's intentions are entirely peaceful, what is wrong with this compromise? Iranian nuclear scientists and engineers could fully master all the technical issues involved in pursuing the "full fuel cycle."

If Iran wanted to be sure that no one country could deny access to the enriched uranium needed to run a peaceful program, then the IAEA could create a multi-nation "uranium bank" from which Iran could draw the enriched uranium needed on the basis of an internationally guaranteed continuous supply.

The Iranian nuclear crisis can be solved fairly easily and quickly by mature and experienced international diplomats, provided that Iran's intentions are truly peaceful and that Iran will stop being defiant.

Truly, Iran should also stop attacking Israel with verbal threats and should stop financially supporting terrorist organizations such as Hezbollah.

The world community would probably step down from crisis mode, as long as Iran were willing to accept reasonably stated IAEA inspection requirements and nuclear program compromises. Regardless of what the political left would like to think, the truth is that the last option the Bush administration or Israel wants is to solve the Iranian nuclear crisis with a military attack of any kind. The military option, if used by the United States, reflects a failure of diplomacy, not a victory of the policy pursued by the international community to resolve the nuclear crisis with Iran.

As yet, diplomacy hasn't done much but buy Iran more time. As the showdown approaches, we might run out of options.

Epilogue

MORAL CLARITY
FOR THE DAYS AHEAD

"I say let Iran go up in smoke, provided Islam emerges triumphant in the rest of the world."

—Ayatollah Khomeini, 1981

On 8 May 2006, President George W. Bush received an eight-een-page letter from Iranian President Mahmoud Ahmadinejad. The missive lectured Bush on the virtues of Islam and rebuked him for not applying the teachings of Jesus Christ to his foreign policy. It was jarringly similar to another letter written in 1989 by an Iranian head of state, Ayatollah Ruhollah Khomeini, to another world leader, Mikhail Gorbachev. The marked difference between the two letters is that in Khomeini's letter, he lets Gorbachev know, "We can help you," whereas Ahmadinejad seems to signal to Bush, "Watch out!"

While the letter received much attention from the secular media, the majority of those who critiqued the message missed one of the most sobering sentences in the letter, the Islamic statement at the end: "*Vasalam Ala Man Ataba'al hod*," which translates as, "Peace only unto those who follow the true path." As an editorial in the *New York Sun* explains, "It is a phrase with historical significance in Islam, for, according to Islamic tradition, in year six of the Hejira—the late 620s—the prophet Mohammad sent letters to the Byzantine emperor and the Sassanid emperor telling them to convert to the true faith of Islam or be conquered." The *Sun* adds, "For Mohammad, the letters were a prelude to a Muslim offensive, a war launched for the purpose of imposing Islamic rule over infidels."[1]

Perhaps Ahmadinejad drew literary strength from Khomeini's letter to Gorbachev and emulated him as a model for proper international correspondence etiquette. Khomeini was a student of the Qur'an and quoted often from those pages in his letter to Gorbachev. Ahmadinejad is a bit less adept at spinning scripture, but both his letter and Khomeini's are replete with insolence and bravado.

Khomeini calls Gorbachev on the carpet for the lack of faith in God in his homeland: "The main problem confronting your country is not of private ownership, freedom and economy; your problem is the absence of true faith in God."

Ahmadinejad takes President Bush to task for what he sees as a failure to follow the Christian teaching: "I fail to understand how such actions correspond to the values outlined in the beginning of this letter, i.e., the teaching of Jesus Christ. . . ."

Khomeini offers help to Gorbachev in the form of Islam: "Let me call on you to study Islam earnestly . . . because Islam has exalted universal values which can bring comfort and salvation to all nations and remove the basic problems of mankind."

Ahmadinejad delivers a veiled warning: "Those with insight can already hear the sounds of the shattering and fall of the ideology and thoughts of the liberal democratic systems."

Given his belief in the Mahdi, we cannot but think that President Ahmadinejad has anything less in mind than the establishment of an Islamic caliphate that would encompass not just Iran but, indeed, the entire world, and that he will move to establish it by military force.

ALREADY AT WAR

Iran has already shown its hand in Israel. That is what the rocket attacks of July 2006 were all about. Iran attacked Israel through its proxy in Lebanon, Hezbollah. Direct evidence may be lacking, but as Daniel Byman, director of the Center for Peace and Security Studies at Georgetown University, says, "Past behavior suggests that Hezbollah wouldn't conduct an operation as significant as the July 12 kidnappings [which provoked the fighting that followed] without Tehran's approval."[2]

"Hezbollah is the long arm of Iran," Knesset Minister Isaac Herzog told me when I visited Israel during the strikes. "On the day of the abduction of the soldiers, the head of the National Security Council of Iran was in negations with G8 in Europe, but instead of flying back home, flew to Damascus, Syria." That he would end up in Damascus is unsurprising considering the close ties between Iran and Syria, which is also a key supporter of Hezbollah.[3]

The distance from which the Iranian proxies are firing missiles must be understood. From Afula, Israel, the distance is 29.4 miles; Carmiel is 10.1 miles; Haifa is 18.6 miles; Kiryat Shmona is 1.7 miles; Naharya is 3.8 miles; Rosh Pina is 8.6 miles; and Tiberius is 20.1 miles. Many rockets, such as the C-802, have a range of 75 miles. The Hezbollah arsenal contains more than 12,000 rockets in Lebanon. But Iran's menace is greater than its proxy. Iran has a rocket with a range of 2050 miles. Today, Iran's missiles can reach Israel and much of Europe. Within a few years, Iran's ICBMs will be able to strike anywhere on the globe.

While in Jerusalem, I interviewed Danny Yatom, former head of Mossad and chief of staff for Prime Minister Yitzhak Rabin. His outlook was grave: "The United States is vulnerable to terror attacks by Iran through proxies. They call the United States the 'Big Satan,' and Israel the 'Small Satan.' Their horrible dream is to destroy *all* of America and Israel. What drives them is their belief they must kill all the infidels, Jews and Christians, and build a new Islamic world. Once, God forbid, Iran acquires nuclear bombs, their proxies will destabilize the Middle East and the West."

Herzog echoed the same sentiment in starker terms. "Iran will have the bomb in the next few months. We should not fool ourselves; Iran with the bomb would be like giving Hitler an atomic bomb."

Indirectly, the strikes against Israel telegraphed Iran's larger ambitions. While in Israel, I also spoke with former Israeli Prime Minister Benjamin Netanyahu, and he saw the connection clearly: "Iran really supported the murder and kidnapping of two of our soldiers . . . to deflect international pressure from its nuclear program. . . . This is undoubtedly a skirmish in the larger war, and the larger war is not against Israel. In the case of the Nazis, they began with the Jews, but the aim was to conquer the world."

When I interviewed retired General Ya-akov Amidror, former Chief of IDF Intelligence, he pointed to two primary connections with Iran. "One, all the weapons systems came from Iran. Not all, 85 percent came from Iran and 15 percent from Syria; they are Syrian-made. Two, who is making the decisions? In the committee who is responsible for the decisions of Hezbollah, there are two formal Iranians, the Ambassador in Lebanon and the commander of the Republican Guard is also a member of the committee. And more than that, [Hezbollah leader Sayyed Hassan] Nasrallah is a formal messenger of the leader of Iran in Lebanon. He is not only the Secretary of Hezbollah; he has direct communication with the leader of Iran. He is the personal envoy."

Frank Gaffney, director of the Washington-based Center for Security Policy, has pointed out the need to take seriously Iran's proxy wars when contemplating the risk of an atomic Iran: "The United States can never win the War for the Free World as long as the most active state sponsor of terrorism is allowed to continue unchecked in its support of violence against freedom-loving nations. . . . We have for too long allowed Iran's nearly three-decade war against the United States to go unanswered. And, unless we deal with it effectively in the immediate future, we will be faced with a nuclear-armed terrorist regime that has shown no reluctance to attack American citizens and American interests throughout the world."[4]

Gaffney lists the following as evidence that Iran "began to wage war against America more than three decades ago and has drawn inspiration ever since from our retreat from Lebanon" in 1983:

- Iran created the revolt in Najaf, Iraq, that was fomented by the radical Shi'ite cleric Muqtada al-Sadr.

- Iran has supported the flow of money, weapons, and terrorists across the Iran-Iraq border and through Syria to attack US troops in Iraq and disrupt the democracy process.

- Iran intelligence has worked to destabilize the pro-Western government in Afghanistan and the regime of Gen. Perez Musharaf in Pakistan; Iran is the patron of Hezbollah, a terrorist proxy that seeks to deny freedom to the people of Lebanon and threatens American and Israeli interests and assets.

- Iran supports the despotic regime in Syria, as well as such Palestinian terrorist groups as Hamas, Islamic Jihad, and Fatah.

- Iran is dedicated to helping Hamas emerge as the dominant p.ower group in the Palestinian areas with the shared goal of destroying Israel; Iran has actively supported al-Qaeda's operations inside Iraq, working with the Jordanian-born terrorist Abu Musab al-Zarqawi.[5]

Iran fully intends to complete its quest for nuclear weapons, and may plan its attacks against American interests to preempt any attempts to destroy its nuclear reactors. This is another reason the

July attacks are so important. Beyond the desire to divert attention during the G8 meeting, the attack was a test to determine US tolerance for terror. If America backed down, you can bet Iran and its proxies would send waves of terrorists to the shores of America with explosives-laden backpacks, just as they have done in Israel. (The materials used in the Katyusha rockets are the same materials used in the suicide bomber's backpack, just in larger quantities.)

If we fail the test, and Hezbollah remains in Iran's terror network on the border of Israel, it will have proven to Iran that America has, indeed, developed a tolerance for terror. Iran will ultimately send proxies across America's borders. Bombers will be assigned to target Americans in malls, restaurants, public transportation, etc., all coordinated to devastate and extract major political concessions from the US. This would force America to back off and allow Iran to build its nuclear arsenal unchallenged.

Targeting major infrastructures such as the mass transit systems (rapid transit, subway, trains, etc.), shopping malls, restaurants, and government buildings would also land a crippling blow to the economy, causing a more severe economic meltdown than was brought about by the events of 9/11. Security measures would demand armed guards and bomb canisters in every storefront, measures now in place in Israel.

These attacks might well be laid at the feet of President Bush because of his support of Israel. What better way to stop Israel than to send Palestine/Iranian proxies into the U.S. so that the media blames the resulting attacks on U.S. support for Israel?

Thousands of miles from the Middle East, the United States is still not safe from an Iranian nuclear missile attack, even given the relatively limited range of Iran's Shahab-3 missile. Even if Iran does not develop true intercontinental ballistic missiles, as I revealed in the fictional prologue, it is very possible for Iran to launch a nuclear weapon over US soil with existing technology. A nuclear weapon exploded at high altitude over the United States would send out an electromagnetic pulse (EMP) of high-energy electrons that could knock out electricity and telecommunications throughout large parts of the continental United States. Power grids, unprotected computers and microchips, all systems that depend on electricity and electronics from medical instruments to military communication, could be disabled or permanently destroyed.[6] At risk would be cell phones, cars and trucks, airplanes and trains, banking and finance, virtually everything that uses or generates electricity, all could be hit in what amounts to an electromagnetic tsunami.

This is the furthest thing from fiction. The EMP threat was assessed in 2000 by a commission created by Congress to evaluate the risk. The EMP Threat Commission reported in the summer of 2004 that terrorists could execute an EMP attack by launching a small nuclear-armed missile from a freighter off the coast of the United States.[7]

Iran has test fired a Shahab-3 missile at sea at high altitudes. Initially, the Western media described the test as a failure because the missile exploded; intelligence experts disagreed, arguing that Iran's intent was to test an EMP attack which would require the Shahab-3 to detonate at high altitudes.[8] If Iran launched a successful EMP attack, the United States might have a very difficult time retaliating. Not only would government and military communications be impaired, we might have difficulty determining who was responsible for launching the attack. An EMP attack would turn one of our major strategic advantages, our technological superiority, into a major disadvantage because our technology is almost entirely dependent upon electronics.

We in America are as vulnerable to Iranian-backed terrorism as the citizens of Israel. What the theocrats of radical Islam hate most is freedom and democracy. We are condemned because we are tolerant of religious differences and open to the advancement of the human spirit. We were vulnerable on 9/11. We will be vulnerable once again, if not this month, then certainly in a month not too distant from now. Given this reality, we need to pose a stark question to appeasers here and abroad. Will the desire for peace at any price enslave us to those whose desire is domination at any price?

THE DESPERATE NEED FOR MORAL CLARITY

In a rally in New York City in the Spring of 2006 (yes, the same New York City attacked by terrorists on 9/11) a group calling itself the "Islamic Thinkers Society" waved banners and flags symbolizing the desire to bring the entire world under Islamic rule. The crowd chanted,

> Zionists, Zionists, you will pay! The Wrath of Allah is on its
>   way!
> Israeli Zionists you shall pay! The Wrath of Allah is on its way!
> The mushroom cloud is on its way! The real Holocaust is on
>   its way!

This diabolical tirade ends with:

> Islam will dominate the world.
> Islam is the only solution!

Such a mindset makes one fact crystal clear. As we proceed, the thing we need more than almost anything else is moral clarity about our foe.

I spoke at the Kennedy School of Law at Harvard and the

World Summit on Terrorism in Jerusalem on the subject of "Winning the War on Terrorism through Moral Clarity." Such clarity is crucial because he who defines the terms controls the debate. We are at war with Islamic fascists. Terrorists are not "freedom fighters," regardless of how aggressively they argue the moral certainty of their cause. Terrorists are not interested in democracy or the God-given inalienable rights Americans traditionally have cherished and to which the rest of the world is entitled. Terrorists are by definition autocrats, and radical Islamic terrorists are theocrats. Islamist fundamentalists—whether in terrorist organizations such as Hezbollah or at the head of regimes such as Iran—are interested in a rigid state where women have no rights whatsoever and the clerics who rule are allowed to exert a degree of arbitrary power that even repressive medieval monarchs would have envied.

1. Moral clarity demands that the present conflict be defined as it really is, World War III.

These men and women believe they are on a mission from God. Their stated goal is not winning in Iraq, or Lebanon, or even Israel. The ultimate goal is to bring America to its knees. They believe they defeated the former USSR in Afghanistan, and can ultimately defeat America in Iraq, and then destroy Israel. The vast majority of Muslims are peaceful people, but there are millions of Islamists worldwide with one mission: killing infidels. The majority are coming from Iran. To win the war on terror, we must expose them, and their ideology must be attacked, like the medical profession going after a killer virus.

As I traveled back from Israel, I couldn't help wondering if we weren't living in a period just like the 1930s. Certainly the comparisons between Ahmadinejad and Adolf Hitler are plentiful—maybe even clichéd. But Hitler had written his intentions clearly in *Mein*

Kampf, and nobody believed him. The thought that Hitler might engage in a Holocaust to rid Germany and Europe of millions of Jews who had lived there peacefully for generations was seen as unlikely. Rather than oppose Hitler when he was weak, the world appeased him. Are we doing the same today with the Iranians? Do we take their radical anti-Semitic ravings as serious statements of their foreign policy intents?

I spoke with Netanyahu about this, and his response was pointed and chilling. "They don't hate you because of us; they hate us because of you. They say we are the small Satan; you are the Great Satan, America. It is important to understand that. They don't hide the fact that they intend to take on the West. The only thing they are hiding is their nuclear program."

2. Moral clarity demands that we recognize the twisted messianic motivations behind Iran's attacks on Israel and its pursuit of nuclear weapons.

What drives Iran is its belief in the Mahdi, the Twelfth Imam. Netanyahu made the connection. "It is a particular creed. . . . They say he disappeared about 1000 years ago and that this Mahdi will come back and bring an apocalyptic war that will claim the lives of many. It almost mandates this kind of conflagration. We really don't want Iran, the only country in the world that is 90 percent Shi'a, and the most extreme of this religious sect, to acquire atomic bombs and missiles to carry out their twisted ideology. This is very dangerous."

Christians believe the second coming of Jesus Christ is a blessed hope. For the West, the second coming of this Muslim messiah is nothing of the sort. This messiah returns in a mushroom cloud over Israel and America.

"They are ordered to do this," Netanyahu elaborated. "It is the danger of this creed. It is not a choice; it is almost a word from Allah. That's why these people are willing to commit suicide. We have a suicidal regime. We have a regime that will actually go to any extreme to achieve this mad, apocalyptic event, believing they will somehow inherit paradise. . . . A normal country with a normal susceptibility to the calculation of cost and benefit would act with a modicum of responsibility. That is not the case. Iran is a militant state that supports militancy worldwide. It is now organizing the rocketing of civilians in Israel. Hezbollah without Iran could not do this. They have been able to whip the people in Iraq into an enormous rage. It's not just Israel."

3. Moral clarity demands that the media cover terrorism as it really is.

Terrorism has worked because media have provided free publicity. Terrorism cannot work without media coverage. Why? For it to work, the terrorists have to reach their objectives:

- Glorify the martyrs through publicity;
- Terrorize masses of people through publicity;
- Raise funds in events similar to a Jerry Lewis-type telethon by showing the acts of successful martyrs, through publicity;
- Recruit more terrorists through publicity;
- Achieve political concessions through publicity.

The oxygen can be sucked out of the terrorists' publicity campaign if those with moral clarity become outraged and refuse to support the media organizations that fuel and feed terrorism.

One of the best examples is Hezbollah using human shields. The press has inadvertently deceived the American people by making it look as if many of those killed in Lebanon were innocent civilians. They failed to report that they were not. Rockets being fired outside of Hezbollah homes were then moved several hundred yards to another home while the Hezbollah supporters and family members acted as if they knew nothing. It was a smoke and mirror show: the theater of the absurd and a festival of hypocrisy. The Hezbollah cowards hid behind civilians and proclaimed their own innocence.

4. Moral clarity demands being able to comprehend that Israel is a Jewish state committed to developing democracy in a region where true democracy as we know it in America has never flourished.

Since 1948, Israel has never known true peace. Always living in a region where most neighbors swore to destroy the Jewish state, a strong military has signified the moral clarity Israel has needed, just to survive. But a nuclear Iran radically alters the power dynamic in the Middle East.

"Iran denies the Holocaust, the murder of six million Jews, while they openly declare their intention to create another Holocaust and destroy the six million Jews in Israel," says Netanyahu with characteristic candor. "Number one, Europe will remain in jeopardy; number two, so will everybody else. In short order, the Western-oriented regimes in the Middle East will fall by the wayside." The shakeup doesn't end there:

"The Middle East will be taken over, and that means the oil spigot of the world would be in Iranian hands," says Netanyahu. "You see oil prices today and what it does to the Western economy, think about tomorrow. Number three, of course, is the ability of Iran to use its nuclear arsenal and its missile arsenal to threaten Europe and the United States directly. Make no mistake about it; in their mad, apocalyptic vision, it would be perfectly possible for them to do it. This is not the Soviet Union; this is not China; these are not rational forces. Whatever you can say about the Soviet Union, they have acted fairly carefully on the world scene. Every time they have made overtures of world domination, when faced with their survival, they have always backed off … in Cuba, Berlin, they have always backed off. They have acted very rationally. But, you can't count on the ayatollahs of the world with nuclear weapons to back off. They often prefer their zeal over their survival. Have you ever heard of a communist suicide bomber? No! A militant will smash into buildings, smash into the Pentagon, smash into US warships, buses, schools, you name it. This is a different ideology and must not be allowed to be armed. These are new barbarians seeking the weapons of mass death. We have all been forewarned. We must wake up."

From 2006 on, Iran's push for nuclear weapons and the world's attempt to stop their progress will be a permanent part of each day's news cycle, until the drama finally resolves. What happens when Iran gets nuclear weapons? What steps will the world have to take if Iran is to be stopped at all costs, as America and Israel have resolved? The prospects either way are bone-chilling and soul-frightening.

The problem is that the moment Iran has nuclear weapons, all bets are off—except the threat of imminent destruction. We will enter a world of nuclear terrorism which we have never before experienced, and that world is nearly upon us. Will the world community be able to stop Iran's nuclear program with diplomacy? Will war be the only alternative for Israel and the United States? If Iran's nuclear program is not stopped, how will the world live with an Iran armed with deliverable nuclear weapons? We might be living on the edge of an era of nuclear apocalypse, whether we realize it or not.

HOPE IN THE MIDST OF CRISIS

When the Jews emerged from Europe, those few who survived the Nazi death camps swore "Never again!" Never again would Jews rely on the world community to have the moral clarity and human compassion to come to their aid in their hour of political peril. What Jews learned in the Warsaw Ghetto uprising of World War II was that armed resistance to evil was the only alternative to survival. Unfortunately, with Iran swearing to wipe Israel from the map, the horror of Nazi-like anti-Semitic violence has raised its ugly head. Facing Iran, Israel has reached its greatest existential crisis since the formation of the state in 1948.

As the showdown with Iran grows closer, Israel knows it must play for keeps. With Iran pursuing nuclear weapons and Ahmadinejad openly proclaiming that Israel needs to be wiped from the face of the earth, Israel knows that war with Iran is inevitable, probably sooner rather than later. Removing Hezbollah as an armed terrorist organization would remove a major weapon from the Iranian arsenal.

Even if conventional war were to expand to Syria and then to Iran, Israel would rather take both countries sooner than later, hopefully before Iran has the short time yet needed to produce deliverable nuclear weapons of its own making. The United States can always exert strong-arm pressure on Israel, but to do so in the showdown with Iran would be to our detriment. By attacking terrorist groups such as Hezbollah and resisting the development of nuclear weapons in Iran, Israel truly is doing the dirty work for the United States.

If the United States is truly serious about waging a successful war on terrorism, the president must give Israel enough time to do the job. No one doubts that the Israel military has the needed skill or force to get the job done. All that is needed now is the political will in Washington to stay the course and back Israel, our only true ally in the region. For the United States, this is the meaning of moral clarity in the Middle East. Truly, the United States has no choice but to support Israel, for if the tiny state of Israel is allowed to be wiped from the map, no democracy is secure—not even our own, at home in the United States.

If we waver now, Israel will only fear doubly that the coming showdown with Iran may be one Israel will have to face alone. The Bush administration should do everything necessary right now to avoid putting this fear into Israel. The more Israel feels isolated today, the more resolved the Israeli government will become that Israel alone must defend Israel, regardless of what anyone, including President Bush, thinks or says. If the United States is going to win the war on terror, Israel must first be allowed to win its war on terror—including the inevitable showdown Israel cannot escape with this radical regime that has truly hijacked both Islam and Persia.

The words I've shared with you in this book are disturbing, but the good news is that the words from the Gospel of John inscribed on a wall in the lobby of the CIA headquarters building are truer today than ever:

AND YE SHALL KNOW THE TRUTH AND THE TRUTH
SHALL MAKE YOU FREE.

Do not think for a moment that it's hopeless. This nation can avoid another 9/11 only if good people with moral clarity stand up and speak up. The truth will set us free.

Truth, as everyone knows, can be stranger than fiction—even more so in turbulent times such as these. As this book goes to press, the Associated Press reports that an ancient twenty-page manuscript dating back to 800-1000 AD has been discovered in the Irish Midlands. "This is really a miracle find," according to Pat Wallace, the director of the National Museum of Ireland.[9]

The book, described as "leather velum, very thick wallet in appearance" was found with its pages open to a copy of Psalm

83—which couldn't be more appropriate, given the current crisis. In a more modern translation (NIV) the passage reads,

> *O God, do not keep silent; be not quiet, O God, be not still. See how your enemies are astir, how your foes rear their heads. With cunning they conspire against your people; they plot against those you cherish. "Come," they say, "let us destroy them as a nation, that the name of Israel be remembered no more." With one mind they plot together; they form an alliance against you—the tents of Edom and the Ishmaelites, of Moab and the Hagrites, Gebal, Ammon and Amalek, Philistia, with the people of Tyre. Even Assyria has joined them to lend strength to the descendants of Lot. (v. 1-8)*

The descendants of those mentioned in Psalm 83 inhabit Saudi Arabia, Jordan, Iraq, Iran, Syria, and southern Lebanon today. The Philistines mainly inhabited what we know now as the Gaza Strip; this could well refer to the Palestinians.

> *Do to them as you did to Midian, as you did to Sisera and Jabin at the river Kishon, who perished at Endor and became like refuse on the ground. Make their nobles like Oreb and Zeeb, all their princes like Zebah and Zalmunna, who said, "Let us take possession of the pasturelands of God." Make them like tumbleweed, O my God, like chaff before the wind. As fire consumes the forest or a flame sets the mountains ablaze, so pursue them with your tempest and terrify them with your storm. Cover their faces with shame so that men will seek your name, O LORD. May they ever be ashamed and dismayed; may they perish in disgrace. Let them know that you, whose name is the LORD—that you alone are the Most High over all the earth. (v. 9-18)*

Tiny Israel may very well have to go it alone and fight America's war with Iran by attacking their nuclear reactors. It is doing that now in Lebanon against the Islamic fascists—enemies of the US that hate America as much as they hate Israel. As Ahmadinejad said, he sees a world without America and Zionism.

The showdown with a nuclear Iran is imminent. Though we might all wish for the crisis to pass, I fear the moment is at hand where the reality of a nuclear-armed Iran is inevitably upon us all. I pray that we get through the coming test with distinction. I pray that the crisis passes and that Israel continues to thrive and the United States of America continues to be strong. Freedom can yet ring throughout the world, but only if we first get through the coming showdown and emerge victorious.

Appendix A

LETTER FROM BUSH
TO SHARON

White House

April 14, 2004

His Excellency

Ariel Sharon

Prime Minister of Israel

Dear Mr. Prime Minister:

Thank you for your letter setting out your disengagement plan.

The United States remains hopeful and determined to find a way forward toward a resolution of the Israeli-Palestinian dispute. I remain committed to my June 24, 2002 vision of two states living side by side in peace and security as the key to peace, and to the roadmap as the route to get there.

We welcome the disengagement plan you have prepared, under which Israel would withdraw certain military installations and all settlements from Gaza, and withdraw certain military installations and settlements in the West Bank. These steps described in the plan will mark real progress toward realizing my June 24, 2002 vision, and make a real contribution towards peace. We also understand that, in this context, Israel believes it is important to bring new opportunities to the Negev and the Galilee. We are hopeful that steps pursuant to this plan, consistent with my vision, will remind all states and parties of their own obligations under the roadmap.

The United States appreciates the risks such an undertaking represents. I therefore want to reassure you on several points.

First, the United States remains committed to my vision and to its implementation as described in the roadmap. The United States will do its utmost to prevent any attempt by anyone to impose any other plan. Under the roadmap, Palestinians must undertake an immediate cessation of armed activity and all acts of violence against Israelis anywhere, and all official Palestinian institutions must end incitement against Israel. The Palestinian leadership must act decisively against terror, including sustained, targeted, and effective operations to stop terrorism and dismantle terrorist capabilities and infrastructure. Palestinians must undertake a comprehensive and fundamental political reform that includes a strong parliamentary democracy and an empowered prime minister.

Second, there will be no security for Israelis or Palestinians until they and all states, in the region and beyond, join together to fight terrorism and dismantle terrorist organizations. The United States reiterates its steadfast commitment to Israel's security, including secure, defensible borders, and to preserve and strengthen Israel's capability to deter and defend itself, by itself, against any threat or possible combination of threats.

Third, Israel will retain its right to defend itself against terrorism, including taking actions against terrorist organizations. The United States will lead efforts, working together with Jordan, Egypt, and others in the international community, to build the capacity and will of Palestinian institutions to fight terrorism, dismantle terrorist organizations, and prevent the areas from which Israel has withdrawn from posing a threat that would have to be addressed by any other means. The United States understands that after Israel withdraws from Gaza and/or parts of the West Bank, and pending agreements on other arrangements, existing arrangements regarding control of airspace, territorial waters, and land passages of the West Bank and Gaza will continue. The United States is strongly committed to Israel's security and well-being as a Jewish state. It seems clear that an agreed, just, fair, and realistic framework for a solution to the Palestinian refugee issue as part of any final status agreement will need to be found through the establishment of a Palestinian state, and the settling of Palestinian refugees there, rather than in Israel.

As part of a final peace settlement, Israel must have secure and recognized borders, which should emerge from negotiations between the parties in accordance with UNSC Resolutions 242 and 338. In light of new realities on the ground, including already existing major Israeli populations centers, it is unrealistic to expect that the outcome of final status negotiations will be a full and complete return to the armistice lines of 1949, and all previous efforts to negotiate a two-state solution have reached the same conclusion. It is realistic to expect that any final status agreement will only be achieved on the basis of mutually agreed changes that reflect these realities.

I know that, as you state in your letter, you are aware that certain responsibilities face the State of Israel. Among these, your government has stated that the barrier being erected by Israel should be a security rather than political barrier, should be temporary rather than permanent, and therefore not prejudice any final status issues including final borders, and its route should take into account, consistent with security needs, its impact on Palestinians not engaged in terrorist activities.

As you know, the United States supports the establishment of a Palestinian state that is viable, contiguous, sovereign, and independent, so that the Palestinian people can build their own future in accordance with my vision set forth in June 2002 and with the path set forth in the roadmap. The United States will join with others in the international community to foster the development of democratic political institutions and new leadership committed to those institutions, the reconstruction of civic institutions, the growth of a free and prosperous economy, and the building of capable security institutions dedicated to maintaining law and order and dismantling terrorist organizations.

A peace settlement negotiated between Israelis and Palestinians would be a great boon not only to those peoples but to the peoples of the entire region. Accordingly, the United States believes that all states in the region have special responsibilities: to support the building of the institutions of a Palestinian state; to fight terrorism, and cut off all forms of assistance to individuals and groups engaged in terrorism; and to begin now to move toward more normal relations with the State of Israel. These actions would be true contributions to building peace in the region.

Mr. Prime Minister, you have described a bold and historic initiative that can make an important contribution to peace. I commend your efforts and your courageous decision which I support. As a close friend and ally, the United States intends to work closely with you to help make it a success.

Sincerely,
George W. Bush

Appendix B

CONVERSATION WITH GENERAL YA'ALON

I n December 2005, I was fortunate to have the opportunity to interview by telephone General Moshe Ya'alon, the former chief of staff of the Israeli Defense Force (IDF). I have always found General Ya'alon's observations to be penetrating, even when he is critical of Israel and the Israelis.

Our conversations covered a wide range of issues. This is the first time I have published our discussions. I am going to try to be faithful to the General's phrasing. I want to make sure we capture the subtleties of his brilliance and his insights.

Question: **How serious is the Iran nuclear program to the State of Israel?**

Ya'alon: No doubt, Iran has military nuclear importance. Today there is no debate about it anymore. Nuclear Iran will be become a threat not just to the State of Israel. It becomes a threat to the Middle East, and to the Western world. But, Iran on the way to defeat the West, as they call it, sees Israel as a state that should be annihilated.

And we just heard recently from President Ahmadinejad at a conference under the title of "World without Zionism and America." His intention is to wipe Israel off the map. It derives from the Shi'ite ideology or belief that in order to encourage the revelation of what they call "The Hidden Imam," or the "Twelfth Imam," the "Mahdi," Israel should be wiped off the map. This belief holds that the Apocalypse must happen first, then the Mahdi will return.

When the Mahdi returns, this Shi'ite cult believes the conditions will be right to impose an Islamic caliphate all over the world. They call it "The nation of Islam." This is a very strong belief.

This president is a follower of Ayatollah Mohammad Taghi Mesbah Yazdi. He believes that he should be pro-active and active, and should do everything to destroy the State of Israel.

Q: **How do you see Iran's role promoting terrorism today?**

Ya'alon: Iran is the main generator today of terrorism against Israel. We continue to see Hezbollah attacks from Lebanon. Hezbollah is an Iranian-made organization supported by Iran. They get about $18 million annually. Iran armed Hezbollah for attacks against Israel, using Lebanon as a platform.

Iran also supports the Palestinian Islamic Jihad. They fully finance this organization. In the Palestinian Authority, Iran finances Fatah activists. They finance the families of those who commit bombing attacks. Families of suicide bombers get $25,000–$40,000 for suicide bombings. That's a lot of money in the Palestinian Authority.

And today, Iran has the connection with Hamas. It is a new phenomenon, this connection with Hamas. Hamas in the past refused to cooperate with Iran, because of differences. Iran is Shi'ite ideology, and Hamas has a conflict. According to the different ideologies, they agree that they should impose a new caliphate all over the world, but Iran believes it should be a Shi'ite caliphate; other Arabs believe it should be a Sunni caliphate. So, they argue about it; meanwhile, their common interest is to destroy the State of Israel.

Q: **Does Iran have a nuclear bomb like Pakistan has, or any nuclear bomb at this time? What would Iran be capable of in terms of nuclear blackmail if they officially had the bomb?**

Ya'alon: Even today, using terrorism, Iran blackmails Saudi Arabia. They try to undermine the Egyptian regime and the Jordanian regime. By having a nuclear bomb, even without using it, just as an umbrella, they will dare to do more in terms of terrorism against Israel. They will dare to do more in provoking Hezbollah in the northern part of Israel. Iran will initiate activities to undermine the moderate regimes to blackmail with the umbrella of the nuclear bomb.

So, this is not the way to reach stability in the region. No doubt that Iran today is behind the scenes acting against American and coalition troops in Iraq as well. They do not help, to say the least, to stabilize the situation in Iraq by providing know-how to the insurgents, the IEDs (improvised explosive devices), by influencing and convincing dissident elements, especially Shi'ite elements, not to stabilize the situation in Iraq.

So, with a nuclear bomb, they probably could do more to harm the Americans and Western interests. They see it as a clash between civilizations. This is the way they see it. It is a clash between cultures. And they want to declare that they should defeat the Western culture. With a nuclear bomb, Iran would be able to do more.

Q: **With the centrifuges producing highly enriched uranium at Natanz, how quickly could Iran create a nuclear bomb, any type no matter how small, if they are unrestrained?**

Ya'alon: Our assessment is that in just about a couple of months, Iran will have the indigenous know-how to build a bomb. On this timetable, we are talking about a couple of years, maybe three, to have a bomb. It's only a question of 3, 4, maybe 5 years to have a bomb.

Q: **The world did not know Pakistan had what they have until it was too late. In 1991-93, a lot of our intelligence was telling us that some 5-kiloton bombs were missing from the Soviet Union. Is there any possibility, even the most remote possibility, that the Iranians already have a bomb?**

Ya'alon: We don't know about it; but in this business of intelligence, we could be wrong. You know what you know; you don't know what you don't know.

In these kinds of activities, no doubt the enemy is trying to hide to use his best capabilities to keep nuclear weapons activity as a covert operation. We shouldn't exclude such an option, because in the past, yes, we underestimated the Libyan capabilities. I'm talking about the Israeli intelligence, what we underestimated. We were wrong in assessing the stages the Libyans had reached in the nuclear arms race. So, we shouldn't exclude Iran getting a nuclear weapon. So far, we don't have hardly any knowledge that they have it.

Q: **If the Iranians have bought from the Russian mafia, if they have any kind of nuclear bomb, no matter the size, your country is a one-bomb state. One bomb in Tel Aviv, no matter how small, could wreak tremendous damage to your country. Is it possible, that through Egypt, the Iranians could move something into the Gaza area that could potentially wreak havoc on your nation?**

Ya'alon: For Israel, no doubt, an Iranian nuclear bomb is a nightmare. An Iranian nuclear bomb is a threat to our existence. No doubt about it. This is the reason that I claim we should stop it. But *we*, and I say *we*, must stop Iran from getting a nuclear weapon.

I consider all the Western world must be involved in stopping Iran because Iran considers Israel as part of the West. Defeating Israel is a stage for Iran on the way to defeating the West. So, we, the West, and of course, Israel, should do our best not to allow this unconventional regime to acquire unconventional capabilities.

213

Q: Because of a diabolical belief in a Jewish world con-
           spiracy, the forged and discredited "Protocols of the
           Elders of Zion" are being embraced by some of the
           major Islamic regimes in the Middle East. Israel was
           kept from joining the coalition President H. W. Bush
           built in the Gulf War in 1991.

           If the US keeps Israel out for appeasement to the
           Arab world, it appears now that the US could very
           well try to deal with Iran through diplomatic means.
           The US is working with a Shi'ite majority in Iraq;
           maybe we could also work with a Shi'ite regime in
           Iran. Is it possible for a regime with such inbred ide-
           ological passions to submit to diplomatic concessions
           and bring about an end to such a serious crisis?

Ya'alon: I am not against political deals, but any political deals
           should be concluded by Iran without nuclear capabilities.

           It doesn't matter if the US or the West use political
           means or economic means, the goal is the isolation of
           Iran. In the end, even economic sanctions might be
           used. We need to reach a deal in which Iran will be
           committed to come under full United Nations inspec-
           tion, involving all of Iran's nuclear capabilities. A polit-
           ical deal can be the conclusion, but we should suspect
           Iran. Iran cheated us in the last decade. Even after
           November 2004, when Iran entered negotiations with
           the IAEA, we still witnessed violations. We should sus-
           pect Iran all the way in dealing with the nuclear issue.

The General's observations came not just from his service as a former chief of staff, but also from thirty-seven years as a former soldier

and officer who since 1968 has been committed to defend the State of Israel. Today, General Ya'alon serves as a Research Fellow in the Washington Institute for Middle East Policy in Washington DC.

I probed General Ya'alon's views on the military strength of Israel, especially in light of the terrorist danger presented by Iran, and now by Hamas, especially after the Hamas victory gaining control of the Palestinian parliament.

Q: **How do you rate Israel's military strength today?**

Ya'alon: Israel is going to celebrate its 58th Anniversary this year. And, no doubt, Israel enjoys the image of the original superpower. When it comes to military strength, Israel is the original superpower in the Middle East. We have very strong armed forces, the Israeli Defense Forces, including a strong airforce, navy, and ground forces, plus extensive intelligence capabilities. All this works to benefit the security of the State of Israel.

Israel is also the original superpower in regard to economic prosperity. You cannot compare the economic situation of Israel with our neighbors. We are state-of-the-art in science and technology. We enjoy a rich cultural life. And, yes, we are a regional superpower. Having said that, to my mind, the core of our security challenge is still a reluctance of too many parties in our region to recognize Israel's right to exist as a Jewish state.

I have heard General Ya'alon comment on this before and I asked him to expand his views on the existential threat Israel continues to experience in the region.

Ya'alon: This is a key point to be understood, even in Israel. Even in Israel, we are confused about this. When Arafat decided to go to war in September 2000 and to launch a deliberate attack using terror capabilities against the State of Israel, he did it because of the reluctance to recognize Israel's right to exist as a Jewish state. By initiating the war, he escaped the final settlement which Israelis were expecting to have as a result and outcome of the Oslo Accords. He escaped the final settlement; he escaped the end of conflict; he escaped a two-state solution. He did not want a two-state solution. And in Israel, we still argue about this. We are still confused about this issue.

We have never seen any Palestinian negotiations that recognize Israel's right to exist as a Jewish state. This goes back to the '30s, with the Peale commission proposal in 1937. Then the UN partition proposal in 1947, and again the Palestinians refused any partition plan. In 2000, it was an Israeli partition plan proposal led by Prime Minister Barak, to divide the land, divide Jerusalem. He was ready to divide everything, but the Palestinian reaction was war. This was the case in any opportunity in which any partition plan was proposed. In the '30s, we faced war; in '47, we faced war; in September 2000, we faced war. The core of this issue is the reluctance to recognize Israel's right to exist as a Jewish state.

Arafat knew that by having the two-state solution, he should recognize Israel as a Jewish state. He escaped it. Today, it is even clearer because we have Hamas-led Palestinian assault. And they say very clearly that the territory from the Jordan River should be one state, and it should be a Palestinian Islamic state, and there is not any room for a Jewish state. Even in Israel today, we argue about it. We might be more moderate; they might be more pragmatic, but there is no way.

Q: **Can Israel win a military war today?**

Ya'alon: When it comes to the military, Israel enjoys deterrence in what we might call "conventional type warfare." This is the outcome of our victories in all the wars—in the Independence War, the Six Day War, the Yom Kippur War. Since 1973, our enemies realized that there is no way to defeat the IDF in conventional type warfare. Since 1973, almost 33 years, Israel has not faced such conventional war. They didn't initiate this kind of attack by armed forces attacking Israel in what we call conventional warfare. But those elements were still reluctant to accept our right to exist as a Jewish state and decided to go to two different types of warfare.

One I call sub-conventional warfare—this involves terror rockets, primitive rockets like the Katyushas. Also, our enemies have explored super-conventional weapons, such as the Iranian Shahab missiles, or the former Iraqi missiles such as the Scuds that Saddam Hussein shot into Israel in 1991. We have also seen weapons of mass destruction—including chemical agents, biological agents, and now the Iranian's determination to acquire nuclear capability.

There is something in common between all these types of warfare: It is simply to avoid the engagement with Israeli Defense Forces and to hit directly the civilian population. This is the case with the suicide bombers. This is the case with the Qassam rockets launched toward our cities, not towards our military installations. It was the case with Hezbollah Katyusha rockets launched from Lebanon toward Kiryat Shmoneh and other cities, and not toward military installations. We have military installations in the north. Hezbollah avoids them, choosing instead to attack directly our civilians. It was the case with Saddam Hussein with the Scud missiles launched toward Haifa and Tel Aviv in 1991. Now the Iranians intend to acquire military nuclear capabilities, and this is part of the same perception.

What General Ya'alon was saying was that terrorism represented a more subtle but more dangerous threat than conventional war.

Ya'alon: Hassan Nasrallah, the head of Hezbollah in Lebanon, said, "Israel is a spider web." What did he mean when he said spider web? He explained he coined this term in his victory speech in June 2000, after our withdrawal from Lebanon. He said, "Israel is like a spider web. A spider web from far away seems very strong, but when you touch it, it dissolves."

No doubt that Israel enjoys the image of regional superpower, having the best airforce, the best navy, the best army in the region. But Israel's society is the weakest link in the Israel national security chain. Israel's society is tired, exhausted from the war. The Israeli people are not ready anymore to fight, to sacrifice lives to protect the State of Israel. They are ready to give concessions, to surrender. It was the explanation after our humiliating withdrawal from Lebanon.

This is not the idea of Hassan Nasrallah, it is my idea. I believe by initiating the war in September 2000, the Israelis began to surrender. We saw that it will be sooner rather than later, but it will be believed when they decided to use terror against Israel in September 2000. Unfortunately, I can't deny it. And when I look to our national security situation today, as I said, we enjoy military strength. The IDF can do everything, as we did in the last five years fighting Palestinian terrorism, enjoying our intelligence capabilities and other capabilities, to resist this enormous challenge.

Q: **How can Israel meet the terrorist challenge?**

Ya'alon: The terrorists deliberately challenge our values, challenge the world order. This is true of Palestinian terrorism as well as al-Qaeda terrorism. They want to blur the borders between combatants and civilians. They use the Palestinian civilian population as human shields. They operate behind the civilians using the neighborhoods as safe havens and shelters. They attack our civilians deliberately. We lost in this war more than 1,080 casualties. Seventy-five percent of our casualties are civilians—and this is done deliberately.

So, for military professionals, it is an enormous challenge. How do we fight terrorists who move among civilians—the "low-profile targets," as we call it? It's not tanks, it is not brigades, it's not military camps—it is terrorists. But, we did it. We enjoyed the intelligence capabilities to be able to intercept terrorists one-by-one. Then we moved from defense to the offense, in the offensive shield operation. But to my mind, we did this too late.

We succeeded in eliminating the terrorists' capabilities, namely arresting and killing the attackers, and keeping our values. We surgically eliminated the targets without causing collateral damage. We were careful not to harm our own values. We need the legitimacy of our own moral and ethical values in our society. It is complicated. In Israel there is a moral and political dispute about it, and we need the legitimacy of our own moral values. And the relatively calm situation that we enjoy today in regard to Palestinian terrorism is because of moving from the defense to the offense.

General Ya'alon's comments concerned me deeply. For Israel to survive, the Israelis will need to remain vigilant. Otherwise, the terrorists will simply keep pounding away, confident they can ultimately win—just by wearing down the Israelis' resolve to keep fighting. The General elaborated on this theme.

Ya'alon: How can Israel meet the terrorist challenge? The problem today is not with how many aircraft we have or should have in order to deter our neighbors. It's not about how many tanks or pieces of artillery we have. The challenge is our capability to stand—our endurance and our resilience—and how not to surrender. This is the key.

Unfortunately, looking back at what has happened in Israel in the last couple of years, in two key issues, we surrendered. One was when Israel withdrew from Lebanon, giving Hezbollah the country. We should be in Lebanon as long as the rockets are fired from Lebanon. We need to protect our cities. We have been deceived by Hezbollah. This is a victory for Hezbollah.

The second event was the withdrawal from Gaza. This is the way the terrorists can hit us, and we shouldn't be surprised that Hamas has been elected to control the Palestinian Authority. Eighty percent of the Palestinians believe that we pulled out of Gaza because of Hamas. And they are partly right. So today, our civilians are on the front lines. The ability of our civilian society to stand is the most important element in our national security situation today. Enjoying the military capabilities, this is the most important factor today in regard to national security.

Repeatedly, General Ya'alon reminded me that the fight against Islam was a fight of cultures, a fight of civilizations. Israel might today be in the lead position, but ultimately radical Islam is at war with America and with the West in general.

Ya'alon: Here we come to look at the future. What we are facing today is not just the challenge of the Israeli-Palestinian conflict, or the challenge of the Israeli-Arab conflict. It has become, in the last decade, a clash between civilizations—a conflict between Islam and the infidels. This is the challenge today, not just for the State of Israel; this is the challenge for the Western world, and we should not ignore it.

Listening to Khaled Mashaal, the Hamas leader, in his victory speech in the Damascus mosque, 12 February 2006, after the elections. He said, "The nation of Islam will sit on the throne of the world, and the world will be full of remorse." He didn't speak just about the Palestinian people; he spoke about the nation of Islam.

He didn't speak just about Israel; he spoke about the West. This is the way the Khaled Mashaal feels, and I'm not surprised. This is the way that the Muslim Brotherhood in Egypt sees this, as a clash between the Western world and Islam. They claim to impose what they call national Islam, a new caliphate to defeat the West, to defeat the Western culture, to defeat the Western values. Not to allow any Christianity or Judaism—no infidels. All the world would be Muslim. And they mean it.

Unfortunately, in the last couple of years, those elements, not just Hamas, are encouraged by the lack of determination on the behalf of Israel and the West. This is the case of Osama bin Laden, without any connection to the Israeli or Palestinian cause whatsoever. He created the al-Qaeda without any connection to the Israeli-Palestinian cause. He planned to defeat the West. And this is the case with President Ahmadinejad. When he said in Tehran that Israel should be wiped off the map, it was in concurrence with his advisors—he saw a world without Israel and without America. It is a strong belief, and it has nothing to do with the Israeli-Palestinian conflict.

Q: **You take seriously then that Ahmadinejad's threat is not just to Israel?**

Ya'alon: You have to listen to what Ahmadinejad is saying. He is talking about a nation of Islam all over the world, defeating the West, and on the way to defeating the West, Israel should be annihilated . . . wiped off the map. He means it.

What they are doing now, all of them, Hamas, al-Qaeda, Iran, is terrorism . . . terrorism against Israel, terrorism against Western targets. That's how al-Qaeda operated in Spain and in London. Al-Zahawiri launched three attacks in Amman, Jordan, just recently. Iran is involved in challenging the coalition forces in Iraq . . . Iranian activities in Syria, sending *mujahedin*, as they call it, to kill coalition troops in Iraq, and to undermine regimes, moderate regimes that lean toward the West; blackmailing regimes like the Persian Gulf states . . . Saudi Arabia . . . they are using terrorism, threatening the regimes with the assassination of their leaders, and this is the Iranian, al-Qaeda, Hamas way to deal with our culture, with our values.

This is the challenge, not just to the State of Israel. We need a wake-up call in Israel, but we need a wake-up call everywhere, in Europe and in the United States, to understand the situation, not to ignore it, but to deal with it. And we are strong enough in the West to deal with it, either to prevent the Iranian nuclear capabilities or at least to demonstrate more determination by forcing Iran to pay the price. Yet if we don't isolate Iran or impose sanctions, the Iranians do not pay the price. They are sure that the West is afraid of them; this is the case. So, this is a challenge, not just for the State of Israel; this is a challenge for the Western world today.

The only way to deal with it is moral clarity, strategic clarity, and strategic decisions.

I left the conversations with General Ya'alon concerned about our resolve as Americans to continue the War on Terrorism. I reflected how quickly we tend to forget the horror of the 9/11 attack, how quickly we return to our lives as normal, as long as there are no more terror attacks here in America.

Deep in my heart, I know General Ya'alon is right. Radical Islamic terrorists are at war with the West. Whether we like it or not, this war will continue as long as countries like Iran have reason to believe they will not be stopped in their pursuit of terrorism to advance their religious cause worldwide.

ACKNOWLEDGEMENTS

I wish to thank my agent, Jan Miller, of Dupree/Miller and Associates for representing me so capably; you are the greatest; and to my publisher at Nelson Current, David Dunham, for your confidence and support of this project. I am especially grateful to my editor at Nelson Current, Joel Miller, whose help has been invaluable.

To my dear friend, Dr. Jerome Corsi, I can only say, what would I have done without you? You have been my right hand. Your help with writing and research on this project has been invaluable. Without you, this book would have been impossible.

My deepest gratitude for those in Jerusalem: Prime Minister Ehud Olmert; Former Prime Minister Benjamin Netanyahu; Lieutenant General Moshe Ya'alon, former Chief of Staff, IDF; Uri Lubrani, Advisor to the Ministry of Defense, Iranian Affairs, State of Israel; Ambassador Dore Gold, State of Israel; Ephraim Kam, Deputy Head of the Jaffee Center for Strategic Studies at Tel Aviv University; Dan Schueftan, National Security Studies Center, Haifa University; Daniel Leshem, Retired Senior Officer, IDF Intelligence (now a member of the Center for Strategic Research at Tel Aviv University); Reuven Pedatzur, Strategic Studies Program, Tel Aviv University; Meir Litvak, Iran Expert, Tel Aviv University; General Yossi Peled (Ret.) former IDF Northern Commander; and Danny Yatom, former head of Mossad and Chief of Staff for Prime Minister Yitzhak Rabin.

I also wish to honor three giants who are no longer with us. They believed in me and are the reason I began this journey three decades ago: Prime Minister Menachem Begin; Dr. Reuben Hecht, Senior Advisor to the Prime Minister; and Isser Harel, founder of Mossad, Israeli intelligence. These great men were my mentors twenty-five years ago. They helped me to understand the extreme seriousness of the subject of Islamic fundamentalism, not only as it relates to Israel but also as it relates to America and the world.

I wish to thank my executive assistant, Lanelle Young. Your amazing and creative assistance to this book was immeasurable. I also wish to thank my good friend, Duncan Dodds, who has been a strong source of encouragement, support, and wisdom throughout this entire process.

Finally, a book project of this magnitude demands a grueling work schedule. Most of all, I'm indebted to my beloved wife, Carolyn. Without her patience, compassion, encouragement, and sacrifice, there is no possible way I could have achieved this.

NOTES

CHAPTER 1

1. Quoted in "The Man Behind the Picture: A Tour Through the History of Emam Khomeini," http://www.worldtrek.org/odyssey/mideast/current/042900monayato.html.

2. The photograph of Khomeini on the 1 February 1979 flight from Paris to Tehran, along with the story of Sadeq Qotbzadeh, can be found at the following address: http://www.iranian.com/Books/1999/June/Khomeini/qotbzadeh.html.

3. John R. Bolton, Under Secretary for Arms Control and International Security, "Iran's Continuing Pursuit of Weapons of Mass Destruction," Testimony Before the House International Relations Committee Subcommittee on the Middle East and Central Asia, 24 June 2005, http://www.state.gov/t/us/rm/33909.htm.

4. Golnaz Esfandiari, "Iran: President Says Light Surrounded Him During UN Speech," Radio Free Europe/Radio Liberty, 29 November 2005, http://www.rferl.org/featuresarticle/2005/11/184CB9FB-887C-4696-8F54-0799DF747A4A.html. A link to a news broadcast where the videotape of Ahmadinejad's conversations with the mullahs over tea can be seen and heard at the following address: http://regimechangeiran.blogspot.com/2005/12/important-video-report-on-hidden-iman.html; See also Scott Peterson, "Waiting for the Rapture in Iran," *Christian Science Monitor*, 21 December 2005.

5. Full text of Ahmadinejad's speech available at the following address: http://www.globalsecurity.org/wmd/library/news/iran/2005/iran-050918-irna02.htm.

SHOWDOWN WITH NUCLEAR IRAN

6. Ali Akbar Dareini, "Iran Leader: Israel Will Be Annihilated," Associated Press, 14 April 2006.

CHAPTER 2

1. Saghand Mining Department, Atomic Energy Organization of Iran, http://www.aeoi.org.ir/NewWeb/Recenter.asp?id=26; See also the National Geoscience Database of Iran (NGDIR), "Mineral Resources of Iran," http://www.ngdir.ir/GeoportalInfo/ SubjectInfoDetail.asp?PID=54.

2. On GlobalSecurity.org; This Internet site contains an extensive discussion of Iran's nuclear facilities, including a site-by-site description, reached by navigating through the following sequence: Iran > Facilities > Nuclear; The discussion of Iran's uranium mines is drawn from the following site: http://www.globalsecurity.org/wmd/ world/iran/mines.htm.

3. "AP: Iran to Extract Uranium in Early 2006," News Max wires, 6 September 2004, http://www.newsmax.com/archives/articles/2004/9/5/115634.shtml.

4. "Esfahan/Isfahan Nuclear Technology Center," available at the following address: http://www.globalsecurity.org/wmd/world/iran/esfahan.htm.

5. "Revealed: Iran's Nuclear Factory," *Sunday Times-World*, 1 May 2005, available at http://www.timesonline.co.uk/article/0,,2089-1592578,00.html.

6. "Natanz [Kashan]," http://www.globalsecurity.org/wmd/world/iran/natanz.htm.

7. "EU Powers to Mull Iranian Nuclear Efforts," *Haaretz*, 9 February 2004, http://www.haaretz.com/hasen/pages/ShArt.jhtml?itemNo=472862&contr assID=1.

8. "Iran Confirms Uranium-to-Gas Conversion," *China Daily*, 10 May 2005, http://www.chinadaily.com.cn/english/doc/2005-05/10/ content_440631.htm.

9. Ibid.

10. Ibid.

11. Tom Baldwin, "Iran Faces Sanctions after Reactivating Nuclear Plant," 9 August 2005, http://www.timesonline.co.uk/article/0,,251-1727066,00.html; See also Seth Rosen, "Iran Restarts Its Nuclear Activities," *Washington Times*, 9 August 2005.

12. Dafna Linzer, "Iran Resumes Uranium Work, Ignores Warning," *Washington Post*, 9 August 2005.

13. "Iran Rejects U.N. Resolution," CBS News, 25 September 2005, http://www.cbsnews.com/stories/2005/09/25/world/main882946.shtml.

14. Jerome Corsi, "Bush Corners the Mullahs," WorldNetDaily.com, 30 September 2005, http://www.wnd.com/news/article.asp?ARTICLE_ID=46592.

15. "Iran Enriches Uranium. Iran Starts Converting New Uranium Batch, Diplomat Says," 27 November 2005, http://www.blog.ca/main/index.php/borisnewz/2005/11/17/iran_enriches_uranium~315692.

16. "Russia Plan Could End Iran Talks Impasse: ElBaradei," 6 December 2005, http://www.iranian.ws/cgi-bin/iran_news/exec/view.cgi/3/11350/printer.

17. Phillippe Errera, "The E3/EU-Iran Negotiations and Prospects for Resolving the Iranian Nuclear Issue: A European Perspective," speech delivered in Tehran, Iran, on 5-6 March 2005, http://www.globalsecurity.org/wmd/library/report/2005/errera.htm.

18. Maria Golovnina, "Russian Announces Completed Nuke Plant," *Washington Times*, 15 October 2004.

19. Tom Walker, "Suspicion Grows on Iran's Uranium," *Christian Science Monitor*, 14 May 2006.

20. Tom Casey, "Designation of National Council of Resistance and National Council of Resistance of Iran Under Executive Order 13244," 15 August 2003, http://www.state.gov/r/pa/prs/ps/2003/23311.htm.

21. "Information on Two Top Secret Nuclear Sites of the Iranian Regime (Natanz and Arak)," December 2002, available at http://www.iranwatch.org/privateviews/NCRI/perspex-ncri-natanzarak-1202.htm.

22. "Disclosing a Major Secret Nuclear Site under the Ministry of Defense," National Council for Resistance in Iran, 14 November 2004, available at http://www.globalsecurity.org/wmd/library/report/2004/new-nuke-info.htm.

23. "Implementation of the NPT Safeguards Agreement in the Islamic Republic of Iran," Report by the Director General, International Atomic Energy Agency (IAEA) Board of Governors, GOV/2006/67, 2 September 2005, http://www.globalsecurity.org/wmd/library/report/2005/iran_iaea-gov_2005-67_2sep05.htm.

24. "Questioning Iran's Pursuit of the Nuclear Fuel Cycle—Iran's Nuclear Fuel Cycle Facilities: A Pattern of Peaceful Intent?" US Department of State, September 2005, http://www.globalsecurity.org/wmd/library/report/2005/iran-fuel-cycle-brief_dos_2005.pdf.

25. David R. Sands, "Army Takes Control of Iran Nukes," *Washington Times*, 5 October 2005, http://www.washtimes.com/world/20051005-121400-6491r.htm.

26. "Abdul Qadeer Kahn 'Apologizes' for Transferring Nuclear Secrets Abroad," http://www.fas.org/nuke/guide/pakistan/nuke/aqkhan020404.html.

27. Attachment A., Unclassified Report to Congress on the Acquisition of Technology Relating to Weapons of Mass Destruction and Advanced Conventional Munitions, 1 July Through 31 December 2003, https://www.cia.gov/cia/reports/721_reports/july_dec2002.htm.

28. "Implementation of the NPT Safeguards Agreement in the Islamic Republic of Iran," GOV/2005/87, 18 November 2005, http://www.globalsecurity.org/wmd/library/report/2005/iran_iaea_gov2005-87_18nov05.pdf.

29. Robert Tait, "Iran Denies Claims about Nuclear Plan," *Guardian*, 14 November 2005, http://www.guardian.co.uk/iran/story/0,12858,1641995,00.html.

30. For a discussion of this controversy, see the following Internet blog posting, "Iran Dope Concerns RV Not Warhead," 14 November 2005, http://www.armscontrolwonk.com/858/sanger-hypes-the-laptop.

31. Tait, op.cit., supra in Footnote #29.

32. William J. Broad and David E. Sanger, "Relying on Computer, U.S. Seeks to Prove Iran's Nuclear Aims," *New York Times*, 13 November 2005, http://www.nytimes.com/2005/11/13/international/middleeast/13nukes.html?ei=5090&en=d5986259aea4ffe9&ex=1289538000&partner=rssuserland&emc=rss&pagewanted=print.

33. Mohamed ElBaradei's comments were reported in the following sources: Anne Penketh, "UN Chief Urges West and Iran to Cool Brinkmanship over Nuclear Programme," *Independent*, 5 December 2005, http://news.independent.co.uk/world/asia/article331219.ece; "UN Nuclear Watchdog: Iran May be Months from Nuclear Bomb," Haaretz Service and Agencies, 5 December 2005, http://www.haaretz.com/hasen/pages/ShArt.jhtml?itemNo=653454&contrassID=1&subContrassID=1; "El Baradei: Iran Only Months Away from A Bomb," Mideast.jpost.com, 5 December 2005, http://www.jpost.com/servlet/Satellite?cid=1132475683499&pagename=JPost%2FJPArticle%2FShowFull.

34. Paul Hughes, "Iran Announces Further Resumption of Atomic Work," 3 January 2006, http://in.news.yahoo.com/060103/137/61twb.html.

35. "Iran to Activate Natanz Nuclear Project in Coming Days," 2 January 2006, http://regimechangeiran.blogspot.com/2006/01/iran-to-activate-natanz-nuclear.html.

36. Paul Hughes, "Iran Announces Resumption of More Atomic Work," 3 January 2006, http://www.iranian.ws/iran_news/publish/printer_11961.shtml.

37. Islamic Republic News Agency (IRNA), "Iran Resumes Nuclear Research Activities," 10 January 2006, http://www.irna.ir/en/news/view/line-24/0601106548122559.htm.

38. "Iran Plans 'Small Scale' Nuclear Fuel Work: IAEA," Reuters/IranFocus.com, 10 January 2006, http://www.iranfocus.com/modules/news/print.php?storyid=5234.

39. "Iran Develops Uranium Separation Technology," AFP, 1 January 2006, http://www.arabnews.com/?article=75617.

40. Jacqueline W. Shire, "Iran to Begin Enriching Uranium. Iran Removes Seals at Nuclear Facility," 10 January 2006, http://www.abcnews.go.com/International/story?id=1488020.

41. Islamic Republic News Agency (IRNA), "Iran 'Unilaterally' Rejects Nuclear Deal, Says France," Reuters/AFP, 5 December 2005, http://www.rferl.org/featuresarticle/2005/12/85A95AD9-E3C3-400B-BD5C-CA66843CA5F4.html; "Iran Will Welcome Proposal for Enrichment inside Iran, Larijani," 8 December 2005, http://www.irna.ir/en/news/view/line-22/0512059184172145.htm.

42. "Iran Body Passes Bill Blocking Inspections of Atomic Facilities," Associated Press, 3 December 2005, http://www.iran-plus.com/de/schlagzeilen/news712.html.

43. Geoffrey Kemp, "Iran and Iraq: The Shia Connection, Soft Power, and the Nuclear Factor," Special Report 156, United States Institute of Peace, December 2005. http://www.usip.org/pubs/specialreports/sr156.html.

44. Arieh O'Sullivan, "Halutz: Sanctions Won't Deter Iran," Israel.jpost.com, 21 November 2005, http://www.jpost.com/servlet/Satellite?cid=1132475589860&pagename =JPost%2FJPArticle%2FShowFull.

45. Julie Stahl, "Strike on Iran Not Easy, Israeli Military Chief Says," http://www.cnsnews.com/news/viewstory.asp?Page=\ForeignBureaus\arc hive\200512\FOR20051205f.html.

46. "Ahmadinejad: Iran Has Joined Nuclear Club," IranFocus.com, 11 April 2006, http://www.iranfocus.com/modules/news/ article.php?storyid=6716; See also, "Iran officially joins nuclear club," Mehr News Agency, 11 April 2006, http://www.mehrnews.com/en/ NewsDetail.aspx?NewsID=310817.

47. Ali Akbar Dareini, "Iran Enriches Uranium to Fuel Reactors," *Guardian*, 3 May 2006, http://www.guardian.co.uk/worldlatest/story/0,,-5796835,00.html.

48. "Israel: Iran 'Months' From Making Nukes," CNN.com, 21 May 2006, http://www.cnn.com/2006/WORLD/meast/05/21/ iran.nuclear/index.html.

49. Dafna Linzer, "Iran Is Judged 10 Years from Nuclear Bomb. U.S. Intelligence Review Contrasts with Administration Statements," *Washington Post*, 2 August 2005, http://pqasb.pqarchiver.com/washingtonpost/access/876186251.html?dids= 876186251:876186251&FMT=ABS&FMTS=ABS:FT&fmac=&date=Aug +2%2C+2005&author=Dafna+Linzer&desc=Iran+Is+Judged+10+Years+Fro m+Nuclear+Bomb.

50. Ibid.

51. Ibid.

52. "Iran Bomb 'Within Next 10 Years," BBC News, 2 June 2006, http://news.bbc.co.uk/2/hi/middle_east/5039956.stm.

CHAPTER 3

1. "Opposition Coalition Calls on Iranians to Boycott the June 17, 2005 Presidential Elections in Iran," June 2005; signed opposition statement published on Internet site of the Foundation for Democracy in Iran, http://www.iran.org/news/2005_06_15boycott.htm.

2. "Iranian Leader Orders Candidates Reconsidered," Radio Free Europe/Radio Liberty, 24 May 2005, http://www.rferl.org/featuresarticle/2005/05/a376750c-3ac9-4bee-b9c5-8aeffeac9bae.html.

3. Safa Haeri, "Boycotting All Elections and Insisting on Referendum: Akbar Ganji," *Iran Press Service*, 22 May 2005, http://www.iran-press-service.com/ips/articles-2005/may-2005/ganji-manifesto-22505.shtml.

4. "Iran to Hold Prez Election Runoff," CBS News, 18 June 2005, http://www.cbsnews.com/stories/2005/06/18/world/main702828.shtml.

5. "Iran Calls for Bush Poll Apology," BBC News, 19 June 2005, http://news.bbc.co.uk/1/hi/world/middle_east/4108452.stm.

6. "Hardliner Ahmadinejad Elected Iran's President," *Iran Mania*, 26 November 2005, http://www.iranmania.com/News/ArticleView/Default.asp?ArchiveNews=Yes&NewsCode=32871&NewsKind=Current Affairs.

7. "Ahmadinejad Elected President," *Iran Daily*, 26 June 2005, http://www.iran-daily.com/1384/2308/pdf/i1.pdf.

8. "Ex-Hostages: Iran's President Was Captor," FoxNews, 1 July 2005, http://www.foxnews.com/story/0,2933,161163,00.html.

9. Ali Akbar Dareini, "Ex-Iranian Agent: Photo Not Ahmadinejad," *Las Vegas Sun*, 2 July 2005, http://www.lasvegassun.com/sunbin/stories/text/2005/jul/02/070200382.html.

10. Kenneth M. Pollack, *The Persian Puzzle* (Random House, 2004), p. 151.

11. Information on the background of Mahmoud Ahmadinejad in this and the following paragraph is drawn from "Mahmoud Ahmadinejad's Biography," on GlobalSecurity.org at the following URL: http://www.globalsecurity.org/military/world/iran/ahmadinejad.htm.

12. Iason Athanasiadeis, "Plainly President: Iran's Ahmadinejad Set Style Early in Life," *Washington Times* (National Weekly Edition), 3 July 2006.

13. These points were vividly made on an Independent Television News report. See "An Important Video Report on the Hidden Imam," 8 December 2005, http://regimechangeiran.blogspot.com/2005/12/important-video-report-on-hidden-iman.html.

14. "Iran, Islamic Republic at a Glance," *World Bank*, 25 August 2005, http://www.worldbank.org/data/countrydata/aag/irn_aag.pdf.

15. Morteza Aminmansour, "Slavery of Children and Women in Persian Gulf Countries," *Persian Journal*, 20 June 2004, http://www.iranian.ws/cgi-bin/iran_news/exec/view.cgi/2/2675; See also Katherine Toliao, "Human Trafficking and Forced Prostitution," IranDokht.com, 27 November 2005, http://www.irandokht.com/editorial/index4.php?area=pro&%20sectionID=12&editorialID=761.

16. N. Janardhan, "In the Era of Ahmadinejad, Do Iran's Youth Offer a Future of Boom or Bust?" *Daily Star*, 13 December 2005, http://www.dailystar.com.lb/article.asp?edition_id=10&categ_id=5&article_id=20706.

17. Golnaz Esfandiari, "Iran: Coping with the World's Highest Rate of Brain Drain," Radio Free Europe/Radio Liberty, 8 March 2004, http://www.rferl.org/featuresarticle/2004/3/C655D456-07DF-405A-8FE9-AAD51173BD66.html.

18. "Iran: Tehran's Stock Exchange Risks Closure," *Adnkronos International*, 5 October 2005.

19. "Iran: New Limits on Travel Abroad," *Adnkronos International*, 19 December 2005.

20. "Iran: New Stock Exchange Head Named," *Adnkronos International*, 22 November 2005.

21. "Iran: New Stock Exchange Head Named," *Asia News*, 23 November 2005, http://www.asianews.ir/en/main1.asp?a_id=1034.

22. "Iran Imports Worth of $4.5b Dollars Gasoline," *Persian Journal*, 29 July 2005, http://www.iranian.ws/cgi-bin/iran_news/exec/view.cgi/3/8323.

23. Alan Peters, "Mullahs' Threat Not Sinking In," FrontPageMag.com, 4 November 2005, http://www.frontpagemag.com/Articles/ReadArticle.asp?ID=20065.

24. Kenneth R. Timmerman, "Is Iran's Ahmadinejad a Messianic Medium?" DailyStar.com, 30 December 2005, http://www.dailystar.com.lb/article.asp?edition_id=10&categ_id=5&article_id=21113.

25. "Iran Government Urging the Hidden Imam to Help," *Iran Press Service*, 21 October 2005, http://www.iran-press-service.com/ips/articles-2005/october-2005/jamkaran_211005.shtml.

26. Scott Peterson, "Waiting for the Rapture in Iran," *Christian Science Monitor*, 21 December 2005, http://www.csmonitor.com/2005/1221/p01s04-wome.html?s=widep; see also Scott Peterson, "True Believers Dial Messiah Hotline in Iran," *Christian Science Monitor*, 4 January 2006, http://www.csmonitor.com/2006/0104/p07s02-wome.html.

27. Islamic Republic News Agency (IRNA), "Full Text of President Ahmadinejad's Speech at General Assembly." The speech took place before the United Nations General Assembly, New York, 17 September 2005, http://www.worldproutassembly.org/archives/2005/09/full_text_of_ir.html.

28. "Iran's Ahmadinejad: Sharon Dead and 'Others to Follow Suit,'" IranFocus.com, 5 January 2006, http://www.iranfocus.com/modules/news/article.php?storyid=5165; the Ahmadinejad quotations in the next paragraph come from this source as well.

29. See, for instance, A. Savyon, "Iran's 'Second Islamic Revolution': Fulfilled by Election of Conservative President," Middle East Media Research Institute (MEMRI), Inquiry and Analysis Series–No. 299, 28 June 2005, http://memri.org/bin/articles.cgi?Page=countries&Area=iran&ID=IA22905.

30. "Iran: Ambassadors Recalled in Major Diplomatic Shakeup," *Adnkronos International*, 2 November 2005, http://www.thewe.cc/contents/more/archive2006/iran_us_confrontation.htm.

31. "Iran President Bans Western Music," BBC.co.uk, 19 December 2005, http://news.bbc.co.uk/1/hi/world/middle_east/4543720.stm.

32. Student Movement Coordinating Committee for Democracy in Iran (SMCCDI), "Hundreds of Bassji and Militiamen in Shiraz," 31 December 2005, http://www.daneshjoo.org/publishers/currentnews/article_2978.shtml.

33. Student Movement Coordinating Committee for Democracy in Iran (SMCCDI), "Female Students Injured by Islamists Using Acid," 4 January 2006, http://www.daneshjoo.org/publishers/smccdinews/article_4486.shtml.

34. "Iran to Hang Teenage Girl Attacked by Rapists," IranFocus.com, 7 January 2006, http://www.iranfocus.com/modules/news/article.php?storyid=5184.

35. "Iran's Islamist Rulers Want Sex Segregation on Pavements," IranFocus.com, 7 January 2006, http://www.iranfocus.com/modules/news/article.php?storyid=5188.

36. R. Nicholas Burns, "U.S. Policy Toward Iran," a speech given at the John Hopkins University Paul H. Nitze School of Advanced International Studies, Washington DC, 30 November 2005, http://www.state.gov/p/us/rm/2005/57473.htm.

37. Peters, "Mullahs' Threat Not Sinking In."

38. Student Movement Coordinating Committee for Democracy in Iran (SMCCDI), "Soccer Game Leads to Another Political Action in Tehran,"30 December 2005, http://www.daneshjoo.org/publishers/currentnews/article_2968.shtml.

39. Student Movement Coordinating Committee for Democracy in Iran (SMCCDI), "Students Slam Repressive Rule in Iran,"13 December 2005, http://www.daneshjoo.org/publishers/smccdinews/article_4456.shtml.

40. "Iran's Crackdown on Internet," News24.com, 22 June 2005, http://www.news24.com/News24/World/News/0,,2-10-1462_1725138,00.html.

41. "President Ahmadinejad: Iran to Continue Cooperation with UN Nuclear Agency," *Payvand News,* 4 January 2006, http://www.payvand.com/news/06/jan/1109.html.

42. Ibid.

43. Ibid.

CHAPTER 4

1. "Iran's Ahmadinejad Says Israel Will Be Wiped Off the Earth," *Iran Focus*, 26 October 2005, http://www.iranfocus.com/modules/news/article.php?storyid=4137.

2. "Iranian President at Tehran Conference: 'Very Soon, This Stain of Disgrace (i.e., Israel) Will Be Purged From the Center of the Islamic World–and This is Attainable," The Middle East Media Research Institute (MEMRI), Special Dispatch Series, No. 1013, 28 October 2005, http://memri.org/bin/articles.cgi?Page=countries&Area=iran&ID=SP1013 05; the remaining quotes from Ahmadinejad's speech come from this MEMRI source.

3. Ibid.

4. Ibid.

5. "Israel's Peres: Iran Should Be Expelled from United Nations," *USA Today*, 26 October 2005, http://www.usatoday.com/news/world/2005-10-26-iran-israel_x.htm.

6. "Iran's Ahmadinejad Says Israel Should Be Moved to Europe," RegimeChangeIran.blogspot.com, http://regimechangeiran.blogspot.com/2005/12/irans-ahmadinejad-says-israel-should.html.

7. "Iran's Ahmadinejad Says Israel Should Be Moved to Europe," Associated Press, 8 December 2005, http://www.breitbart.com/news/2005/12/08/051208164944.y49anqze.html.

8. Salah Nasrawi, "Iranian President Jabs at Israel Again," *ABC News International*, 8 December 2005, http://abcnews.go.com/International/wireStory?id=1387162.

9. Edwin Black, "Denial of Holocaust Nothing New in Iran—Ties to Hitler Led to Plots Against British and Jews," *San Francisco Chronicle*, 8 January 2006, http://www.sfgate.com/cgibin/article.cgi?f=/c/a/2006/01/08/INGODGH99Q1.DTL.

10. "Iran's Ahmadinejad Says Holocaust a Myth," Reuters, 14 December 2005. Also: "Holocaust Is a 'Myth': Iran's Ahmadinejad," Associated Press, 14 December 2005, http://www.breitbart.com/news/2005/12/14/051214075349.kfyauqdq.html.

11. Amos and Yoav Stern, "Two People Killed in Moshav Meron Rocket Attack," Haaretz.com, 14 July 2006.

12. "US to Sell Bunker Bombs to Israel," BBC News, 28 April 2005, http://news.bbc.co.uk/2/hi/middle_east/4493443.stm.

13. "Guided Bomb Unit-28 (GBU-28)," http://www.globalsecurity.org/military/systems/munitions/gbu-28.htm; this site includes technical specifications and photographs of the GBU-28.

14. "Vice President Cheney on Inauguration Day," MSNBC, 20 January 2005, http://www.msnbc.msn.com/id/6847999/page/2/.

15. "President Bush Sworn-in to Second Term," 20 January 2005, http://www.whitehouse.gov/inaugural/.

16. "Bush Goes Soft during Second Term," *Korea Herald*, 28 February 2005, http://www.ksg.harvard.edu/news/opeds/2005/022805_nye.htm.

17. "Remarks by the President at Concert Noble," White House Press Release, 1 February 2005, from Brussels, Belgium, http://news.bbc.co.uk/1/shared/bsp/hi/pdfs/21_02_05bush_belgiumspeech.pdf.

18. "Ahmadinejad Calls on Moslems to Boost Vigilance Against Israel," Deutsche Presse-Agentur, 17 December 2005, http://news.monstersandcritics.com/middleeast/article_1069719.php/Ahmadinejad_calls_on_Moslems_to_boost_vigilance_against_Israel.

CHAPTER 5

1. "Iran's President Criticizes Détente Foreign Policy," *Iran Focus*, 3 January 2006, http://www.iranfocus.com/modules/news/article.php?storyid=5117.

2. "Iran President Says Anti-Israel Comments 'Awakened' Muslims," *Iran Focus*, 3 January 2006, http://www.iranfocus.com/modules/news/article.php?storyid=5123.

3. Ibid.

4. Ibid.

5. "Iran Says Anti-Israel Diatribe Is 'Deliberate Strategy,' *Iran Focus*, 3 January 2006, http://www.iranfocus.com/modules/news/article.php?storyid=5138.

6. Peter Schweizer, *Victory: The Reagan Administration's Secret Strategy That Hastened the Collapse of the Soviet Union* (Atlantic Monthly Press, 1994), p. xv.

7. Ibid., p.140.

8. Ibid., p. 141–143.

9. Ibid., p. 234.

10. Mike Eckel, "Russia Reportedly to Sell Missiles to Iran," *Guardian*, 2 December 2005.

11. Ali Akbar Dareini, "Iran Seeks to Master Space Technology," ABC News International, 8 December 2005, http://www.abcnews.go.com/International/wireStory?id=1355870.

12. "Russia to Launch Iranian Satellites within Months," MissileThreat.com, A Project of the Claremont Institute, 2 February 2005, http://www.missilethreat.com/news/200502021445.html.

13. The statistics on China's oil consumption in this paragraph and the next are drawn from the US Department of Energy, Energy Information Administration (EIA), "China: Country Analysis Brief," http://www.eia.doe.gov/emeu/cabs/china.html; the EIA last updated the China Country Brief in August 2005.

14. "China, Iran Sign Biggest Oil & Gas Deal," CRI.com, 31 October 2004, http://www.china.org.cn/english/2004/Oct/110808.htm.

15. The statistics on Iran's oil industry come from the EIA website, "Iran: Country Brief" http://www.eia.doe.gov/emeu/cabs/iran.html; the EIA last updated the Iran Country Brief in March 2005.

16. "China Signs $70 Billion Oil and LNG Agreement with Iran," *Daily Star*, 30 October 2004, http://www.dailystar.com.lb/article.asp?edition_id=10&categ_id=3&article_id=9713.

17. "China to Develop Iran Oil Field," BBC News, 1 November 2004, http://news.bbc.co.uk/2/hi/business/3970855.stm.

18. John C. K. Daly, "UPI Energy Watch," *Washington Times*, 7 July 2004.

19. Iran's nationalized control of the country's oil and national gas resources are documented on the "National Iranian Oil Company" section of the Ministry of Petroleum's website: http://www.nioc.org/subcompanies/nioc/index.asp.

20. "Southwestern Asia and the Middle East," Radio Free Europe/Radio Liberty, 19 October 2004, http://www.rferl.org/newsline/2004/10/6-SWA/swa-191004.asp; original story reported by Radio Farda, http://www.radiofarda.com/iran_article/2004/10/5d215c23-eed2-41bf-9b63-c4a64e395734.html.

21. M.K. Bhadrakumar, "India Finds a $40bn Friend in Iran," *Asia Times Online*, 11 January 2005, http://atimes.com/atimes/South_Asia/GA11Df07.html.

22. "Economy and Politics of Sino-Russian Oil Deals," China Business InfoCenter, 13 January 2005, http://www.cbiz.cn/news/showarticle.asp?id=2208.

23. "Yukos at a Glance," http://www.yukos.com/About_us/yukos_at_a_glance.asp.

24. Ibid.

25. "India, Pakistan to Build Iranian Pipeline," *BusinessWeek Online*, 19 December 2005.

26. "China and Russia Issue a Joint Statement, Declaring the Trend of the Boundary Line between the Two Countries has been Completely Determined," Ministry of Foreign Affairs of the People's Republic of China, 14 October 2004, http://www.fmprc.gov.cn/eng/wjdt/2649/t165266.htm.

27. "Iran Says Does Not Need Permission for Nuclear Work," Reuters, UK, 26 December 2006.

28. For a statement of this argument against America's War on Terrorism, see Stephen J. Sniegoski, Ph.D., "America's 'War on Terror': A Prescription for Perpetual War," *Current Concerns*, 25 December 2005, http://www.currentconcerns.ch/archive/2005/06/20050601.php.

29. Jephraim Gundzik, President of Condor Advisors, "The Ties That Bind China, Russia, and Iran," *Asia Times Online*, 4 June 2005, http://www.atimes.com/atimes/China/GF04Ad07.html.

30. Anadolu News Agency, Cihan News Agency, Tehran, "Visits to Ankara Disturb Tehran," ZamanOnLine, 27 December 2005, http://www.zaman.com/?bl=international&alt=&hn=27965.

31. "Cicek: 'CIA Head's Visit is a Natural Outcome of Developments,'" TurkishPress.com, 27 December 2005.

32. The PKK is profiled on the website of the Federation of American Scientists, at the following web address: http://www.fas.org/irp/world/para/pkk.htm.

33. See, for instance: BBC News, "PKK 'Behind' Turkey Resort Bomb," 17 July 2005, http://news.bbc.co.uk/1/hi/world/europe/4690181.stm.

34. "Iran Accused of Aiding Turkey Islamic Violence," IranMania.com, 19 December 2005, http://www.iranmania.com/News/ArticleView/Default.asp?NewsCode=38929&NewsKind=Current%20Affairs; see also Michael Riazaty, "Iran's Qods Operations in Turkey," reported by Gary Metz on 19 December 2005, http://regimechangeiran.blogspot.com/2005/12/irans-qods-operation-in-turkey.html.

35. Islamic Republic News Agency (IRNA), "Rafsanjani Underlies Need to Bolster Ties with Turkey," 27 December 2005, http://www.irna.ir/en/news/view/line-24/0512252842164857.htm; also Kumar Choudhary, "Iran-Turkey Cooperation Promotes Regional Stability: Rafsanjani," KeralaNext.com, 26 December 2005.

36. Cumali Onal, Cairo, "Gul: There Is No Demand from US to Support Iran," ZamanOnLine, 27 December 2005.

37. Ibid.

38. Ian O. Lesser, "Turkey, Iran, and Nuclear Issues," in Henry Sokolski and Patrick Clawson (Editors) *Getting Ready for a Nuclear-Ready Iran* (Strategic Studies Institute, October 2005), p. 89.

CHAPTER 6

1. Mark T. Clark, "Small Nuclear Powers," in Henry D. Sokolski, Editor, *Getting MAD: Nuclear Mutual Assured Destruction, Its Origins and Practice* (The Strategic Studies Institute, November 2004), p. 279.

2. Quoted in Taheri, *Holy Terror*, p. 24.

3. See Taheri, *Nest of Spies*, p. 271.

4. The Middle East Media Research Institute (MEMRI), "Iranian Pilgrims in Mecca at Anti-American Rally: We Express Our Hatred & Disgust to the Center of Evil, the Criminal America ... 'Death to America,'" Special Dispatch Series, No. 1067, 10 January 2006.

5. Quoted in Michael Eisenstadt, "Deter and Contain: Dealing with a Nuclear Iran," included in Henry Sokolski and Patrick Clawson (Editors) *Getting Ready for a Nuclear-Ready Iran* (The Strategic Studies Institute, October 2005), p. 227.

6. Ibid., p. 228.

7. Islamic Republic News Agency (IRNA), "Rafsanjani: Iran Will Get Its Nuclear Rights with Wisdom," 11 January 2006.

8. The Santorum Resolution (Senate Resolution 336) on Iran was reported by Gary Metz, on RegimeChangeIran.blogspot.com, "Underreported US Senate Resolution on Iran Reveals a Lack of Conviction," 21 December 2005.

9. Susan Krause, "U.S. Sanctions Nine Companies Under Iran Nonproliferation Act," 28 December 2005, http://usinfo.state.gov/is/Archive/2005/Dec/28-303284.html.

10. The Eleventh Annual International Oil, Gas, and Petrochemicals Exhibit, held by the Iranian Ministry of Petroleum, scheduled for 20-23 April 2006, http://www.iran-oilshow.com/en/index.htm; A list of exhibitors for the Tenth Annual Conference held in 2005 is available on the Internet at http://www.iran-oilshow.com/en/exh_list10th.aspx; those exhibitors registered for the Eleventh Annual Conference in 2006 are also listed on the Internet at http://www.iran-oilshow.com/en/exh_list11th.aspx.

11. Dafna Linzer, "Russia Won't Block U.S. on Iran," *Washington Post*, 12 January 2006.

12. "Diary of the Dispute," BBC News, 24 May 2001, http://news.bbc.co.uk/1/hi/world/asia-pacific/1270365.stm.

13. "President Bush Meets with President Hu of the People's Republic of China, Oval Office," White House Press Release, 20 April 2006, http://www.whitehouse.gov/news/releases/2006/04/20060420-1.html.

14. "US Accepts Draft on Iran That Omits Use of Force," IranMania.com, 3 June 2006, http://www.iranmania.com/News/ArticleView/Default.asp?NewsCode=43360&NewsKind=Current%20Affairs.

15. Ali Akbar Dareini, "Iran Foreign Minister Welcomes U.S. Talks," Examiner.com, 1 June 2006.

16. For a technical description of the Eros-B satellite, see ImageSat International, Owners and Operators of the EROS Family, at http://www.imagesatintl.com/files/Media_Kit/ ImageSat_Company_Profile.pdf.

17. "Israeli Spy Satellite Launched to Watch Iran," Associated Press, 25 April 2006.

18. "Interview with Yitzhak Ben Yisreal, Head of the Israeli Space Agency, Discussing the New Israeli Satellite to Spy on the Iranian Nuclear Program," TMCnet.com, 26 April 2006.

CHAPTER 7

1. "Mordechai Vanunu: The *Sunday Times* Articles," TimesOnLine.co.uk, 21 April 2004.

2. A thorough discussion of the Dimona facilities can be found at "Dinoma: Negev Nuclear Research Center," GlobalSecurity.org at the following URL: http://www.globalsecurity.org/wmd/world/israel/dimona.htm.

3. Warner D. Farr, "The Third Temple's Holy of Holies: Israel's Nuclear Weapons," The Counterproliferation Papers, Future Warfare Series No. 2, USAF Counterproliferation Center, Air War College, Air University, Maxwell Air Force Base, Alabama, September 1999, http://www.globalsecurity.org/wmd/library/news/israel/farr.htm; see also "Israel: Nuclear Weapons Stockpile," http://www.globalsecurity.org/wmd/world/israel/nuke-stockpile.htm.

4. For technical descriptions and photographs of the Popeye Turbo cruise missile, see "Popeye Turbo," http://www.israeliweapons.com/weapons/ missile_systems/air_missiles/popeye_turbo/Popeye_Turbo.html.

5. "Israeli Submarines," http://www.fas.org/nuke/guide/israel/sub/ index.html.

6. Sammy Salama and Karen Ruster, "A Preemptive Attack on Iran's Nuclear Facilities: Possible Consequences," a CNS research story on the website of the Center for Nonproliferation Studies, http://www.cns.miis.edu/pubs/week/040812.htm.

7. "F-16I Soufa Fighter and Ground Attack Aircraft, Israel," http://www.airforce-technology.com/projects/f-16i/; in addition to technical specifications, the website also has photographs of the F-16I. For technical specifications and photographs of the F-16I, see Israeli-Weapons.com at the following URL: http://www.israeli-weapons.com/weapons/aircraft/f-15i/F-15I.html.

8. This point is made by Anthony Cordesman, a senior researcher at the Center for Strategic and International Studies in Washington DC. Cordesman is quoted in "Iran's Military Called No Match for U.S. But Its Missiles Pose Threat to Israel," GeoStrategy-Direct.com, week of 4 January 2005. See also Anthony H. Cordesman, Arleigh A. Burk Chair, *Iran's Developing Military Capabilities, Main Report*, (Center for Strategic and International Studies), Working Draft, 14 December 2004, referred to hereafter as the *CSIS Report*.

9. US Energy Information Agency, Depatment of Energy, "Persian Gulf Oil and Gas Exports Fact Sheet," http://www.eia.doe.gov/emeu/cabs/pgulf.html.

10. "Iran Threatens Retaliation on Persian Gulf Arab Oil if Attacked by U.S.," WorldTribune.com, 4 March 2005.

11. *CSIS Report*, p. 39–40.

12. Ibid. For additional Internet reports concerning Iran purchasing Sunburn cruise missiles, see "A Weapons Analysis of the Iran-Russia-US Strategic Triangle," on TBRnews.org, at http://www.thetruthseeker.co.uk/print.asp?ID=2439; also, see Mark Gaffney, "Iran a Bridge Too Far?" http://www.informationclearinghouse.info/article7147.htm.

13. Reported by Bill Gertz and Rowan Scarborough, in their column "Inside the Ring," under a subtitle "Fighters Deploy," *Washington Times*, 13 January 2006, http://www.washtimes.com/national/20060112-113400-5198r_page2.htm.

14. Websites of the military installations discussed are as follows: Ft. Rucker, Alabama, at http://www-rucker.army.mil; Hulburt Field, Florida, Hulburt Field, Florida, http://www.29palms.usmc.mil/; the authors acknowledge an unpublished paper by Paul L. Williams, "U.S. Invasion of Iran Now 'Imminent,'" as identifying the importance of these bases in preparing for a US military attack on Iran.

15. Iran's nuclear facilities are detailed at GlobalSecurity.org, including in many instances satellite photographs, http://www.globalsecurity.org/wmd/world/iran/nuke-fac.htm.

16. "Iran Profile: Iran Missile Facilities," NTI.org, http://www.nti.org/e_research/profiles/Iran/Missile/3876_4104.html.

17. See, for instance, http://www.globalsecurity.org/military/world/iran/.

18. Robert Coram, *Boyd: The Fighter Pilot Who Changed the Art of War* (Little, Brown and Company, 2002), p. 42.

19. Described in Bijal Trivedi, "Inside Shock and Awe," *National Geographic Channel,* 14 February 2005.

20. "A Day of Sirens, Bombs, Smoke and Fires," CNN.com, 21 March 2003, http://www.cnn.com/2003/WORLD/meast/03/21/sprj.irq.aday/; a comprehensive listing of the weapons, armaments, and war action in the 2003 Iraq War can be found at "War in Iraq," http://www.cnn.com/SPECIALS/2003/iraq/.

21. Robert Tait, "Iran Issues Stark Warning on Oil Price," *Guardian,* 16 January 2006.

22. Reuters, "200 Sign Up to Be Martyrs," *Pittsburgh Tribune-Review,* 17 April 2006.

EPILOGUE

1. "Iran Declares War," *New York Sun,* 11 May 2006, http://www.nysun.com/article/32594.

2. Daniel Byman, "Proxy Power," Slate.com, 26 July 2006.

3. Daniel Byman, "Strange Bedfellows," Slate.com, 19 July 2006.

4. Frank J. Gaffney and Colleagues, *War Footing: 10 Steps America Must Take to Prevail in the War for the Free World* (Naval Institute Press, 2006). The quotation comes from Step 9, "Launch Regional Initiatives," in the essay entitled, "Defend and Foster Freedom in the Middle East and Its Periphery," p. 157; the following are listed as contributors: Lt. Gen. Tom McInerney, USAF (Ret.); Maj. Gen. Paul E. Vallely, USA (Ret.); Alex Alexiev; Kenneth R. Timmerman; Dr. Michael Rubin; Caroline B. Glick; and Christopher Brown.

5. Ibid., p. 151–152.

6. Curt Weldon and Roscoe Bartlett, "Counter the Mega-Threat: EMP Attack," in Gaffney, *War Footing*, op. cit., p. 100–112.

7. "Report of the Commission to Assess the Threat to the United States from Electromagnetic Pulse (EMP) Attack," http://empcreport.ida.org.

8. Joseph Farah's G2 Bulletin, "New Congress Warning on Nuclear EMP Threat," WorldNetDaily.com, 20 June 2005, http://www.worldnetdaily.com/news/article.asp?ARTICLE_ID=44866.

9. "Medieval Book of Psalms Unearthed," CNN.com, 25 July 2006, http://www.cnn.com/2006/WORLD/europe/07/25/ireland.psalms.ap/index.html.

If you desire to receive regular intelligence briefings, simply join the Jerusalem Prayer Team at www.jerusalemprayerteam.org. You may also visit the Evans Institute of Middle East Studies at www.eimes.net.

INDEX